How to **Start** a Business:
Mac Version

10 Essential Business Steps for Startups using a Mac

Kevin Cullis

Denver, CO

TX 007512666 1/16/2012
20130708

ISBN-13:   978-1-4495423-68
ISBN-10:   1-4495423-60

Contents

Chapter Four   111

Step 4: Business Model to Actions Steps 111

Chapter Five   133

Step 5: Your Business & Mac Software.................133

Chapter Six   177

Step 6: Mac Hardware Tools 177

Chapter Seven   193

Step 7: Marketing Plan - Customer Funnel 193

Chapter Eight   213

Step 8: Sales Plan - Meet The Demand.................213

Chapter Nine   229

Step 9: Operation Plan - Work it 229

Foreword by Dave Taylor

It's not easy being green
It seems you blend in with so many other ordinary things
And people tend to pass you over 'cause you're
Not standing out like flashy sparkles in the water
Or stars in the sky.

It's Not Easy Being Green, lyrics by Joe Rapposo

The hardest part of starting a business shouldn't be the technology on your desk or in your pocket. Successful businesses grow out of successful execution, out of paying attention to your marketplace, your customers and your competitors, perhaps not in that exact order.

Still, every morning, every invoice, every purchase order, every email query, you're firing up that computer and working with the digital tools at hand, and if they aren't good, you're going to spend hours every day pushing that huge Sisyphean rock up hill. Not good, and not a smart use of your energy and enthusiasm.

Heck, I know this firsthand because while I'm really good at running my business, I don't generally pay much attention to my P&L statements (profit and loss, you'll know what that is by the time you're a week into your biz, trust me) because it requires me to actually do something other than focus on the fun parts of my business: interacting with my customers and marketplace.

That's why I was enthused to watch Kevin turn an idea into the book you are holding in your hands: every businessperson needs to find that sweet spot between doing what you love and running the business itself. Every biz needs to file taxes, pay employees, respond to customer complaints, and take care of the thousand other bits and pieces that differentiate what you're doing from a hobby, a side project that might make money but isn't essential to your financial well being.

I'm also an avowed Mac bigot (we call 'em "fanboys," actually) so a book that looks at the process of creating, building and running an actual business that's unabashedly pro-Apple is a nice break from the constant drumbeat of Windows, Windows,

Windows. It's not that Microsoft's platform is bad but that too many small businesspeople end up spending much of their time dealing with computer weirdnesses, whether it's avoiding viruses and spyware or just trying to figure out why it takes ten minutes to boot, five minutes to start Quicken and why that darn PC never shuts down any more. And backups? Fuggetaboutit!

By contrast, I have a small network for my business that is built around an Apple Time Capsule and includes a desktop and laptop system. Everything's in sync -- including my Apple iPhone, thanks to Apple's iCloud remote sync services -- and I always have backups going, while being able to keep everything secure and safe at the same time. I can understand how it works so I know when I'm safely connected to a public wifi network (I write this while sitting at a Starbucks on their public network) I still know my data connection is secure.

How do I know about all this pain from small business owners and their computer systems? I run a tech troubleshooting site – AskDaveTaylor.com – and over a million people a month find help from my Q&A articles, while I collect usage and analytic data to see just what doesn't work well and how people fix it, and I can tell you that even though I have more Mac than Windows articles, there are a lot more people using a PC looking for answers than Mac users…

However you slice the data, it's clear that when you're running a business you want to focus on what you're good at, what you enjoy doing, and what is really the benefit you bring to the marketplace and have as your strategic differentiator. If you can't find that, you don't have a business, you have a commodity, and that's a tough, painful way to proceed.

Find your muse, gain that inspiration, and fire up that Mac. With Kevin's help you can turn your savvy business idea into a thriving, successful business and change your life, the lives of those around you and, most importantly, improve the lives of your customers.

Now go! Succeed!

Dave Taylor
Boulder CO

Acknowledgments

No man can rise to fame and fortune without carrying others along with him. It simply cannot be done. Napoleon Hill

A portion of book sale profits will be donated to Wounded Wear (woundedwear.org) which support wounded servic members and veterans with special clothing and to Junior Achievement (ja.org) to help over 9 million kids in 122 countries worldwide to achieve their fullest potential in business. JA was started in 1916 and its first chairman, Mr. Vail, Chairman of AT&T, stated his ideals for JA in a speech: "The future of our country depends upon making every person, young and old, fully realize the obligations and responsibilities belonging to citizenship…The future of each person rests in the individual, providing each is given a fair and proper education and training in the useful things of life."

There are some people that I'd personally like to thank for their help and encouragement: Ruth Ann Cullis, my wife of over 26 years who has stood by me, through thick and thin. My mother Midge Cullis who was always looking forward for what's around "the next bend" in life. My dad Harry Cullis who sees details that I may not see and without his support this result would have never happened. My brother Drew Cullis whose creativeness astounds me every time I watch him at work. And my sister Jill Cullis, who's the best, who always is willing to give a helping hand and the best school teacher for encouraging kids to be their best! Most of all, Mary McLean whose encouragement and belief in me *early* in my writing this book was a key motivating factor in my determination to finish it. I will forever be thankful for her mentorship and insights.

Also, all of my past customers who asked me questions about using a Mac. Thank you for your business. Others that have had a direct or an indirect comments toward me or this book, whether it was an encouragement, idea, suggestion, or just displayed their talents in action, a heartfelt thanks to you all: Pete Faber, Will Stevenson (poweredbywill.com), Tony Lonsinger, Jennifer Starry Stout, Suzanne Khetagurova, Elizabeth Lewis (eclewis.com), Ron

Aclan, Shawn C. White, Brian Povlsen (chimac.net), Michael Lloyd, Dave Taylor (askdavetaylor.com), James Tummins, Rob Koehn, Zach Ankenman, Merle Snyder, Casey Rellaford, Gary Barnes (garybarnesinternational.com), Will Stevens, Lynn Mitchell (surfaceindesign.com), Dan Beaury, Laz (chernik.com) and Echo Chernik (echo-x.com), Matthew Gallizi (entrepreneurenclave.com), Michael Ibarra, Laura Compton, Robert Castro, Chris Eichenberger, Craig Lindsey, Bob Withers (bobwithers.com), Michael Linde, Dan & Joyce Miller (permissionacquisition.com), Paul Basker, Derek George, Richard Harris (harrisfamilylaw.com), Mike Hance, David Downes, Peter Cranstone (5o9inc.com), Darin Hagre, Rachael West (rachaelwesttalent.com), Rachel Perry Schrank (playaweddings.com), Grady Herndon, Laura Compton, Roger Denton (sharedplan.com), Bryan Carter, Tyler Hardie, Betsi Shields, Jeanine Swatton (swattonlive.com), Michelle Guasto, Walton Mendelson (12on14.com), Josh Thomas, Amber Ludwig (insightfuldevelopment.com), Betsy Rubner, Jon Gates, Amy McKnight (themacspa.com), Xavier De Leon, Rod Billingsly, Tom Aspenwell, Raymond Scott, David Veal (vealcreative.com), Travis Heath, Ted Hodges, Jackie Risley, Jen Goode (jgoodedesigns.com), Mark Labriola, Ted Wahler (tedwahler.com), Melissa Harris, Holly Macgregor, Col. Robin Wohnsigl, Julian Long, Robert Gray, Jeremy Miles, Mark Fukami, Alan Warner (trionpromo.com), Dan Burcaw, Lindsay Giachetti, Christine Comaford-Lynch (mightventures.com), Andy Carr, Saquib Doctor, Jon Wilson, Vicky Gundrum, and finally Amalia Starr (amaliastarrspeakerautism.com) for her insights into health issues that entrepreneurs can help solve. Others that I may have worked with whether above, below, or beside me in some capacity in whatever job or industry I was in. Lastly, all the writers in the book section below whose encouragement and ideas contributed to where I am and where I'm going.

There are many more people that I would like to have named here and my sincere thanks to all of you and your various talents and how you positively affected my life.

Kevin Cullis
Denver, CO

Chapter One

Step 1: "You Had Me At..."

The turning point in the lives of those who succeed usually comes at the moment of some crisis through which they are introduced to their "other selves." Napoleon Hill

A 14 year-old-son brought his mother into an Apple store to see if Macs could help her clothing boutique business. She said, "My son says I should get a Mac to run my business, so why should I?" I told her, "Let's show you why!"

I then gave her a Mac demo. Starting with Garage Band, I created a 30-second advertisement that sounded like a newscast. She could create her own music and save both the ad and music as audio files. In PhotoBooth, I recorded a short video while she talked about her boutique. The video and audio files, along with several pictures from iPhoto, were dropped into an iMovie project; I exported the finished project to iTunes and transferred the file onto an iPod. She could now take her iPod to her retail store and stream her own commercials through her store's stereo or video system. We took her boutique pictures and created a marketing flyer in iWork Pages and a catalog in Numbers so she could send these direct mail pieces to her customers at just the right marketing time.

Her face betrayed her astonishment at what I was able to do, and she told me that about 40 percent of her marketing budget was in outsourcing advertising to others she could do it herself, she could save money. "This is what I can do in five minutes," I said, "Think how much more you could do. So, what do you think?"

"You had me at GarageBand," she said (true story).

She already had a successful business and learned the Mac could help save her time and money by bringing outsourced marketing. In *Good to Great,* author Jim Collins says the correct view of using any technology that it "becomes an *accelerator* of momentum, not a *creator* of it (emphasis added)." Macs are just tools to help you with your business. Better tools can increase your creativity and produce better results in your business, saving you time and money. One thing is certain: Macs have cool tools.

Mental Toughness: A winning mindset

Starting a business begins with the first step. It starts with a decision and it begins where you are, with what you have and don't have. Decide. You build a business one decision, one action, and one brick at a time. Take action.

Mindset to confidence foundations. No one is born a winner. Mental preparation, learning, training, and the constant sharpening of your mind is 99% the essence of a winning mindset; taking action is the other 1%. Pushing oneself beyond one's *perceived* mental, physical, emotional, and spiritual limits, including letting go of bad habits or various traumas in one's life, is part of that 99%. Hold onto your past or grab your future; you can't do both. So getting the right

> People don't fail because they want to fail. They fail because they don't know how to succeed.
> - Mark Twain

mindset is the start of your journey into business.

In Deu 6:5 it states: "You shall love the LORD your God with all your heart and with all your soul and with all your might." Then in Lev 19:18b, "but you shall love your neighbor *as* yourself (emphasis added); I am the LORD." When you read Proverbs 11:18, we're reminded, "The wicked earns deceptive wages, but he who sows righteousness gets a true reward." How does an entrepreneur or business person reconcile business with morality?

Rabbi Lapin in his book *Thou Shall Prosper* writes,

> *Chanukah is the expansion of the Hebrew word for education. … Joining together the themes of the candles and the money, we find the reason for the custom of giving children money for each of the eight nights of Chanukah is amounts that are proportional to the success of their studies. The money is a reward for the* **light** *[education, understanding] they have gained during the past year. … not only is money not bad, but it often can be a result of self-improvement. … You receive money in proportion to how helpful you can make yourself to other people.*[1]

Most Christians are not aware that Jesus understood Chanukah, too. In John 10:22-23 it says, "At that time the *Feast of the Dedication* (emphasis added) took place at Jerusalem; it was winter, and Jesus was walking in the temple in the portico of Solomon." So Jesus had an understanding of Lapin's comment about Chanukah.

Lapin writes further,

> *Jews always viewed putting one's capital at risk to enable someone else to make a profit as an honorable way to earn a living and to help others. The Jewish hierarchy of charity regards lending someone money to go into business as more noble than simply giving him the money. … This way his dignity is preserved, and he retains the psychological self-image so necessary to conducting business successfully.*[2]

In the Christian New Testament, 2 Thess 3:10b states, "if anyone is not willing to work, then he is not to eat, either." God requires us to work for our living. In the parable of the Talents (Matt 25:14-30), you find five statements about business that stand out. Verse 15, "And to one he gave five talents, to another, two, and to another one, *each according to his own ability*." In verse 19, "the master of those slaves came and *settled accounts* with them." Verse 26 says, "But his master answered and said to him,

---

[1] *Thou Shall Prosper* by Rabbi Daniel Lapin, pg 24-25

[2] *Thou Shall Prosper* by Rabbi Daniel Lapin, pg 25-26

'You wicked, lazy slave, you knew that *I reap where I did not sow* and gather where I scattered no seed." And lastly in verse 27, "Then you ought to have *put my money in the bank*, and on my arrival I would have received *my money back with interest* (emphasis added)." The parable takeaways:

▸ the *attitude* of the two "slaves" was being "in business for themselves" and putting their master's capital to good use, not viewing their station or "title" in life as a slave;

▸ each slave had different levels of talents, aptitudes, and skills (thus different potential for pay/income/rewards);

▸ the master *entrusted* different amounts of capital for each, but each slave had an *equal and full opportunity* to perform at their maximum ability using *all* of their unique talents and skills;

▸ the master was a capitalist, not directly doing the work, but invested in his slaves and looked for their individual *results*;

▸ if the lazy slave had put the money in a bank (a viable business) means *the capital would have been put to work* serving others;

▸ so, the lazy slave was fired because he/she did not do the work, but fearfully and secretly hoarded the capital.

It is your calling, duty, responsibility, or purpose to use all of your talents, gifts, skills in the pursuit of serving others. The idea here is this: when looking to God for blessings, you're really praying for the chance to serve someone. When service is rendered, money is usually the result of that exchange, and the higher quality or quantity of people you serve, the more money you make.

> The person born with a talent they are meant to use will find their greatest happiness in using it. - Johann Wolfgang von Goethe

This theme of knowing oneself and doing good is echoed by another story, but it gives an internal picture with an external result. An old Indian Chief was teaching his grandson about life. "A fight is going on inside of me," he told his grandson. "It is a terrible fight between two wolves."

4

"One is evil—angry, envious, sorrowful, regretful, greedy, arrogant, self-pitying, guilt-ridden, resentful, lying, full of false pride, superiority and ego driven," the Chief continued.

Then the Chief paused and said, "The other wolf is good— joyful, peaceful, loving, hopeful, serene, humble, kind, empathetic, generous, truthful, compassionate, and faithful."

"The same fight is going on inside of you, Grandson, and in every other person," said the Chief.

The grandson thought about this for a moment, turned to the Chief, and asked, "But, Grandfather, which wolf will win?"

"The one that you feed," the old Cherokee replied.

Building confidence. Feeding oneself good information is the start of having a good mindset. Having a strong personal and entrepreneurial mindset and conviction of one's principles prepares oneself for one's purpose and life endeavor. It's knowing to expect it (failure, change, growth, etc.), being prepared for it, and being able to handle it. It's doing good, for yourself, and equally for others: i.e. business.

> Don't measure yourself by what you have accomplished, but by what you should have accomplished with your ability.
> - John Wooden

Mental toughness can be defined as: remaining calm when others are overcome with fear or panic; a person's ability to defeat the voice in their mind that is telling them to quit; adversity brings out the best in them and knowing there's always a way to win; and mentally tough individuals aren't immune to fear, they simply refuse to let it affect them in a negative way.[3] There are six sequential steps to creating or having mental toughness.

1. **Capability - innate and learned talents and skills.** What are your talents and skills? Find out what you're made of, because everyone has multiple talents and skills. It may mean trying something you've never done before, or pushing yourself beyond your current limits. Get the book *Strength Finder* by Tom Rath to help find your strengths to operate in.

---

[3] *Navy SEALS Training Guide: Mental Toughness* by Lars Draeger

2. **Cause - serving something bigger than yourself.** It's finding *a calling* with your talents that helps others in their lives, whether it's engineering, arts, administration, the military, or it's finance. It's about using all of your talents and skills in helping and serving others.

3. **Commitment - take on or give up something to accomplish your Cause.** Another word for commitment is discipline; it takes discipline to change yourself, the market, and society. The discipline to take on more responsibilities or bigger goals or enhance your talents and skill sets. Or, you give up watching TV or unhealthy eating habits or delegate to others some tasks. Commit to a cause/vision, using your talents and skills you take multiple, small-step actions toward your vision, even if it's finishing one task in the next 60 seconds. It begins with preparing oneself with the mindset of "refuse to lose" so that when the right opportunity comes along you're at the right place with a solution for the right customer.

> Amateurs work it until they get it right; professionals work it until they can't get it wrong.

4. **Confront - facing your fears and faults and favorable results.** Why do you fail to take actions or make the same mistakes and repeatedly payed huge consequences for your actions? While you may or may not "shout out" about your successes, you may not "call out" your mistakes and debrief both good and bad actions. A *debrief* is a real "face your faults and fears" where you lay all of your issues, good and bad, out. Then outline how to improve or fix them, do it, then follow up with an honest "hot shower" relief after the mental and/or physical workout making the change is over. We naturally want to minimize our mistakes because then we feel better about ourselves. HALT! Be honest and accountable. Do what's necessary to reduce and/or eliminate mistakes from ever happening again, improve failures into successes. Being open and honest about them forces you to admit that maybe you don't know everything and maybe it's time to

change your habits, tactics, or life's new path. REPEAT this step, as often as necessary.

5. **Competence - knowledge learned, training applied, experience gained.** Competence is taking one's talents and skills (#1 above) and using and building on them one success after another; it's allowing "failures" to become stepping stones to a greater success. Does a parent stop a baby from walking after its hundredth fall? Do Olympic hopefuls quit when faced with a single failure? You *learn and train* to become better. Ultimately you become the "go to" expert using your talents, skills, and various tactics in serving others. Your confidence comes from the natural and/or developed skill set you constantly improve to be both effective (getting the job done) and efficient (in the least amount of time, and at the most profit).

> Failure should be defined as failing to learn from failure.

6. **Confidence - quiet confidence.** Customers pay you. Confidence comes from many turns "at bat" even though one may have many strike outs, it means an entrepreneur never stops their mission to change their world.

A successful entrepreneur employes a number of elements: at the top is mental toughness. This toughness is knowing the DNA of you, the whole person. It's that combination of innate talents, learned skills, and the ability to drive on to be effective, and through repetition, honed to be efficient.

Roadmap: From idea to grand opening

Levels of thinking in business. There are multiple ways of thinking about a business and Illustration 1 three levels of such thinking. Most entrepreneurs only think like technicians; good entrepreneurs work at all levels.

Business growth stages. Illustration 2 shows a desired growth path, but it does not always work out this way. A critical business point: Once a business reaches cruising altitude, the

Thinking Levels	Issues
Business Owner	finance, marketing, taxes, customers, competition
Project Management	project, process, and task time, costs
Technician (clerk, bookkeeper, etc.)	technical issues, producing invoices, emails, phones

Illustration 1: Thinking levels

business owner lets others take over, much like a pilot uses autopilot to fly the aircraft. Otherwise, what's the sense?

The "Big Picture" of your business and Mac. Each entrepreneur decides which business habits are good for their business and which to apply to become a successful entrepreneur.

Business roadmaps are available that will pull some of these pieces of information together, but *How to Start a Business: Mac Version* is unique in that it combines both a practical list of startup business steps and information about the Mac. These are woven together into a step-by-step guide to starting a business using a Mac, shown in Illustration 3. Starting at letter A, you read and progress through to the letter N, and at each letter you are guided through each stage.

Principle: Define your business needs > find your Mac software solutions > decide the Mac hardware to run them. Your

Startup Stages	1 Flight Planning	2 Preflight, Taxi	3 Takeoff	4 Climb Out	5 Cruising Altitude
Focus	Idea, start, prototype	Need customers	Retain customers	Grow	Others and outsourced
Income	Self funded, outside work	Burning $, outside work	Regularly breaking even	Income higher than bills	High Income
Emotion	"Cool"	"Sell, sell"	"Keep moving, can't stop"	"Still on a treadmill"	"Off the treadmill, others take my place."

Illustration 2: Basic stages of startup growth over time

business requirements narrow down the Mac software you need to run your business and which Mac hardware is best fitted to run your business.

Whether your business is working from home, retail, consulting, system administration, graphic arts, software development, writing, law, or medicine, you can benefit by using a Mac. Marketing, selling, and operations function similarly in all those businesses. Size, processes and other details will change. Using this book, you can learn ways to integrate the Mac applications and technology into your business processes.

A business startup is much like a meal; you start gathering a pantry full of ingredients, and through trial and error, some basic cooking knowledge, or a cookbook at your side: your goal is to make a delicious dinner. You decide if your business "recipe" is

Stepping Through "How to Start a Business: Mac Version"

Letters **A** - **N** in the below graphic are the "You Are Here" pointers as you begin to read this book of the various thinking perspectives and skills. It walks you through the essential actions steps from your **Initial Idea** all the way to **Open for Business**.

Level of Thinking Needed	Initial Idea					Open for Business			
CEO/Business Owner	A				E	H	K	N	
Project Management		B			F	I	L		
Technician			C	D	G	J	M		
Chapter Number	3	4	5	6	7	8	9	10	

Business Research to Model — Business Model to Action Steps — Your Business & Mac Software — Mac Hardware Tools — Marketing Plan - Customer Funnel — Sales Plan - Meet The Demand — Operations Plan - Work It — Next Steps

Illustration 3: Stepping through the book

9

American, Italian, or Japanese. Your decisions about how you put together the right ingredients in the right order at the right time will determine how your recipe will turn out—just make sure you don't substitute tuna as a substitute for meat in a lasagna recipe; it will look and taste lousy.

Start your story and legacy right

There are many things that need to be considered before you start a business. Some important things to think initially about are:

▸ **Support from family and friends**: Starting a business takes a great deal of time and requires sacrifices from you and from your family and close friends. It's important that you allot time for them and not exclude them from your new endeavor.

▸ **Finances:** Just like buying a new house, consider the timing for making any major buys or changes in your financial situation. Any significant changes in your financial situation could raise red flags to financial institutions if you intend to pursue funding for your startup.

▸ **Legal issues**: Wills, business ownership and continuity. Consider discussing your plans with a legal professional. If you plan for your business to continue beyond your lifetime, you should plan your business future and how it will affect your family and business partners.

Legacy
Legacy |ˈlegəsē| noun (pl. -cies) a thing handed down by a predecessor. What will you leave behind when you're gone?

"I have to try." Sold computers for a number of years. Drawing from that experience, I just started writing about computers and business. A customer suggested I turn my writings into a book, which resulted in my first draft in 2004 covering Windows, Mac, and Linux. In 2006, I changed direction and focused on only Mac computers and my first book become my second book. From that version came this, the third version focusing on startups.

During that time, I continuously answered the same computer questions from business people. My wife is in real estate, and she would ask me the same questions, as well. All of them wanted to use the computer as a tool to help with their work, their passions, and their dreams. They didn't want to become computer geeks. Just like buying a car, they just wanted to get in, start it up, and drive.

I looked at all the business books and there were many with good info, but while the words change, the business processes rarely change. I researched computer books. All of them were hundreds of pages long (some close to a thousand) for each specific task or bundle of applications. Most business people would not read them—not because they didn't want to, but because they didn't have time. That's the reason I wrote this version of the book, help steer through the open sea of solutions (true story).

> Fear means you have butterflies in your stomach, courage makes them fly in formation.

"Will you try?" Do you love what you do? In the book *Now Discover Your Strengths,* Marcus Buckingham says that *only one in five employees feel fully engaged* at work?

Is this you?

Do you feel like the four out of five?

Or, maybe you've just lost, quit, or changed jobs, and can't find one that totally engages you.

Now what do you do?

Get angry?

Cuss?

See only the negative?

Naw. Nope. Nada. Nyet.

Getting it done. Here are the eight levels on the "take action" spectrum:

1. I won't do it - fears, inaction, keep you from believing.
2. I can't do it - doubts and excuses for why you can't do it.
3. I want to do it - it is possible, but you have reservations.
4. I'll figure out how to do it - neutral, taking a longer look.
5. I'll try to do it - take actions and see the possibilities.
6. I can do it - seeing the probabilities.

7. I will do it - seeing the finish line.

8. I did it - crossing the finish line!

In a January 2009 *Wired* magazine interview about his book *Tribes,* Seth Godin said, "The Internet means geography isn't so important, so if you can find the 1,000 or 5,000 or 50,000 people out there who want to make a certain kind of change and can connect them and show them a path, they want to follow you. You can use that tribe, that group of people, to make change that matters."

Do you have the next big idea? What do you imagine your legacy will be?

Go create a tribe and a movement with your ideas!

Chapter Two

Step 2: Overview of Business

Just so the wealth of the country, its capital, its credit, must be saved from the predatory poor as well as the predatory rich, but above all from the predatory politician.-- James J. Hill

Business in the U.S.

Entrepreneurship and small business

There is a difference between small businesses, inventors, and entrepreneurs. An *inventor* designs something new, may not go into business, but sell it to a business. A *small business* starts a familiar business that most people recognize, such as a restaurant. An *entrepreneur* creates something totally new, where the product or service never existed before, or is radically more convenient, which changes the current market.

Two illustrations describe entrepreneurship and the role it plays in a nation's economy. First, before a good farmer plants a crop, he ensures that he is prepared for the growing season. He has to have seed, the soil is tilled, and any other elements are ready to promote a healthy crop growth and to maximize the quantity and quality of the yield. In the business environment, the seed is the entrepreneur's idea and the various elements to make a business grow. It includes having a good community of customers and suppliers and the right role and level of the local, state, and federal government as a significant part of the "soil" for economic growth around a business idea.

The second illustration describes the economy as a horse and rider. The horse's owners are the American people, the economy/business is the horse, and the government is the rider. Both the rider and owner need to have good intentions and positive actions to enable the horse to perform. Imagine if the rider is too small or untrained (unable to handle the horse), abusive (confuses, hinders, hurts, or disables the horse), or is overweight (too large for the horse to perform at optimum, or perform at all). The horse's productivity is hindered. Just as a farmer tests new ways for increasing crop yields, so also a horse rider must maintain optimal weight, obtain good training, see a veterinarian, and feed and exercise the horse to achieve the positive results.

Entrepreneurs don't get good school grades for resourcefulness, guts, curiosity, honest failure, agility, connecting the dots, and tenacity.

Entrepreneurs challenge the status quo.

Entrepreneurs earn success.

The better the business environment or climate, the better one can build a successful business. The three areas that make up the business environment are the marketplace, the government, and the people. Each of these areas affect competition, taxes, regulations, accurate and right educational content, laws, resources, and the public support of commercial ventures, all of which must be favorable to create a positive business environment. It is this foundation that creates the economic engine that makes a country prosperous.

> The man with a new idea is a crank until the idea succeeds.
> - Mark Twain

Capitalism in America didn't just happen over night, but was a new economic garden cultivated over time. Hernando de Soto in *The Mystery of Capital* shows evidence that throughout the world, everyone, including the very poor in third world countries, is capable of running a small business and becoming an entrepreneur. It is America which has created a proper system and leading the rest of the West and the world to take advantage of potential capital. "The poor inhabitants of these [third world] nations—five-sixths of humanity—do have things, but they lack the process to represent their property and create capital. They have houses but not titles; crops but not deeds, businesses but not statues of incorporation." He goes on, "Only the West has the conversion process required to transform the invisible to the visible," i.e. connecting land, assets, and inventories (the visible) with property documents (the invisible), thus creating capital.[4] So how did it happen?

In 1828, the French word entrepreneur[5] meant "one who undertakes or manages." Later, the Americans changed the term to mean "manager or promoter of a theatric production." It wasn't until 1852 that it came to mean "business manager" and today's definition a person who organizes, operates and assumes the risks for a business venture. The change of the word's definition in the early 1800s only followed the changing nature of business in America.

> *The first thing is to get the business, and the next thing is the way you transact your business.*
> *- J. P. Morgan*

When Adam Smith published *The Theory of Moral Sentiments* (1759), referring to the "invisible hand" to describe the apparent benefits to society of people behaving in their own interests, and *An Inquiry into the Nature and Causes of the Wealth of Nations* (1776), offering one of the world's first collected descriptions of what builds a nation's wealth, it helped change the new economic blueprint and the American nation.

In Smith's economic vernacular, "sell dear, buy cheap" is the basis for the business equation of: supply = demand. Sellers want a high price, buyers want a low price, and it is the competition between sellers for the buyers attention which creates a market of

---

[4] *The Mystery of Capital* by Hernando de Soto, pg 6-7

[5] etymonline.com

the right item for the right price that is agreeable to the parties.[6] So, any shortcomings, restrictions, or failures of the business environmental conditions results in the vacillation of the economics of a society creating artificial bubbles and recessions/depressions than the natural market would automatically correct.

Essential to Smith's book *The Wealth of Nations* did not deal with the *absence* of government from business affairs, but its *proper role* in the economy. He states, "Commerce and manufactures can seldom flourish long in any state which does not enjoy a regular administration of justice; in which the people do not feel themselves secure in the possession of their property; in which the faith of contracts is not supported by law."

Startup Nation America

The newly transplanted English colonists of the 1600s in the New World of America brought some of the old world governance and business habits to the new land. They considered themselves very much British citizens, but ultimately the distance, time, and the various actions between America and England allowed Americans to begin to redefine their views of governance and business models. Thus begins the American experiment and new national direction. From these new beginnings today's entrepreneurs can learn much.

The American Revolution sparked innovation and the Founding Fathers proposed not just a new nation, but a *new nation with a new set of national principles*; a society where heredity status, entitlements, and class distinctions would be erased. Citizenship only required allegiance to the republic and its principles, and all individual rights were immune to legitimate revocation.

Guilds, Mercantilism, Corporations, and Monopolies. Words may remain, but the meaning or definitions may change.[7] During the fourteenth and fifteenth centuries, guilds were associations of craft workers or merchants, often having considerable power granted to them by monarchs. They were

---

[6] *American Entrepreneur* by Larry Schweikart, pg 3-13

[7] etymonline.com

chartered primarily to enforce a monopoly in certain industries or geographic regions and were the precursors to corporations. The word corporation came into being during the mid 1500s, defined as "persons united in a body for some purpose." Its meaning was similar to guilds and were also chartered by monarchs.

The Plymouth and Jamestown colonialist's economic view was mercantilism, the "economic doctrine that government control of foreign trade is of paramount importance for ensuring the prosperity and military security of the state during the 1700s and 1800s." [8] These mercantilist legal entities, laws, class, and societal norms set the pace of the economic development in America, but it was not to remain.

"Merchant" was the business term and title in that day and it was not until the 1830s that the American version "business man" supplanted it as Americans tired of mercantilism and all that it brought to the people. This new American entrepreneurial mindset and economics propelled the national economic trajectory such that the nation would eventually equal and/or eclipse the European "Old World" businesses and economies in most industries by the late 1800s.[9]

> *Market processes aren't races, with winners and losers. When two parties voluntarily agree to exchange, they do so because they both expect to benefit, not because they hope they will win and the other will lose.*
> *- Tom Palmer*

In essence, the mercantilism mindset held that wealth was fixed and controlled, because the European view of wealth consisted only of gold and silver. The more of this precious metals a government had in their vaults (stored, not put to good use), the richer and powerful it became, and the poorer others became.[10] It also meant getting permission from the government to start a corporation, because it was an "elaborate scheme of state-sponsored monopolies and

---

[8] http://en.wikipedia.org/wiki/Mercantilism

[9] *Triumphant Democracy* by Andrew Carnegie, whole book showcases it

[10] *Patriot's History of the United States* by Larry Schweikart, pg 11-12

protections of businesses from competition (through protectionist tariffs, for example)."[11] In Smith's *Wealth of Nations*, he wrote: "In the mercantile system, the interest of the consumer is almost constantly sacrificed to that of the producer," i.e. the business. Large corporations with substantial revenue and cash reserves support this system of regulations as it over burdens small businesses and deters new competitors with high costs, thereby restricting commerce.[12]

The prevailing British monarchial and "political" attitudes saw the American colonies merely as a source of raw materials for England, rather than a more economically opportunistic place for creating manufacturing businesses.

The colonists had fled class-ridden conformity or outright tyranny and started fresh in a new land and created a culture of those willing to dare, to take a risk. Not just to be innovative, creating a new idea, but inventive, *putting the innovations to good use*. Colonialists became more than inventors, they became entrepreneurs.[13] Israel Kirzner writes:

> *Only in a society where entrepreneurs are free to make errors, can we expect an outpouring of entrepreneurship to lift its economy to new, hitherto unglimpsed, heights of prosperity. Only where potential entrepreneurs are free to follow the lure of profits as they see them, will there be the unleashing of entrepreneurial vision, daring, and judgment that creates profits in fact—and in **so doing, creates new, more valuable ways of utilizing resources** (emphasis added).[14]*

As some businesses became more successful, monarchs, aristocrats, and others got involved. For example, the East India Corporation was chartered in 1600 in England and ultimately its corporate shareholders were wealthy businessmen and aristocrats.

---

[11] *How Capitalism Saved America* by Thomas DiLorenzo, pg 44

[12] *How Capitalism Saved America* by Thomas DiLorenzo, pg 43-48

[13] *They Made America* by Harold Evans, pg 10-11

[14] *The Economics of Errant Entrepreneurs* by Israel Kirzner

The East India Company was struggling in the mid 1700s to survive financially and was given a "tax break," a subsidy of £1,000,000, and a monopoly in the Tea Act in 1773.[15] Over time the American's saw the British colonial policies changed in: taxes, occupation by a standing army, and 150 years of commercial regulations becoming more discriminatory.

Americans realized the Tea Act of 1773 was a dangerous precedent that threatened free trade and the tax was a scheme to ease the colonists into an imperial tax burden. Some towns took protested. On the other hand, Boston answered more dramatically with the Boston Tea Party, dumping a total of 90,000 pounds of tea into the harbor. In addition, the tea tax was to be used to pay for the support of royal governors and other royal officials in America, thus redirecting accountability of the royal administration to the crown instead of answering to the people they were governing.[16]

> FEAR can have two meanings:
> Forget Everything And Run;
> Face Everything And Rise

Some colonists, including Ben Franklin, condemned the flagrant destruction of property in the Boston Tea Party and called for Bostonians to refund the substantial value of the tea. Such restitution might have helped to resolve the growing colonial crisis. The British view of the near sacred status of property—where courts were known to hang paupers for stealing a loaf of bread—saw the Boston Tea Party as worse than a riot, and parliament sought not restitution, but retribution with the Intolerable Acts of 1774, ending local self government and closing down Boston's commerce.[17]

It was the parliament's economic sanctions that stifled and upset the Americans. "Increasing numbers of colonists wished to have greater control over their destiny, and steadily more of the

---

[15] http://en.wikipedia.org/wiki/East_India_Company

[16] *Independence* by John Ferling, pg 44-41

[17] *Independence* by John Ferling, pg 41-42

best educated and the affluent were growing restive with the limitations for advancement that they faced simply because they were colonists. By 1773 many Americans had come to think like Samuel Adams, who had recently written that it was 'the Business of America to take care of itself.'"[18] All the various legislative changes concerning America convinced the Americans they were being reduced to absolute despotism. They outlined their list of grievances in the Declaration of Independence.

America's Yankee business and economic know-how was created over decades of accumulated and "closely held" knowledge and these skills and experiences would be brought to bear in the new nation, then later against the world with a national view in their limited global competitive environment. The Yankees were throwing off the burden of government and embracing capitalism. And all economic activity, capitalism, can then be summarized with a question—"How have you served your fellow man?"—and an imperative—"Prove it!"[19]

Pilgrims. The Jamestown settlement started in 1607 and the Pilgrims landed in Plymouth in the fall of 1620 knowing all about the early economic disasters at Jamestown.[20] The Plymouth investors wrongly assumed that establishing a form of communal labor was the most profitable arrangement to return their investments. However, under this approach each worker attempted to exploit their fellow workers by freeloading. After working under this approach over the course of many months, most of the settlers grew destitute. Plymouth governor William Bradford wrote in his classic *Of Plymouth Plantation,* that,

> *They began to come into wants, many sold away their clothes and bed coverings; others (so base were they) became servants to the Indians, and would cut them wood and fetch them water, for a cap full of corn; others fell to plain stealing, both night and day, from the Indians, of which they grievously complained. In the end, ... some starved and*

---

[18] *Independence* by John Ferling, pg 38-39

[19] *American Entrepreneur* by Larry Schweikart, pg 11

[20] *How Capitalism Saved America* by Thomas DiLorenzo, pg 57-67

died with cold and hunger. One in gathering shellfish was so weak as he stuck fast in the mud, and was found dead in the place.

Bradford's comments made it clear that communal labor, where everyone was expected to work and contribute for the common good, demoralized the community far more than other issues. Pilgrims laboring for other Pilgrims caused most of their conflicts. The industrious were forced to subsidize the slackers.

How was this identified as the problem? What was the solution? How does an elected leader encourage individuals and a community to be more productive? After about two years of failing at this approach, Bradford changed course. Rather than having a communal plot of land that all Pilgrims farmed, he writes:

And so assigned to every family a parcel of land, according to the proportion of their number for that end, only for present use (but made no division for inheritance), and ranged all boys and youth under some family. **This had very good success; for it made all hands very industrious, so as much more corn was planted then otherwise would have been by any means the Governor or any other could use, and saved him a great deal of trouble, and gave far better content. The women now went willingly into the field, and took their little ones with them to set corn, which before would allege weakness, and inability; whom to have compelled would have been thought great tyranny and oppression** *(emphasis added).*[21]

Bradford's switch made all the difference in individual, and thus the community's, productivity. This change redefined the Pilgrim's economic experience and the motivational change was between three views on a continuum: *selfish*-interest on one end, *self*-interest in the middle, and *slave*-interest on the other end. Selfish-interest is only helping the community of me, myself, and I, an "I win, you lose" perspective. Self-interest can be seen as primarily taking care of oneself, with an eye for self-reliance and

---

[21] http://mith.umd.edu//eada/html/display.php? docs=bradford_history.xml #210, #216, #217

self-sacrifice to get ahead, and then secondarily helping others, such as family and friends. Slave-interest is everyone contributing to the common good with little to no opportunity to better one's or one's family's economic situation.

American Revolution, Founding Fathers, and economic liberties. The Pilgrims' newly found economic freedom allowed the colonists to take full advantage of the abundant resources that were around them and the Yankee know-how to get it done was soon engrained into the American psyche. That is, until the mid 1700s when the British began their economic policies of "taxation without representation" and other legislation to help fund their wars and wrest economic control from the soon-to-be rebellious colonialists' hands.

By 1775, the American economy was a hundred times larger than the 1630s (whaling and fishing generated a boom in ship construction, the U.S. was the world's third largest maritime fleet), so much so that some colonists had even accumulated enough wealth to be millionaires by today's standards. Thus, during the mid 1700s, the ever increasing economic restrictions of the Molasses (1733), Sugar (1764), Stamp (1765), Townshend (1767), and Tea (1773) Acts enacted by the British increasingly provided fuel for the American Revolution. The British attempt to control the Americans came through taxes to aggrandize funds for British war debts. The spark came during the Battle of Lexington and Concord as the "shot heard 'round the world."[22]

In Andrew Carnegie's 1886 book *Triumphant Democracy,* he writes about America's colonial experience:

> *During the colonial period the industries of America were cramped and repressed by the illiberal policy of the imperial government. The occupations of the people were necessarily confined to those connected with the cultivation of the soil. The varied pursuits which now distinguish the Republic were unknown. 'The colonies have no right to manufacture even so much as a horseshoe nail,' was the dictum of a leading English statesman; and in accordance with this doctrine, the early settlers were hampered by restrictions which, but for their injurious effect on American industries, would appear*

---

[22] *How Capitalism Saved America* by Thomas DiLorenzo, pg 67-78

ludicrous to us of modern times. The manufacture of hats was forbidden; the making of paper gave offense; and even the weaving of homespun cloth for domestic use was regarded as indicating a rebellious spirit. Iron could not be manufactured beyond the condition of pig; and none but British vessels were permitted to trade with the colonies.[23]

Samuel Adams stated, "Wealth had corrupted the mother country ... and had driven Britain's rulers to try to get their hands on American revenue in order to feed their wastrel habits."[24]

The Americans had a devotion and abiding love toward their mother country Great Britain, and the British merchants and people petitioned for a conciliatory tone toward America's plight. Even King George said of the American crisis, "I do not want to drive them [Americans] to despair but to Submission," but most of the British press and the British policies changed from the initial carrot and stick attitude to a small stick and large stick approach.[25] American attitudes responded in kind.

America's Colonial population split about into thirds, political conservatives, the British Loyalists (Tories), wanted most to avoid war and the threats of economic boycotts, while the liberals (Whigs) were pushing for independence, with moderates in between.[26] However, the small Jewish American population split as well, but overwhelmingly favored and ultimately supported the Revolution, seeking freedom of opportunity, until then severely restricted in other nations. Haym Salomon, part of the Sons of Liberty, helped finance the war and later died penniless, while the Jews of St. Eustatius (Carribean island) became a major arms center for the Americans. The supplies and the island's business class were destroyed by British Admiral Sir George Rodney, whose goal was to cut off aide to the American rebels.[27]

---

[23] *Triumphant Democracy* by Andrew Carnegie, pg 76

[24] *Independence* by John Ferling, pg 54

[25] *Independence* by John Ferling, pg 91-99

[26] *Independence* by John Ferling, pg 71-77

[27] http://jewishmag.com/80mag/usa3/usa3.htm

Over time, the British heavy-handed legislative actions were seen as: restricting the American dream of pecuniary gain; relegating Americans to second class citizens by the British government; and the American's desire for greater autonomy increased. These and other grievances constantly pushed more Americans toward liberalism, liberty, and independence.[28]

Of the 56 signors [29] of the Declaration of Independence, 13 were merchants (businessmen), seven were large land speculators, 11 speculated on large securities, and 14 owned or managed large plantations. While 35 had legal training, most did not practice law. During the American Revolution, some of the British Loyalists (around 20 percent of the total U.S. colonial population) left for Canada or the Caribbean. They later came back, but the effect of American Revolution damage was done. "The departure of so many royal officials, rich merchants and landed gentry destroyed the hierarchical networks that had dominated most of the colonies" until that time, but this change allowed a new upward economic mobility and wealth for others. This new attitude was carried into the early 1800s and beyond.[30]

> One person's trash is another person's treasure.

When Benjamin Franklin exited the Constitutional Convention he was asked, "Sir, what have you given us?" Franklin's immediate response was, "A republic, Ma'am, if you can keep it."[31] Those at the Convention did not see their new perspective of government as one of political *parties*, but of political *power*, that continuum between two extremes: tyranny (100% power) on one end and anarchy (0% power) on the other. The American Revolution shifted power from King George's monarchy (ruler of one) and it's smaller governmental brother

---

[28] *Independence* by John Ferling, pg 71-77

[29] http://en.wikipedia.org/wiki/
Founding_Fathers_of_the_United_States

[30] http://en.wikipedia.org/wiki/Loyalist_(American_Revolution)

[31] http://www.wimp.com/thegovernment/

Oligarchy (ruled by a few), moved past Democracy (rule by majority) but stopped just short of reaching Anarchy (rule by no one). America's Declaration of Independence started this process, but it would take a little over a decade before the right path was achieved, forming a Republic (rule of law).

Initially America's Declaration of Independence started a new form of government resulting in the drafting of the Articles of Confederation, a sort of "Committee of States" having no executive, judiciary, taxing, nor enforcement power. It was a step away from Anarchy, but was too loose of a form of government with states holding all the power with little to no "federal" or centralized elements to help shape national issues among the states. General Washington saw over 2,000 soldiers die at Valley Forge and elsewhere because of this constitutional weakness of the lack of a central government in the Articles of Confederation. To fix this problem, Congress debated for months over what the Constitution should provide and compromised in 1787 and formed a Republic (rule of law) which included the Executive, Judiciary, Legislative branches and other elements.[32]

> A people however, who are possessed of the spirit of commerce, who see, and who will pursue their advantages, may achieve almost anything.
> - George Washington, 1784, Letter to Benjamin Harris

The Declaration of Independence, the US Constitution, and the Bill of Rights were designed as a package to ensure there were "check and balances" of this new addition of federal power. The Constitutional Convention created the House (size based on US population) and the Senate (two Senators per state) that balanced representation between the small and large states. In addition, if Americans decided they elected the wrong representatives, it allowed for a quick legislative course change with House elections occur ever two years and the Senate every six years. The House/Senate compromise created a balance between changing too fast and too slow, and large versus small.

---

[32] *The 5000 Year Leap* by W. Cleo Skousen, pg 9

America's attitudes about what they were fighting for in the young nation is best described by an American Revolutionary General named Francis "Swamp Fox" Marion. In the early 1780s he had hid in the hills and swamps of South Carolina with his militia. On being approached by a British officer to discuss an exchange of prisoners, Marion invited him to stay for dinner and the officer accepted the offer. Seeing no visible provisions and the Americans take out cooked sweet potatoes from the fire, the British officer laughed heartily. He wondered out loud if the Americans were getting better food or pay for doing this, right?

"Worse" said Marion about their food and pay.

"How can you stand it?" asked the British officer.

"I would rather fight to obtain the blessing of freedom for my country, and feed on roots, than desert the cause."

When the British officer returned to his commander he was asked why he looked so serious, "I have cause, sir, to look so," was his reply. "Why," said his commander, in alarm, "has Washington defeated Sir Henry Clinton?"

"No sir: but more than that. I have seen an American general and his men without pay, and almost without clothes, living upon roots, and drinking water, *and all for liberty* (emphasis added). What chance have we against such men?"[33]

The same attitude can be said for entrepreneurs and the various economic or business opportunities that come within their reach. It's the opportunity and the freedom to better both the entrepreneur's and their customer's life.

While the Declaration of Independence was signed in 1776, the US Constitution was finally ratified in 1787. Even then, when some of the larger states threatened to reject the Constitution, they were asked to ratify the current version and then invited to suggest any amendments: submitting over two hundred, almost one hundred were unduplicated. James Madison reduced them to twelve and ten were finally ratified by the states with Madison playing a significant role in the creation of what has become America's Bill of Rights.[34]

---

[33] *Life of Washington* by Anna C. Reed, pg 156-159

[34] usconstitution.net/madisonbor.html

During the 1700s, the British Loyalists and the American "aristocracy" saw no conflict of interest economically in using public office to enrich themselves, and that only they should be entrusted with America's economic stewardship. The end of the American Revolution at the end of the 1700s brought a new sense and view of both entrepreneurship and economics (although those specific words were never used) to the young new American nation: individualistic, self-determining, competitive, and anti-aristocrat.[35] This new social, philosophical, and economic outlook caught on and soon became a contest and race between the ideas of the old government-granted mercantilist monopoly of chartered corporations and the new burgeoning free enterprise system: It was all about an earned success, not selected, given, or inherited.

A postscript about the American Revolutionary War: If the Americans had lost, some serious consequences would have changed America's national makeup. England had discussed and suggested a plan: Parliament would have power to tax within America, the Church of England would be established in the thirteen colonies as the state church, and a hereditary aristocracy would be established. Unbeknownst to Americans, this was sketched out in 1763 before the American Revolution.[36]

America in the 1800s. While the American Revolution somewhat disengaged it's political and economic trajectory from England's, corporate (business) charters still were the lay of the business landscape in America. Individual states could still create the charters and select and carve up which part of a state's economy each of any prestigious "aristocratic" families would receive, but the Revolutionary War had "let the cat out of the bag" and the American public grew ever more hostile to continuing with the old economic idea of mercantilism. Older, less adaptable merchants saw they could no longer freeze out new entrepreneurs thus business competition had begun.

---

[35] *The First Tycoon: Life of Cornelius Vanderbilt*, T. J. Stiles, pg 41, 95

[36] *How the British Gun Control Program Precipitated the American Revolution* by David Kopel, Charleston Law Review Dec 2012

Then, in 1824 the Supreme Court landmark decision *Gibbons v. Ogden* held that the power to regulate interstate commerce was granted to Congress by the Commerce Clause of the United States Constitution. Deciding in favor of Gibbons, the decision struck down the states' right to grant monopolistic charters, thus opening the competitive floodgates in the travel and other industries. Chief Justice Marshall said, "Commerce, undoubtably, is traffic, but it is something more; it is intercourse." Marshall could see into the future and see commerce, free and abundant, moving across state boundaries, and gave voice to what Americans now believed was a basic right.[37]

America's Founders came to the realization of the now classically liberal principle that government had no "legitimate business interfering with a person's *right to earn a living* unless doing so was necessary to protect the public health and safety" (although this principle was often violated in practice).[38] While America's economic shift from a few "chosen" corporate chartered businesses to individual and entrepreneurial ones was a fresh beginning in the American economic mindset—the idea that some governmental subsidies to businesses were legitimate policies was still just below the surface of the national debate. That is, until these governmental subsidies created havoc with many state taxes and budgets after the Civil War.[39]

Until the year 1800, there were sixty-nine private road building companies chartered by the states, building and operating turnpikes in America.[40] For most of the first half of the 1800s, the arguments for using government-subsidized investments in America's roads, canals, and railroads for so-called "internal improvements" were in the minority, but over time they grew more vocal. The decades-long discussion between using public money to finance public works projects and letting the private sector handle the investment was a constant battle.

---

[37] *The First Tycoon: Life of Cornelius Vanderbilt*, T. J. Stiles, pg 63-65

[38] *The Right to Earn a Living*, Tim Sandefur, pg 39-49

[39] *How Capitalism Saved America*, Thomas DiLorenzo, pg 91

[40] *How Capitalism Saved America*, Thomas DiLorenzo, pg 84

President Andrew Jackson said of these "corporate welfare" subsidies that they were "saddling upon the government the *losses of unsuccessful private speculation* (emphasis added)." Jackson's comments were ignored as many of the states took on debt to finance these new projects, but his words would come to haunt these state decisions. By 1875 the failures of these subsidies were so pronounced that all the states except Massachusetts had amended their constitutions to prohibit any further internal improvement subsidies.[41]

Railroads were a part of these improvements during the mid to late 1800s. Most promising the Union Pacific and Central Pacific railroads building the Transcontinental Railroad. Federal and state governments, in the "need for speed" laying tracks, created various production incentives such as land grants and sizable governmental loans per mile of track laid. These metrics used for the subsidized railroads incentivized poor building workmanship: winding, circuitous, extended routes to collect for more mileage; choosing cheap and light wrought iron rails (failed to handle heavy rail traffic); using lower quality wood for rail ties (required quicker replacement); laying rails on top of snow and ice during winters (required to be rebuilt in the springtime); and made the roads in farm and unsettled land (causing farmer and Indian skirmishes).[42]

> *Work, hard work, intelligent work, and then more work.*
> *- James J. Hill, when asked by a reporter to reveal the secret of his success*

The evidence of the comparison between subsidized and private investments for profit came to a head. All the major railroads that were started and received U.S. government land grants and other subsidies suffered bankruptcies during the 1893 Panic, except for the Great Northern (GN) railroad, which was privately owned and operated by James J. Hill and was one of the best constructed and most profitable of the world's railroads.

---

[41] *How Capitalism Saved America*, Thomas DiLorenzo, pg 79-92

[42] *Myth of the Robber Barrons* by Burton Folsom, pg 22-23

Hill bought the bankrupted Minnesota railroad that had been run into the ground by the government-subsidized Northern Pacific (NP), which was recklessly built. Hill's decisions to use higher quality rails and ties, lower topographical grade routes (finding the cost-saving "Lost Marias Pass" over the Continental Divide), his win/win vision with his rail customers, and superior strategic business decisions allowed him ultimately to beat his subsidized competitors with a more effective and efficient railroad transportation system for his customers.[43]

Hill's motto, "We have got to prosper with you or we have got to be poor with you," was a significant part of his overall customer and business strategy. He provided free seed grain; imported sheep, cattle, and hogs; and helped create "model farms" to educate his farmer customer base on the latest developments in agricultural science. He also knew that monopolistic price gouging of his customers would equate to killing the goose that lays the golden egg. Thus he believed in having a community of interest.[44]

During the middle to late 1800s, most Americans began to know the names and avidly followed the "captains of industry," such as Cornelius Vanderbilt, John D. Rockefeller, Andrew Carnegie, James J. Hill, Charles Schwab, and the Scrantons. There was no higher goal for a young American male than to become a "self-made man,"—to make their way through hard work.

Vanderbilt's view of business and his personal life was as such: "I manage it [a railroad corporation] just as I would manage my individual property."[45] Not until the post Civil War era of the late 1870s did the rise of the populist movement, emphasizing the individualistic values of self-reliance that they believed were being threatened by industrial-age capitalism, and the progressive movement, emphasizing unity and collectivism, begin to take root in America.[46]

---

[43] *James J. Hill* by Michael P. Malone, pg 131

[44] *James J. Hill* by Michael P. Malone, pg 198

[45] *The First Tycoon: The Epic Life of Cornelius Vanderbilt* by Stiles, pg 443

[46] *The Right to Earn a Living*, Tim Sandefur, pg 44

Carnegie writes in his 1886 book *Triumphant Democracy*, when the mother United Kingdom created the child America, what America initially received was great tutelage. But once America realized the freedom of being grown up and the yoke of heavy-handed bondage of the British government's unfair taxes and aristocracy was thrown off, America began to out produce the rest of the world in nearly all industry sectors within 100 years of its birth. Industries such as watches, newspapers, lumber, pig-iron, shipbuilding, mining, agriculture, art, music, literature, railroads, textiles, and others. "So it is in every branch of manufacture, so rapidly is the child land dwarfing her illustrious mother. One has only to have faith in the Republic. She never yet betrayed the head that trusted, or the heart that loved her."[47]

Carnegie also writes, "In Mr. Pidgeon's clever book, 'Old World Questions and New World Answers,'[48] which is, upon the whole, the best book of its kind that I know of, we find the author unerringly placing his finger upon the one secret of the Republic's success, viz.: *the respect in which labor is held* (emphasis added)." Throughout his book Carnegie shows how the freedom of labor is respected and that respect transcends throughout America, versus England's caste system: "The parent land will become in Europe what the Republic is upon the American continent—the unselfish, the true and trusted counsellor, guide,

> Head service or hand service, it is heart service that counts. - Andrew Carnegie

friend, of its less powerful, less advanced nations. It is not by wicked conquest over other States, but by honest, peaceful labor within its own bounds and with the good will of all its neighbors that the Democracy builds up the State."

Carnegie summarizes the results of the new American nation's attitude, "Thank God, these (natural resource) treasures are in the hands of an intelligent people, the Democracy, to be used for the general good of the masses, and not made the spoils

---

[47] *Triumphant Democracy* by Andrew Carnegie, pg 163

[48] archive.org/details/oldworldquestion00pidgiala

of monarchs, courts, and aristocracy, to be turned to the base and selfish ends of a privileged hereditary class."[49]

However, the rise of both populism and progressivism in the late 1800s represented a shift in American political philosophy. From a free-market and entrepreneurial approach, with customers voting with their money, to corporatism: "corporate welfare," "industrial policy," or a "partnership/collaboration between business and government" with politicians and special interests deciding which projects would being subsidized, influenced, and in some cases controlled by citizen tax dollars and political forces. With no skin or personal investments in the game, politicians rarely picked winning industries to invest in, usually putting increasingly good money into bad investments to disguise squandered tax dollars.

There has always been a time in America when there has been a mixture of both free-market entrepreneurs and political entrepreneurs, or neomercantilism, with parties using government force to control the market, but it is a matter of how much of a free market there is. As American and world history has shown, government aid and subsidies breed inefficiencies, which create consumer wrath. Consumer wrath leads to government regulation, and government regulation leads to more government involvement and dependence. Thus, governments can both create problems and then try to solve them, mostly with unintended consequences: New bad laws don't fix old bad laws.

As written in Smith's chapter of Of Merit and Demerit in his book *Moral Sentiments*, the qualities of deserving reward and of punishment shows how the actions and conduct of a business are both rewarded and punished by their customers. When a business has the right incentives in place, effective and efficient business results are rewarded ultimately with sales and profits, ineffective and inefficient results are penalized with less business or losses. Sometimes the wrath of consumers is ignited over a major business issue and all businesses can be targeted, sometimes erroneously. If a consumer makes a wrong choice, they can change their buying habits and shop elsewhere. However, if a

---

[49] *Triumphant Democracy* by Andrew Carnegie, pg 182

government official, bureaucrat, or worker makes a mistake, the taxpayers suffer the consequences.

Early 1900s: Growth of Government. From the birth of the American nation, the size of the our state and federal governments has grown and shrunk depending on needs, remaining mostly small and limited. During the late 1800s and early 1900s, the populist and progressive movements together with scientific and religious groups cause social reform fervor to grow. It culminated with passing the sixteenth through the nineteenth amendments during the 1910s. The sixteenth amendment allows the federal government to collect income tax; with the initial tax rates from *one to seven percent.*

During WWI, the government raised income taxes to a high of 77% to help pay U.S. war expenses. Because most people considered war to be short term, they willingly suffered through the economic hurt, convinced they would be building their lives and communities back up again once the war ended. In most cases, high tax rates rarely cover the true cost of war and once the war ended, Wilson and others maintained that the high tax rates were needed to pay down the war debt.

In the 1920 election, Wilson lost to Harding and his "Return to Normalcy" platform. Harding picked wealthy banker, industrialist, and philanthropist Andrew Mellon as his Secretary of Treasury, who saw the solutions to paying down the national debt and increasing economic activity much differently than Wilson. Mellon, who stayed through Hoover's administration, outlined his economic government policy plan in his 1924 book *Taxation: The People's Business* :

The problem of the Government is to fix rates which will bring in a maximum amount of revenue to the Treasury and at the same time bear not too heavily on the taxpayer or on business enterprises. A sound tax policy must take into consideration three factors. It must produce sufficient revenue for the Government; it must lessen, so far as possible, the burden of taxation on those least able to bear it and it must also remove those influences which might retard the continued steady development of business and industry on which, in the last analysis, so much of our prosperity depends...Any man of energy and initiative in this country can get what he wants out of life. But when that initiative is crippled by legislation or by a tax system which denies him the right to receive a reasonable share of his earnings, then he will no longer exert himself and the country will be deprived of the energy on which its continued greatness depends...The Government is just a business, and can and should be run on business principles...If the spirit of business adventure is killed, this country will cease to hold the foremost position in the world. And yet it is this very spirit which excessive surtaxes are now destroying. Any one at all in touch with affairs knows of his own knowledge of buildings which have not been built, of businesses which have not been started, and of new projects which have been abandoned, all for the one reason high surtaxes. If failure attends, the loss is borne exclusively by the adventurer, but if success ensues, the Government takes more than half of the profits. People argue the risk is not worth the return...The real problem to determine is what plan results in the least burden to the people and the most revenue to the Government. [50]

Those in government after the war feared losing tax revenue if tax rates were reduced, but as an experienced financier, Mellon was able to persuade Presidents Harding and Coolidge and legislators to cut the top marginal tax rate (from 73% to 58% in 1922 down to 24% in 1929) and reduce other tax rates, as well. (Note: FDR campaigned on fiscal conservatism against Hoover, but actually increased the tax rate to 79% in 1937; his governmental policies, control, and spending were commensurate with the added taxes raised.)

Mellon "compared the government setting tax rates on incomes to a business owner setting prices on products, 'If the price is fixed too high, sales drop off and with them profit.'"[51] His winning argument to substantially cut the tax rates in lower brackets was to relieve the tax burdens of those in middle-class to poor households. Mellon as the nation's top government financier and any experienced business person knows, reducing

---

[50] http://archive.org/details/taxationthepeopl033026mbp , pg 22

[51] *The Myth of the Robber Barons* by Burton Folsom, pg 109-110

government tax rates and spending below the levels of tax revenue creates tax revenue surpluses.

With the size of government slimmed, and its spending and tax rates reduced, the revenue surplus generated by Mellon's fiscal policies and actions reduced the overall public debt (the national debt skyrocketed from $1.5 billion in 1916 to $24 billion in 1919 because of World War I obligations) from a high of $33 billion in 1919 to about $16 billion in 1929.[52] The Tax Revenue Collected table and graph illustrates Mellon and Coolidge's sound fiscal and tax policies for the American government and populace. Not only do the rich pay more, but the poor paid less, thus relieving the middle class and poor from the burden of unfair taxes and shifting the tax burden to the rich.

Mellon also championed preferential treatment for "earned" income relative to "unearned" income:

Tax Revenue Collected by Income Grouping		
before and after 1926 tax cuts (in millions of constant 1929 dollars)*		
Income	1921	1926
<$10,000	$155.1	$32.5
$10-25,000	$121.8	$70.3
$25-50,000	$108.3	$109.4
$50-100,000	$111.1	$136.6
>$100,000	$194.0	$361.5
Total	$690.3	$710.3
* *The Myth of the Robber Barons* by Burton Folsom, pg 108		

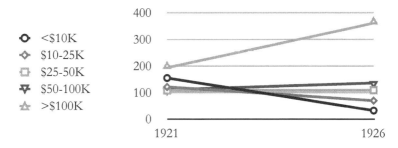

Chart 1: Tax Revenue Collected by Income Grouping

---

[52] usgovernmentdebt.us

The fairness of taxing more lightly income from wages, salaries from investments is beyond question. In the first case, the income is uncertain and limited in duration; sickness or death destroys it and old age diminishes it; in the other, the source of income continues; the income may be disposed of during a man's life and it descends to his heirs. Surely we can afford to make a distinction between the people whose only capital is their mettle and physical energy and the people whose income is derived from investments. Such a distinction would mean much to millions of American workers and would be an added inspiration to the man who must provide a competence during his few productive years to care for himself and his family when his earnings capacity is at an end.[53]

In between the progressive and restrictive economics of the Wilson and the Hoover/FDR presidencies was Coolidge and Mellon's highly successful economic policies, creating the Roaring Twenties. But it was not until ten years after the Wall Street crash of 1929 and under the FDR administration's economic policies, FDR's Secretary of the Treasury, Henry Morgenthau, Jr., told the House Ways and Means Committee in May 1939:

We have tried spending money. We are spending more than we have ever spent before and it does not work. And I have just one interest, and if I am wrong...somebody else can have my job. I want to see this country prosperous. I want to see people get a job. I want to see people get enough to eat. We have never made good on our promises...I say after eight years of this administration we have just as much unemployment as when we started...And an enormous debt to boot![54]

Mellon's view, based on his years of business and government experience, echoed what Bradford learned about motivating the Pilgrims 300 years earlier. The principle that the right setting and environment has a lot to do with motivating others to work and to take risks; the basis for any entrepreneur starting a business is

[53] http://archive.org/details/taxationthepeopl033026mbp

[54] *New Deal or Raw Deal?* by Burt Folsom Jr., pg 2-3

to better their lives. So the right to earn a living comes with the responsibility of the government to allow each person the right to pursue "life, liberty, and the pursuit of happiness."

Carnegie best concludes about life in America:

> *Americans have been praised for their energy, their devotion to education, and to religion, their inventiveness, their resolute payment of debt, and for other qualities, but who could have believed that a leading statesman of Britain would cite their high courage and stubbornness to the old bulldog race of Britons. Mr. Chamberlain, however, in my opinion, does the original race injustice. Men decreed by the laws of a State unworthy at birth to be equal citizens thereof, have no reason to fight very hard and sacrifice much for its maintenance. Give them the rights of the American, my dear Mr. Chamberlain, and you will then see in Britain what patriotism means.There is not yet in Britain a government **of** the people but a government **and** a people.[55]*

Yankee know-how: Your right to earn a living

Thomas Jefferson penned these words, "We hold these truths to be self-evident, that all men are created equal, that they are endowed by their creator with certain inalienable Rights, that among these are *life, liberty and the pursuit of happiness.*" Those last seven words comprise the essential motivation for individuals and most certainly for any entrepreneur. In *Wealth of Nations,* Smith furthers this thought and writes, "Whoever offers to another a bargain of any kind, proposes to do this. Give me that which I want, and you shall have this which you want, is the meaning of every such offer; and it is in this manner that we obtain from one another the far greater part of those good offices which we stand in need of. *It is not from the benevolence of the butcher, the brewer, or the baker that we expect our dinner, but from their regard to their own interest* (emphasis added)." It is this harmony and agreement between the butcher, baker, and brewer and their customers by which commerce is done. Or, in today's vernacular, Zig Ziglar said,

---

[55] *Triumphant Democracy* by Andrew Carnegie, pg 345

"You can get everything in life you want if you will just help enough other people get what they want."[56]

After escaping slavery via the Underground Railroad, Frederick Douglass became an American social reformer, orator, writer, statesman, and leader of the abolitionist movement. He was a face, the black face, of a man and an honorable segment of American society who understood an individual's right to earn a living is a moral case. In 1838, Douglass reached New York and found work carrying coal into a white woman's house, earning two silver half dollars. He wrote, "I was not only a freeman, but a free-working man, and no Master Hugh stood ready at the end of the week *to seize my hard earnings* (emphasis added)."

You have a natural right as a talented, skilled, and free person to earn a living. Earning a living comes down to two basic issues: receiving a just reward for your *labor* and being able to own *property* (both physical and intellectual property). Both labor and property are intertwined as an employee, but as an entrepreneur, it's more so and the drive or motivation that propels one to do more. "If morality is to be a guide for human survival, it must place special emphasis on those productive virtues by which such wealth is created." "One has the right to provide a better life for oneself through work, trade, and commercial enterprise" because *nature does not give it to human beings; it must be earned* through applying one's mind and body to a task or endeavor.[57]

Profit (or loss) = a compass and reward. Profit is the ultimate goal for the entrepreneur, and it is both a compass (*where should I spend my time and efforts?*) and a reward (the greater the *reward* means the greater the profits). It also means that any mistakes made by the entrepreneur show up in smaller profits or even losses. Benjamin Franklin said, "The way to wealth is as plain as the way to market. It depends chiefly on two words, industry and frugality; that is, waste neither time nor money, but make the best use of both. Without industry and frugality nothing will do; with them, everything."

---

[56] *Secrets of Closing the Sale* by Zig Ziglar

[57] *The Right to Earn a Living* by Tim Sandefur, pg 3

Labor (employee versus entrepreneur). Finding a *job* is different from finding *work;* the word job is limiting and specific while finding work is more opportunistic and open. Using your labor to make a table, create a marketing brochure, or mowing a lawn exists in the context of being paid hourly or a salary. The fruits of your labor are your property; you either sell them to an employer as a job or work, or you sell them as an entrepreneur.

Property. The Pilgrims solved the motivational issue of working and being productive with Bradford's solution of giving everyone their own property to work as they pleased. And pleased them it did, as their self-interest took hold and they became more productive.

When you work for an organization, it normally owns what you create under its direction. However, if you create a solution that does not compete with your employer, you can sell that, as long as you were never tasked with solving that problem by your employer. In this instance, creating this product or service becomes your property and it's your property to sell.[58] The issues surrounding work continue, whether it's being motivated, doing the work, or protecting your ideas and work through various laws. Motivation is the key.

Motivation. Benjamin Franklin said of the poor, "I am for doing good to the poor, but I think the best way of doing good to the poor, is not making them easy in poverty, but leading or driving them out of it. I observed that the more public provisions were made for the poor, the less they provided for themselves, and of course became poorer. And, on the contrary, the less was done for them, the more they did for themselves, and became richer." The motto of the day was: if you don't work, you don't eat. Once the Pilgrims under Bradford changed the rules the Pilgrims lived by, the results improved, but there was something else afoot during our Founding Father's time as more wealth was created.

> *Having been poor is no shame, but being ashamed of it, is.*
> *- Benjamin Franklin*

---

[58] Consult with intellectual property professionals.

John Adams sent a letter to Thomas Jefferson on December 21, 1819 in which he posed the question, "Will you tell me how to prevent riches from becoming the effects of temperance and industry? Will you tell me how to prevent riches from producing luxury? Will you tell me how to prevent luxury from producing effeminacy, intoxication, extravagance, Vice, and folly?"[59]

In other words, the Founding Fathers were asking very important questions: How does one prevent the poor and the rich from quitting working: the former by just giving up, feigning sickness, or preying on those by force or crime; the latter, to use their wealth to restrict competition with legislation and laws or using their wealth to take another's wealth by force?

Right environment breeds prosperous entrepreneurs

The conclusion to be made from the above historical information is that a small, smart role of a government body means the greater potential there is for economic growth and prosperity. It also means the greater need for high morals, ethics, good citizenship, and laws with which to conduct business: a win/win/win (consumers, businesses, and governments) for a society. At any time, if one of those three segments gets an upper hand to dominate or to rule, they will ultimately use laws to take advantage of the other two. That is why America's Founding Fathers chose to structure and limit our federal government in such a fashion that no overly powerful part of our government would be able to control the people with impunity.

Most Americans had a similar view about this governmental foundation. John Adams said of the efforts to establish a new government, "Our Constitution was made only for a moral and religious people. It is wholly inadequate to the government of any other." George Washington said, "Human rights can only be assured among a virtuous people. The general government . . . can never be in danger of degenerating into a monarchy, an oligarchy, an aristocracy, or any despotic or oppressive form so long as there is any virtue in the body of the people." Benjamin

---

[59] *The Adams-Jefferson Letters* Edited by Lester Cappon, pg 551

Franklin made a similar statement regarding virtue, "Only a virtuous people are capable of freedom. As nations become more corrupt and vicious, they have more need of masters."

Testifying before the Bank and Currency Committee of the House of Representatives, in an exchange between Samuel Untermyer, a corporate lawyer, and J. P. Morgan, American financier, Untermyer asked, "Is not commercial credit based primarily upon money or property?"

"No sir," replied Morgan. "The first thing is character."

"Before money or property?"

"Before money or anything else. Money cannot buy it."

Untermyer said, "So that a man with character, without anything at all behind it, can get all the credit he wants, and a man with property cannot get it?"

"That is very often the case."

"That is the rule of business?"

"That is the rule of business, sir...Because a man I do not trust could not get money from me on all the bonds in Christendom."

"That is the rule all over the world?"

"I think that is the fundamental basis of business," replied Morgan.[60]

> If you want children to keep their feet on the ground, put some responsibilities on their shoulders.
> - Abigail Van Buren

As a whole, America believed people's character was tied to liberty, and liberty to property and all three were needed for success. The "surest way to ensure the presence of good character was to keep God at the center of one's life, community, and ultimately, nation. 'Separation of church and state' meant freedom *to* worship, not freedom *from* worship. Yet virtue and character alone were not enough. It took competence, skill, and talent to build a nation." Compared with other nations, it was only in America, "where one was *permitted* to do almost anything,

---

[60] Testimony of J. P. Morgan, Dec 18-19, 1912, before the Bank and Currency Committee of the House of Representatives

but *expected* to do the best thing," did America's virtue germinate and take root.[61]

Entrepreneurial Framework: The US Constitution

We can see from the trend lines of our American history and from comments from our Founding Fathers that there is a real purpose of government for entrepreneurs, individuals, and the community and nation at large. James Madison in Federalist #62wrote, "A good government implies two things: first, fidelity to the object of government, which is the happiness of the people; secondly, a knowledge of the means by which that object can be best attained. Some governments are deficient in both these qualities; most governments are deficient in the first. I scruple not to assert that in American governments too little attention has been paid to the last."

The Law. We all have a natural right—from God, not a government—to defend our person, our liberty, and our property, with the added responsibility of preserving, developing, and improving them. It is up to each of us to apply our individual talents and capabilities to convert our various natural and developed resources into solutions that help man. Since life, liberty, and property came first, the rule of law is the collective organization of the individual's right to lawful defense. The rule of law is intended to protect property and to punish plunder, both the legal (legal taking, eminent domain, etc.) and illegal (crime via fraud, theft, etc.) seizing and consuming of the production of the labors of others.

The law is obligated to be *defensive* in nature, protecting equally every individual's property and rights, preventing harm against others, and to prevent injustice from reigning. It is when the law goes on the *offensive* with legal plunder that the rule of law becomes a weapon of every kind of greed by government, officials, bureaucrats, and corporations using the government to do their bidding. Instead of checking crime, the law itself is guilty

---

[61] *A Patriot's History of the United States* by Larry Schweikart, pg xxii-xxiv

of the very evils it is supposed to punish, defending all forms of plunder and participating in it.

The law becomes perverted by the influence of two entirely different causes: stupid greed (taking/taxing from the many to give to the few), and false philanthropy (doing for others, specifically the poor, what they should be doing for themselves). It is when the law and morality contradict each other, the citizen has the cruel alternative of either losing his moral sense or losing his respect for the law.[62]

The role of government. America's Founding Fathers understood the *sovereignty of the monarch*, but reversed this top-down controlling approach and recognized the *sovereignty of the individual* was the best design and framework for all individuals, to pursue their own happiness. The concentration of power into fewer and fewer people meant a return toward a monarchy, an anathema to the Republic they designed and for which they fought and sacrificed.

Here is how the founders designed the U.S. constitutional framework [63]:

▸ **Separation of Powers. Separation of Powers**. The whole purpose of the separation, rather than balance, of powers is to purposely frustrate government actions of the few against the many. No one person could *make* (Legislative Branch), *interpret* (Judicial Branch), or *carry out* (Executive Branch) the laws. James Madison said it best, "The accumulation of all powers, legislative, executive, and judiciary, in the same hands … may justly be pronounced the very definition of tyranny."

▸ **Consent of the Governed (Popular Sovereignty).** This Popular Sovereignty is granted by God and comes from the Declaration of Independence clause that reads, "All men are *created* equal." This is different from the Divine Right exercised by monarchies with a propensity for wanting more power. Consent of the governed is not by conquest or claimed to divine right. The ninth and tenth amendments to

---

[62] *The Law* by Frederic Bastiat

[63] billofrightsinstitute.org

43

the Bill of Rights were written to limit any future government controls of the people that were not previously enumerated.

▸ **Representative/Republican Government.** The word democracy, rule by a majority, is used quite often to describe the U.S. form of government. The problem with a democracy is that the majority can overrun the minority. Unfortunately, a majority cannot be trusted with all the people's rights any more than a minority or a monarchy can. Democracy is often described as two wolves and a lamb voting on what to have for lunch, while liberty is a well-armed lamb contesting the vote. A representative- or republican-styled government is one where the people elect representatives to carry out their governmental needs and ensure that none are oppressed.

▸ **Rule of Law.** The purpose of the rule of law is manyfold, but the main reason is to protect the common man, because the rich and powerful have always had the wherewithal to manipulate the system for their benefit. The rule of law's *primary purpose is for economic development for people to be secure in the property rights and contracts are enforced.* For the rule of law to work in a nation, laws must be:

- *Known* - Laws are intended to be known by all;

- *Transparent* - Everyone should have access to the process of determining laws;

- *Stable* - Laws are intended to be stable, not vacillating from one extreme to another; this provides a known entity for the people to operate under;

- *Written* - Laws are written down so that they can be reviewed, debated, and changed and are not arbitrarily changed per the whim of one or a few people;

- *Common Man* - The intent is to allow the common man to have their say in court, not to be railroaded by the government, the wealthy, or big businesses;

- *Commitment* - Everyone should have respect for the Rule of Law. This means possessing the ability repeal or replace laws that the citizens do not want.

The phrase "No one is above the law" is a statement of what the constitution outlines for all American citizens and the process by which it was framed and ratified reflects the rule of law, and many of its protections ensure that the United States is, as John Adams explained, "an empire of laws and not of men."

Historical short list of US entrepreneurs

Below is a short list of some prominent Americans who "made it big." As with all individuals, each entrepreneur had faults and/or character flaws which they exhibited starting and building their businesses. There are multiple reasons why these entrepreneurs are here, but the primary reason is that they helped make America with their devotion to equal rights, freedom, and liberating others with their products and services.[64]

> *Success is a learned behavior, so find the best, then learn their behaviors*

Benjamin Franklin (1706–1790, printer, inventor, writer). Franklin was primarily a printer, but was also a leading author, political theorist, politician, postmaster, scientist, musician, inventor, satirist, civic activist, statesman, and diplomat. No one more exemplifies an American entrepreneur than Franklin. In 1758, Franklin wrote an essay, *The Way to Wealth,* a collection of adages and advice to propel others to success.

Thomas Paine (1737–1809, writer, businessman). Paine failed at two marriages (his second wife paid him to leave her) and two businesses, but arriving in America, became a writer during the American Revolution (*Common Sense* and *The American Crisis*). He sold almost half a million copies by 1800, donated all of his profits to the Revolution, and died penniless.

John Jacob Astor (1763–1848, real estate magnate, investor). As a German-American business merchant, he was the first in the U.S.

---

[64] *They Made America* by Harold Evans, whole book about entrepreneurs

to become a millionaire. He financed explorations to find the Northwest Passage after hearing the results of Thomas Jefferson's funding of the Lewis and Clark expedition.

Paul Cuffe (1759–1817, abolitionist, sea captain). Patriot/Quaker businessman, Cuffe sailed ships along the Atlantic coast and to Europe.

Samuel Finley Breese Morse (1791–1872 painter, inventor). Morse began as a painter, commissioned to paint Marquis de Lafayette, who served under Washington during the Revolutionary War. Morse also contributed, with Joseph Henry, to the invention of the single-wire telegraph in 1836. Henry was a scientist, but Morse worked out the practical implications and brought the invention to the marketplace. Morse co-invented Morse Code, which lasted until the late 1990s.

Cornelius Vanderbilt (1794–1877, shipping/railroad magnate, industrialist, philanthropist). Vanderbilt throughly disliked politics and government intervention in business, preferring to compete honorably in the marketplace. He helped the North during the Civil War by donating his $1,000,000 passenger ship, the *Vanderbilt,* to the Federal government. After the war, he was taxed $1,500,000 while the *Vanderbilt* sat rotting in the San Francisco Bay, on which he commented, "Why don't you give me back my ship and I can put it back into service in my business and we can call it even!"

Johns Hopkins (1795-1873, entrepreneur, abolitionist, philanthropist). Johns was a Quaker businessman who sold wares and in payment took corn whiskey. He made most of his money, though, investing his profits in other ventures, including the highly successful Baltimore and Ohio (B&O) railroad. He eventually became a B&O Director, then Chairman of the Finance Committee. His will gave bequests to be used in medical research and training (Johns Hopkins Hospital), and an orphanage.

William Leidesdorff (1810–1848, shipping magnate, hotel and warehouse owner). Leidesdorff was one of the earliest mixed-race U.S. citizens and a highly successful, enterprising businessman in San Francisco. He was a West Indian immigrant of African Cuban, possibly Carib, Danish, and Jewish ancestry.

Samuel Colt (1814–1862, armament manufacturer). Overhearing soldiers talk about the success of the double-barreled rifle and the impossibility of a gun that could shoot five or six times without reloading, he decided he would solve this. On a voyage, he viewed the ship's wheel clutch keeping the wheel locked in place, which gave him an idea for his revolver. Over many years, and many good and bad business and financial issues (lavish spending habits), he was finally successful in making a quality revolver. It was less of his revolver design, but his combination of interchangeable parts, assembly line production, and being a pioneer in the fields of advertising, product placement and mass marketing that helped him succeed against competitors.

P. T. Barnum (1810–1891, entertainer, showman, businessman). Barnum was best known for being a promoter, namely of General Tom Thumb, English singer Jenny Lind, and various celebrated hoaxes. He later founded the circus that became known as the Ringling Brothers and Barnum & Bailey Circus. He was known as a fair businessman, paying Thumb and Lind a base rate for each show and offered profit sharing to both.

Levi Strauss (1829–1902, businessman). Born in Germany to an Ashkenazi Jewish family, Strauss immigrated with his family to America to join his brother's business in New York, later opening a branch of the family's dry goods store in San Francisco. In the 1870s, Jacob Davis, a tailor who designed men's work pants using a combination of denim, stitching, and copper rivets, sought out Strauss as a partner. Strauss left bequests to a number of charities, such as the Pacific Hebrew Orphan Asylum and the Roman Catholic Orphan Asylum.

Philip Danforth Armour (1832–1901, mining support owner, wholesale grocery owner, meat packing industrialist). Armour was a serial entrepreneur whose extensive Armour & Company enterprises helped make Chicago the meatpacking capital of the world.

Friedrich Weyerhäuser (1834–1914, timber magnate, papermill owner, landowner). Weyerhäuser, a German-American, successfully turned around a failing sawmill and went on to found the Weyerhäuser Company in 1899 with the help of James J. Hill.

Andrew Carnegie (1835–1919, steel mogul, philanthropist). Carnegie led the expansion of the American steel industry in the late

1800s, creating U.S. Steel. He became one of the nation's most well-known philanthropists of his time by donating much of his wealth to libraries, schools, and scientific research.

J. P. Morgan (1837–1913, finance). Morgan was an American financier, banker, philanthropist and art collector who dominated corporate finance and industrial consolidation during his time.

James J. Hill (1838–1916 railroad magnate). Hill was the owner of the Great Northern Railroad who always paid a dividend to his stockholders. He was also the only railroad magnate who never went bankrupt.

John D. Rockefeller (1839–1937, oil baron, philanthropist, medical R&D funder, education funder, public health researcher). Rockefeller founded Standard Oil Company; its kerosine replaced whale oil to light and heat homes. While other companies threw away the refined waste (gasoline) of kerosine, he invested his profits in R&D to find sellable products from this waste (petroleum jelly, lubrication oils, grease, etc.) to make additional profits. Rockefeller was also known early on for his continual 10% giving throughout his life, even after retirement. His strategic areas of philanthropy included education (major funding for an African-American college later becoming Spelman College), medical research (hookworm and yellow fever solutions), scientific research, the arts, and public health.

Benjamin Altman (1840–1913, retail magnate). At the age of 25, Altman founded what would become B. Altman & Company, one of New York City's premier and most successful department stores.

Thomas A. Edison (1847–1931, inventor). Edison started out an inventor, later becoming a businessman, but is most well known for his 1,093 patents. The phonograph invention gave him notoriety, while his Menlo Park facility was the first industrial research lab. Nikola Tesla's AC current was the adversary to Edison's DC current technology. Edison waged a propaganda war over which current was better; Tesla's AC current won out because of the better quality electric power distribution.

Alexander Graham Bell (1847–1922, telecommunication inventor). Bell's life was surrounded by the study of sound (elocution and speech), as both his mother and wife were deaf. His natural curiosity was encouraged by his first job at the age of 12, dehusking wheat at a flour mill. He was able to invent a simple machine to make the job easier. Although his school record was undistinguished, marked by absenteeism and lackluster grades, his first patent was for the telephone in 1876, and he started Bell Telephone Company in 1877. In 1915, Bell made the first transcontinental telephone call between New York and San Francisco.

Asa Candler (1851–1929, soft drink producer, real estate magnate, banker, philanthropist). As an American business tycoon, Candler started his business career as drug store owner and manufacturer of patent medicines. He is best known, though, for making his fortune selling Coca-Cola. Purchasing the Coke formula in 1887, his success was built on his aggressive marketing. That success allowed him to make him millions, which he reinvested in Central Bank and Trust, real estate, a funding for the Methodist Church (what would become Emory Hospital), and endowments to numerous schools.

George Eastman (1854–1932, photographer). Eastman was an American innovator and entrepreneur who founded Eastman Kodak and invented roll film, helping to bring photography to the mainstream.

Andrew William Mellon (1855–1937, banker, industrialist, philanthropist). Mellon was an American banker, industrialist, philanthropist, art collector, and Secretary of the Treasury from 1921-1932. In 1924, he wrote *Taxation: The People's Business*[65] which he applied to American economic policies. His ideas helped turn around America's economy after WWI and created the economic boom of the Roaring Twenties.

Henry Parsons Crowell (1855–1943, real estate magnate, oat mill owner, stove inventor). Crowell was the son of a successful merchant who died when Crowell was nine, but he knew he had a talent for business. At the age of 26, with profits from previous real estate sales, he bought the failing Quaker Mill. Crowell, with his partner Frances Drury, started the Perfection Stove Company and in 1901 they were approached by business associates of John D.

---

[65] http://archive.org/details/taxationthepeopl033026mbp

Rockefeller to cross-market each other's products using Standard Oil's salesforce, Crowell's line of stoves, and Rockefeller's kerosine. As a result of his Quaker Oats Company, for more than 40 years he donated over 70 percent of his earnings.

Richard W. Sears (1863–1914, retail mogul). Sears was the founder of Sears, Roebuck and Company, along with his partner, Alvah C. Roebuck. While a railroad station agent, Sears purchased a refused watch shipment and sold the watches for a profit to passersby. Reaping a hefty profit, he moved to Minneapolis and started writing ad copy for rural and small-town farm publications and selling products by mail-order. Sears hired Roebuck as his watch repairman, who later left the company. Sears then hired clothier Julius Rosenwald. Having been raised on a farm, Sears knew what his customers were looking for, and in 1888 his first catalog was published.

> *Thoughts lead to acts, acts lead to habits, habits lead to character, and our character will determine our eternal destiny.*
> *- Tyron Edwards*

Henry Ford (1863–1947, automobile mogul). There were over 3,000 other car companies before Henry Ford started his counter-revolution Ford Motor Company, liberating transportation for the common man ("You can have any color as long as it's black"). His company fought alone in the face of legal warfare by monopolists intent on keeping transportation prices high.

George Washington Carver (1864–1943, scientist, botanist, educator, inventor). With a Masters degree in agriculture, Carver is best known for his focus on economic development and education of sharecroppers. His research into crop rotation and the promotion of alternative crops to cotton, such as peanuts, soybeans, and sweet potatoes stabilized their livelihoods. However, crop surpluses caused prices to drop, angering farmers. So, Carver developed over hundreds of products derived from peanuts, sweet potatoes, and pecans thus ensuring farmers of their livelihoods.

Charles H. James (1864–1929). C.H. James established the nation's oldest black-owned company that evolved into a wholesale fruit and produce distribution house serving independent grocers and restaurants.

Madam C.J. Walker (1867–1919). The first African-American female millionaire. "I am a woman who came from the cotton fields of the South. From there I was promoted to the washtub. From there I was promoted to the cook kitchen. And from there I promoted myself into the business of manufacturing hair goods and preparations…I have built my own factory on my own ground."[66]

Wilbur (1867–1912) and Orville (1871–1948) Wright, (inventors, aviation pioneers). The Wright brothers each had unique abilities, Orville more business, Wilbur more initiatives, both collaborated immensely. The U.S. government refused to purchase the Wright's flying machine because the Army spent $50,000 and the Smithsonian gave $20,000 (totaling over $1,600,000 in 2012 dollars) to develop Samuel Langley's Aerodrome piloted airplane and did not want further embarrassment.

Amadeo Pietro Giannini (1870–1949, banker). Giannini did so well as a youngster at business that he retired at the age of 31. He was asked by local businessmen to serve on the board of a small Savings and Loan that catered to the Italian-American community. Banks only leant money to large businesses and other assorted rich folks, Giannini challenged this unwritten rule and founded the Bank of America, the people's bank.

Pierre Samuel du Pont (1870–1954, chemist, businessman). Pieree was named after his great-great-grandfather Pierre Samuel du Pont de Nemours, who was a French economist who emigrated to America in 1799 after surviving the French Revolution. A family member, Eleuthere Irenee du Pont, founded the DuPont company in 1802, and descendants would form one of the richest American business dynasties of the ensuing two centuries.

Garrett Augustus Morgan Sr. (1877–1963, inventor, entrepreneur). As an African-American, he invented a traffic signal and a hair-straightening preparation, but is most renowned for creating a type of respiratory protective hood. He helped save workers

---

[66] madamcjwalker.com

trapped in a tunnel system filled with fumes after other rescue attempts had failed at Lake Erie in 1917.

Florence Nightingale Graham (1884–1966). *Graham* went by the business name Elizabeth Arden. She opened a New York-based beauty salon in 1908 and revolutionized cosmetics. Her "makeovers" promoted the "total look," matching lip, cheek, and nail polish colors. Because Arden failed to financially prepare for business continuity, the taxes due at her death required the selling of her business assets and estate to pay them.

Arthur George Gaston (1892–1996, insurance salesman, motel magnate, financier). An African-American businessman who formed the Booker T. Washington Insurance Company, Citizens Federal Savings and Loan Association (the first black-owned financial institution in Birmingham), and the A.G. Gaston motel.

Economic Trading and Business Game

This short game demonstrates the differences between a centralized, planned economy and a free market economy.

Preparation. Buy vending machine snacks for the number of participants in the game. All need to be the same price (example, $0.75 each), and no items should be duplicated. Also ensure that you can separate a number of participants into sections or tables to be used in this game as you'll progress from individuals, to tables, to room, simulating various economies.

Steps.

1. *Leader/helper hands out individual items, tally values (Initial)*. Participants do not swap or exchange their items with others as the Leader/helper hands out items to each participant randomly, simulating a centrally-planned economy. Write down the name of the participant (can be skipped to save time) and ask each individual to put a value from 1-10 on what they were given (1 being the worst, 10 being the best).

2. *Leader/helper swaps individual items with other tables (Swap)*. Gather each table items; leader/helper takes Table 1 bag to Table 2, not letting participants take what they want. Swap Table 2 with Table 3, 3 with 4, etc. Revalue items and tally them.

3. *Individual participants swap items and revalue items at their table (Table).* Ask each table to now exchange their item with individuals at their table/row, revalue and tally the numbers.

4. *Individual participants swap items and revalue items in the room (Room).* Individuals exchange items in the room. Revalue and tally.

5. *Discuss and enjoy.* Discuss the steps and enjoy the snacks.

Discuss. Ask who? What? Where? Why? When? And how? As a final question, what would a business do if they had this information? To make more sales? To reduce costs?

Example. The table and chart below is real data from a High School Junior Achievement class. Notice the totals of all tables, their values, and

> Give all the power to the many, they will oppress the few. Give all the power to the few, they will oppress the many.
> - Alexander Hamilton

the upward trends. The Initial and Swap steps may be close, while the Table and Room steps will be on an upward trend. Use the Initial/Swap and Table/Room as an illustration of a planned versus free market economy (city, state, nation, international). The principle: the freer the trade, the more satisfied the people, regardless of price.

	Initial	Swap	Table	Room
Table A	38	25	30	44
Table B	19	31	31	33
Table C	22	36	44	46
Table D	23	17	17	20
Table E	24	29	37	41
Totals	**126**	**138**	**159**	**184**

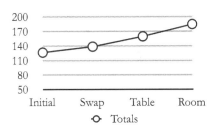

Chart 2: Economic Trading and Business Game Data

Entrepreneurs: Saints, citizens, or scoundrels?

Entrepreneurs, more citizens than saints or scoundrels. Entrepreneurs are explorers. They travel through uncharted economic territory searching for answers to problems both they and others encounter. When you look at the history of entrepreneurs, a few are saints, and they have their faults. So while there are business snake oil salespersons that don't deliver on what is promised, and even business scoundrels and criminals that are unscrupulous and commit fraud, the vast majority of entrepreneurs have ideas which provide solutions and do good with what they provide to the public. That being said, many entrepreneurs have also given away their wealth, more visibly the rich ones: John D. Rockefeller always gave 10 percent or more yearly to charity, amounting to millions of dollars. Andrew Carnegie devoted the later part of his life donating his wealth to various causes, and Bill Gates has donated his wealth and uses his expertise in various causes.

Citizen Entrepreneurs: Sell no harm. All too often, an entrepreneur's need to build and grow a new business overtakes the need to get involved in any local, state, or federal legislation. Failing to get involved, though, can put entrepreneurial businesses at greater risk of adverse affects or unintended consequences. Businesses may have to relocate, slow their business growth, or obey various regulations, legislation or government oversight that could ultimately close their business down.

Thomas Jefferson said to Charles Hammond in 1821, "When all government, domestic and foreign, in little as in great things, shall be drawn to Washington as the center of all power, it will render powerless the checks provided of one government on another and will become as venal and oppressive as the government from which we separated."

It is not the PR or marketing claims that ascertain the true worth of an entrepreneur's contributions to a society; only through the historical lens of time can we judge an individual's contributions as truly worthy of the accolades that they receive. As entrepreneurs and citizens of their state and nation, they have a responsibility to ensure that the products and services that are produced do no harm to others. This also means getting involved in your local politics to ensure that laws and regulations are fair to all and favor no one or any demographic.

Booker T. Washington, an African-American educator, author, orator, and advisor to Republican presidents, once said, "You can't hold a man down without staying down with him."

Entrepreneurs need to follow the Golden Rule: Treat others as you would like to be treated. The same is said in the Jewish Torah and Christian Bible in Leviticus 19:18, "but you shall love your neighbor as yourself; I am the LORD." In other words: Entrepreneurs as citizens should sell no harm to others.

Craft of your business, business of your craft

First, the *craft of your business,* is about your talents (what you *love* to do) and your skills (what you *can* do). You learn everything about your craft: doctors learn about medicine, coffee baristas about coffee, and plumbers about plumbing. Your craft is defined as what you eat, breathe, live and love. It's what comes natural to you, while being difficult for others to do. Do not take your talents for granted; work them. It's who you are.

Using your talents, you provide relief of *pain,* a solution to a *problem,* a present of *pleasure,* or a pound of *prevention.* Your solution(s) must be: pressing (urgent, compelling), practical (beneficial, useful), distinct (different, unique), and in "hungry crowd" quantities.

Second, the *business of your craft,* is serving your customers with your talents and skills. Rather than "starving artist" survival or "grabbing all you can get," your goal should be a sustainable, win/win, long-term income based on relationships. The business of your craft is also understanding customer relationships and psychology, process, profit, markets, sales, taxes, rule of law, basic free market economics and finding the sweet spot between your talents/skills and your market. It's answering the question: Is there a market for what you love and can do?

Starting a business is a matter of blending the love of your craft with the business of your craft so that neither one overpowers the other. This allows you to make more sales of more products so the expenses of running a business are less than your revenues. With each sale you hope to create a win/win/win for your customers: a win for you, your family, and the vendors you serve.

Alexander Hamilton said it best, "Men give me some credit for genius. All the genius I have lies in this: When I have a subject at hand, I study it profoundly. Day and night it is before me. I explore it in all its bearings. My mind becomes pervaded with it. Then the effort which I make the people are pleased to call the fruit of genius. It is the fruit of labor and thought."

Craft Issue #1: Starting a business is about you, so describe the reason you are your own business. You need to start a business for the right reasons. Do you have the personality and guts to make it happen? Do you have the talents and skills needed? If not, are you willing to learn? Get to know yourself better before you become your own boss. The bigger your *why* for starting your own business, the smaller the *how* to reach your goals becomes, because you'll figure out a way to get it done.

The U.S. military has what's called a "gig line." This line is where your uniform's shirt, pants and tie are "lined up" to look sharp. In your *personal world,* it means preparing yourself and lining up your mental, physical, spiritual, and emotional self to handle the rigors of the business world. In the *business world*, you line up your resources, money, time, people, and effort to create and sell a product or service to make a profit.

Entrepreneur and author Guy Kawasaki says, in *Art of the Start,* that if you make meaning (the *why)*, you'll make money; in fact, this is the only way. To make meaning with your startup you do one of three things: you improve quality of life, you right a wrong, and/or you prevent the end of a good thing.

The first question to answer for any entrepreneur is not what can I create, but how do I serve my ideal customers with my talents and passions so that customers are willing to pay for my efforts?

Next, describe your positive and negative reasons for going into business, especially looking at the extremes. If you have any negative reasons, they will either stop you from getting started or limit your business growth. For example, a negative reason may be that you're tired of working for your current boss. When you work for yourself, you still report to someone else, your customer, because as an entrepreneur, every customer becomes a new and different boss.

If you have a positive reason, "it's always been my dream," you may need to weigh your dream against the reality of the type and amount of work you'll have on your own. Do your homework. If you want to open up a coffee shop or a bakery, then work at one for three to six months to see if you like it. If you still love doing it and can't wait to go to work every day, then pursue it. You can hire someone or outsource to others some of the tasks that need to be done.

If, on the other hand, you find that you don't like what you thought was your dream, you've learned something about yourself and hopefully earned a little money along the way. You also haven't spent much money on a dream that was more "pie in the sky" than a true business passion.

Keep evaluating your ideas until you find the right fit for what you love to do and what customers need that you can turn into a business and make a profit.

Craft Issue #2: Describe what it means to be successful, to make it in the art and game of entrepreneurship. How do you see your business in the longterm? A business is not intended to be a win-lose contest with your customer, though it may be with your competitors. For your customer, you need a win-win result. If it's not win-win, then either you or your customer gets the short end of the stick. The loser may not want to work with the other party again. Your ultimate goal is serving your customers; then, both you and your customer will profit.

> Unconsciously, everyone expects a startup to be like a job, and that explains most of the surprises.
> - Paul Graham

Making it at the game of entrepreneurship also means having a work and life balance. Starting a business and keeping it in perspective with the rest of your life is important. A work-life balance allows you to connect with both networks in ways that recharge your battery. It also helps you avoid entrepreneurship burnout that can lead to business failure and problems with your family and friends. You can learn valuable lessons about other industries in your "off-hour" discussions with others that can translate into your area of business.

Craft Issue #3: Describe how much you'll commit to your dream. What are your critical points of time? Sometimes you have the luxury to think long-term, such as five or ten years ahead. Other times you can't see beyond a year, a month, or even a week. Sometimes you may not be able to see beyond tomorrow, especially if you have critical financial needs. Your current situation may overrule longer-term thinking, but short-term thinking should not become a long-term habit.

What are your long-term goals for your business? Do you want to find out, in the short-term, if the market likes your product? Do you want to make a living, or do you want your business to survive you? Do you want to sell it to another company so you can start another business? Do you want to be a business owner, serial, or parallel entrepreneur? Answering these questions will set the stage for how you continue down the road of building your business.

Business Issue #1: Define the things that you love, like, tolerate, and dislike about running a business. Create lists of your talents, skills, and various business tasks. You have to learn how to do everything it takes to run a business. Once you learn to do those things yourself and understand what it takes to get them done, you can then outsource to others the work that:

Can be performed by someone else with that talent;

Costs less to do by outsourcing;

Frees up your time in order for you to concentrate on more business-critical things.

Business Issue #2: Invest in your future; it's not about you. Investing in your future takes many forms. First, learn more, become a constant learner and concentrate in areas that will get you the best results. Second, invest in your retirement, which means pay yourself first. Invest in areas to start your business and then invest in long-term savings for large items, etc. What's the reason to put aside some of your profits? It provides an economic cushion during down times and gives you confidence when tough times hit. See the "Secrets of Money" section below to get a clearer picture of your life long view.

In the beginning, you *start* your own business from the perspective of "it's about me" and set up your business around your talent and passion. When it comes to how to *run* your business, "it's about you and your life" and what it takes to run your business without sacrificing your other interests. When it comes to your *future*, it finally becomes "it's not about you." You don't want another full-time job; it would always be needing you. On the other hand, when you think of your future you can take time off, sell your business, or start another business. You will be able to choose how to live your life by the choices you make now. Having your own business, rather than another full-time job, creates opportunities for more choices.

While it starts out being "all about you," it ends up becoming "all about your customers."

Your Idea: Spark + Air + Fuel = Business

There is a strong parallel between starting a fire and starting a business, and for each you need three elements:

▸ **Spark = Idea.** Most people understand a spark gets a fire started, and it's the same for a business. As with any spark, whether for a fire or an idea for a business, if you don't have or provide the other two elements of air and fuel, your spark and idea will fizzle out rather quickly. Before you think your idea is worth millions, take this quick idea test: how much would you pay for a package of strawberry seeds? Now how much would you pay for strawberries after they've ripened? You'll pay next to nothing for the seeds, but in exchange for the time and effort put into producing fruit, you'll pay much more. Your business idea is the same. Your idea's worth is not in the idea itself, but in taking actions, sometimes massive actions, to grow your idea into something worthwhile that people are willing to buy. Most people do not want to buy seeds; they want the fruit. Take it one step further: how much would you pay for a bottle of strawberry jam or a strawberry fruit dessert at a restaurant?

▸ **Air = Beliefs/Aspirations.** Once you have your idea, it is a matter of having the belief, self confidence, and aspiration to take your idea to market and make sales. You do not need much belief to get started, just enough belief to take some starting actions. Your belief grows as you progress forward in your business journey.

▸ **Fuel = Actions.** The three kinds of wood -- tinder, kindling and timber -- are the necessary stages that allow a fire to grow. Actions and initiatives are force multipliers, just like the three types of wood fuel. You take a single step, then multiple steps, and finally have multiple projects going on at the same time to propel your idea off the ground. Both a fire and your business require constant "stoking," taking many actions, otherwise, the fire and business will be snuffed out.

As with any idea, the spark and ensuing growing fire, fueled by taking many actions, creates a larger fire which requires more fuel. Mark Zuckerberg of Facebook and Steve Wozniak of Apple fame both wanted something that was not yet available to them, so they created it by and for themselves. They each created an organic idea that grew over time. Notice that they "scratched their own itch" by creating their own product which ultimately turned into a business. This process is *typical of most startup businesses*. What starts out as an idea eventually grows into a business later on, after the business "Aha" moment hits the founder. It was only until after fueling each of their ideas with many actions that they saw that they could create a business out of each of their ideas.

To continue with your business idea, see the "Strategy Search" section below to expand your idea into a business.

Perspectives of various business startups

There are always four things associated with startups: 1) it will take longer; 2) it will cost more; 3) it will be undercapitalized; and 4) you will fail many times. All four of these will cost you time and/or money.

There are three typical tracks that startups follow:

▸ **A "Start Now!" Business** - Take the "bull by the horns" when you meet it and ride it until you tame it! Christine Comaford-Lynch, author of *Rules for Renegades,* started a business within minutes of hearing of an opportunity, and had 35 employees soon after. Seize an opportunity; strike while the iron's hot: utilize no planning at all; you'll fix, organize, or improve things along your journey. You can't steer a parked car, can you?

▸ **Everything In Between** - Think it up; draw up some actions steps, then take some actions. Do it!

▸ **Planning to Start a Business** - Create a business "flight plan" to move you from where you are to your destination. In his book, *Losing My Virginity*, Richard Branson tells how he started Virgin Atlantic. While on vacation at Virgin Island/ Beef Island, Richard and Joan were left stranded because of a canceled local flight. Richard made a few calls to airline charter companies and chartered a plane to Puerto Rico for $2,000. He divided the price by the number of seats, borrowed a blackboard, and wrote: "Virgin Airways, $39 single flight to Puerto Rico." Richard then walked around the terminal and soon filled every seat on the charter plane. As they landed at Puerto Rico, one passenger said to Richard: "Virgin Airways isn't too bad. Smarten up the service a little, and you could be in business." Richard laughed. "I might just do that." Entrepreneurs solve problems, their own, and once finding others with the same problem, create a business around the solution. Branson's airline opportunity came in 1984.

> *Results: Because you* **win** *does not make you great just as* **losing** *does not make you a failure. Improve the* **how** *you get results to increase your results.*

Whichever route you follow above, businesses will fail or succeed. There is no correct formula for what is right or successful; there is only listening to the market and seeing what it's willing to pay for. It's up to you to change your business plan's course and increase your chances of success.

Startups work out risks to build a business

Being an entrepreneur means that you take risks. You can't avoid risks, but you can calculate the boundaries of your project scope and the risks involved. Most small businesses are constantly preparing and looking for growth, but they seldom prepare for unforeseen things that happen to a business. Emergencies can hinder or stop a business cold and business continuity is preparing to continue operating despite problems or disasters that occur.

Types of risk costs. Costs associated with risks and disasters "double dip" into businesses at two levels:

‣ **Loss of sales and profit** - Some to all of your business sales or profit can be lost during disaster downtime. This can be the result of a PR or customer satisfaction disaster, poor marketing, a competitor coming out with a similar product, or a host of other situations that cause a loss of sales.

‣ **Recovery costs** - Hard drive crashes, mistakes and errors by vendors, etc., deplete your cash reserve or increase your debt.

Manage your business risks. Understand the amount of risk that you are exposed to regarding reputation, legal affairs, product, market, etc., in the context of how much you could lose in any of those areas when making or not making a decision.

Keeping your business going when disaster strikes is not just backing up your hard drive to protect your data, but continuing your business during and after a disaster strikes.

Types of various risks. Disasters, accidents, or drastic changes come in many forms: identity theft, scams, fraud, natural disasters, terrorist attacks, cyber attacks, fires, chemical spills, human mistakes, competition, changes in tax laws, changes in culture and market conditions, computer bugs, and, of course, hard drive crashes. These are just some of the more visible risks; their chances of occurring are shown in Illustration 4[67]. The premise of business continuity, being able to continue in business after a disaster, is: The better prepared you are for disaster, the

---

[67] http://www.drj.com

better you will be able to continue business, and the less you'll be negatively affected by events that come your way.

Risk management and business continuity mean that over time you prepare for contingencies in most of your critical business areas that affect your business revenues.

Economic cycles will go up and down. Weathering a slow or

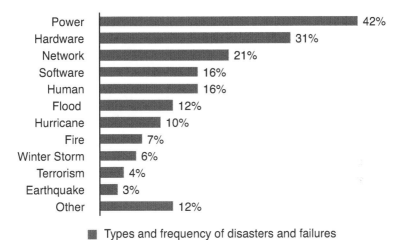

Power	42%
Hardware	31%
Network	21%
Software	16%
Human	16%
Flood	12%
Hurricane	10%
Fire	7%
Winter Storm	6%
Terrorism	4%
Earthquake	3%
Other	12%

■ Types and frequency of disasters and failures

Illustration 4: Types and frequency of disasters

down economy helps you better prepare for the next one. Be ready to change repeatedly at every downturn because no downturn cycle is ever exactly the same. Microsoft's Bill Gates had one year's worth of income in the bank so he could still pay his employees in an economic downturn.

You and your team: Mentors to networking

No one ever builds a business alone. You'll need key vendors such as a lawyer, a bookkeeper, or a CPA to handle legal and accounting needs. There are graphic artists, web hosting, and design companies among many others.

Your team, your money. Those you intend to work with, whether hiring them for single task, joint venture, or temporary work, do only one of two things for you and your business:

1. **Make money = Increase sales.**

a. *More quantity* such as contacting more people or marketing more, increasing a six-pack to a case, using MS Office (more features/options) instead of Apple's iWork.

b. *Higher quality*, add value to your product, remove obstacles that prevent sales, drop a low-profit product.

2. **Save money = Reduce costs.**

a. *Less quantity* by finding a less-costly solution, iWork (fewer features) versus MS Office, reducing the size of your product (from a case of 24 to a six-pack).

b. *Lower quality*, i.e., going from perfect to good enough without sacrificing profits, removing non-added value features from your product, improving process-reducing production time or costs.

Customer feedback can help with making and saving money. If potential vendors cannot tell you how they can contribute to the above, they don't have an entrepreneur's attitude; don't hire or work with them. You have to set that expectation up front with them, as well. Also, if you're so controlling that you have an attitude of "I think, you do!" and won't allow them to be engaged in contributing to your business, then you are the problem, not those you intend to hire.

Building your team. Hiring others to help means that you either do not have the time to get things done or that you don't have the necessary skills or knowledge to perform those tasks. At first, you may need to do as much as you can, yourself, to keep your costs down. Unless you have tons of talent, at some point you'll need to hire more professional talent to do what you need. Delegate less critical tasks to others. Finding an intern to help with the smaller tasks can be helpful and can free up your time. You'll need to pay for professional services to handle your more important tasks.

Mentors, masterminds, networks, coaches, and fans.

Getting good advice from someone is great, but it is essential that you thank them, return the favor and/or help others. Do not be a sponge, willing to take anything given without thanking others or looking to give back or contribute to others. You won't be in business for the long haul if you are not a giver. It's a matter of having a hand up for a mentor and a hand down to help someone else.

Mentors are like-minded individuals that have the same attitude toward growing businesses and are willing to help you with your business. You meet with them, such as a mentor from Score.org, on a consistent and frequent basis to focus and strategize your efforts to move your company forward.

Coaches, such as an accountability coach, is someone you pay to help find the many methods or approaches to remove, go around, or go through the many obstacles in your way. Their purpose is to keep you moving consistently ahead toward your goal.

A *mastermind* is a group of individuals from a diverse industry background that you meet with on a regular basis, usually monthly, to help grow your business. These people could be a local Meetup.com group, a group of people that want the same for you, someone from your local Chamber of Commerce (asbdc-us.org) who provides assistance, or a group of people that has banded together for mutual support. It is essential to have mentors and a mastermind group; you won't get far without them.

> Mastermind definition: Coordination of knowledge and effort, in a spirit of harmony, between two or more people, for the attainment of a definite purpose.
> - Napoleon Hill

Network is both a noun and a verb. As a noun it is an organized group of individuals with whom you connect or have an affinity. As a verb, you network by attending various events or meetings to connect with others to enlarge your number of connections.

Fans or Community. A fan base or a community is a dedicated group of leaders around your company's products and services. You can use social networks such as Twitter, Facebook, LinkedIn, or a Mac support group such as a Mac User Group (MUG, apple.com/usergroups/) to connect. Tapping into these groups will give you sources of inspiration and feedback, and they are great bunch of people with whom to keep in touch.

Customers. These are individuals or groups who purchase your product and do only that: buy and use it. They do not become a part of your fans or your community. They only want to buy the product to solve their problem and move on.

The best way to learn a subject is to teach it to someone else. In the beginning, making connections is important to get feedback about your efforts. At some point you'll need more devoted people who will both offer you timely advice and to whom you can give great advice, as well.

Decide now! T-30, 29, 28...days and counting

Yes, today, now, is the time to start a business. You can get up and running in just a few days and begin making money. However, there are a few things that you need to consider now that affect your business startup.

Date your startup. The earlier you date things, especially when it comes to registering your business, the better off you are. This becomes true when determining startup expenses versus operating expense tax deductions. You have to put a stake in the ground when you start your business because you need to begin tracking the amount of money, time, and use of equipment for tax purposes, even though you may not be open for business. From the IRS tax perspective, the date your business opens is not when a customer pays you, but when you are able to perform your services or have begun the necessary steps to start a business. It also includes dates of any intellectual property patents or trademarks that you need to file, because for these types of issues, the early bird gets the worm.

> We have a system that increasingly taxes work and subsidizes nonwork.
> - Milton Friedman

Choose and register your business, the earlier the better. You'll need to name and set up shop by registering your company. This registration date becomes important with financial and legal issues. While you can start now and name your company, you more appropriately begin when you file the papers with the various government agencies and begin to track what you are doing. Even though not all companies need to register with governmental authorities, it can be a lifesaver if your business goes under and creditors attack your personal assets and income in seeking payment for business debt. Registering your business protects your personal belongings if you ever have to go to court, keeping them separate from your business.

Determine your company structure and other legal issues. Should you register your company as a Limited Liability Company (LLC), S or C Corporation, or other? This decision is where your long-term view of your business will determine your structure. Even though it may not be critical to the life or death of your company, if you make a wrong structure decision, it could create difficulties later if problems arise. Talk with a business attorney to see what is best, but the decision is yours. Where you want to go with your business will determine your company's structure. Other issues to consider are signing intellectual property papers for trademarks, copyright, and patents and especially business ownership if the business owner dies. Who gets to run the company or own the copyrights or trademarks if the owner leaves or sells the company?

> *You may never know what results come of your action, but if you do nothing there will be no result.*
> *- Mahatma Gandhi*

Think long-term. Your legal structure, legal continuity (wills, etc.), and branding are important to your business. Starting a business in two days is easy, and can move you forward very quickly. But if you are considering expanding your number of brick and mortar stores, going national or even international, it will become more complicated to change your business processes and elements once you've started. You'll run into difficulty with a competitor business if it has a similar name, logo, trademark, or online handle (domain name, Twitter, Facebook, LinkedIn, etc.). Changing these various business elements and issues is time consuming as you move from a local to a national or international perspective. Most importantly, changes will cause customer confusion and affect your sales negatively, so think long term.

Financial issues. Because you are starting up a business, you may have any number of these financial issues:

▸ **Startup expenses.** There are limits to what you can declare as a business startup expense and these are determined by the date you registered your company. Startup expenses can include things such as getting business cards, website domain names, email accounts, and other necessary items.

▸ **Capital expenditures.** These are items that depreciate, such as Macs, printers, vehicles, some office equipment, etc.

▸ **Bank/PayPal accounts.** You'll also have to open up various banking and vendor accounts for your business to monitor what you are spending and track the money you spend for tax purposes. It keeps your books separate when having to explain things to your bookkeeper, accountant, Certified Public Accountant (CPA), or Enrolled Agents (EA). The same goes for your time. You'll need to monitor your time and effort in your new business for tax purposes. If you use personal equipment, such as a truck or computer, there are tax issues surrounding these, so consult with your tax professional.

▸ **Saving money for your startup.** If you can, begin saving money for your business. Set up your retirement accounts to begin putting some of your profits into those accounts. Don't consider saving $1 or $5 as chump change. It's the *habit of saving* that is most important to start here, not the amount. There is a benefit to the present value of money via compounded interest over time when beginning to build your retirement income.

Why a Mac? Which Mac? Budget for a Mac?

Make, save, manage money with your Mac

Most people see this phrase from only one perspective: making a living using their Mac. Can you see the other perspectives? There are four ways of thinking about money when it comes to your Mac:

1. **Always be serving first.** This is the first rule of startups and entrepreneurship. Your Mac is only a tool that helps you with your startup. Don't place your Mac, your business model, or yourself above your potential customer. Focus on your customer and how to solve their problems because you can only make money by taking action for your customer. Taking action to solve a customer's problem that they are willing to pay money for will make money; ideas are a dime a dozen. Which makes more money, a package of seeds, or a ripe and picked crop? Yep, ready to pick and eat makes more money.

2. **Make money with your Mac.** Use your Mac and all its hardware and software tools to make money as a writer, graphic artist, video editor, web designer, application developer, or database programmer. The primary function here of the Mac is to help make you money. Here's a short list of what you can do creating a company around these business themes.

   a. iLife ideas:

      i. Create audio podcasts for businesses or consumers.

      ii. Interview family members for video scrap books or create a DVD for grandparents, parents, and kids.

      iii. Create How-To videos for various industries or startups.

      iv. Create business calendars or cards in iPhoto to sell.

   b. iWork ideas:

      i. Create newsletters for organizations.

      ii. Write ads or engage in marketing copywriting.

      iii. Sell freelance writing.

      iv. Create catalogs of products for companies.

> v. Create presentations for smaller companies, and design projects and other plans using Numbers.

3. **Manage money with your Mac.** When you manage money with your Mac, it helps you keep your business running smoothly. Think of a retailer that uses a Windows Point of Sale (POS) machine as a cash register, but uses a Mac to track business information and results. Most Windows applications allow you to export data into an Excel spreadsheet or a Bento or Filemaker Pro database for slicing and dicing the data. You can find golden nuggets about your business to help you sell more or cut your business costs. Most people who manage money with their Mac refer to No. 4 below. Using Mac technologies saves money because it saves time.

4. **Save money with your Mac.** How you use the Mac and its tools can save you time, which in turn can save you money. In most cases, the time savings allows you to concentrate on building your business. If you talk with most Mac users, especially those who have switched from Windows to a Mac, you'll find that 95 percent of them have an attitude of "once we've switched to a Mac we'll never switch back!" They then pass that passion on to others.

Why use a Mac for business? Because by using a Mac you'll find that:

▸ It's about the user experience, being productive, not cheap.

▸ It saves time.

▸ It costs less (more included and tightly integrated applications).

▸ It's easier to use.

▸ It has few to no software viruses, trojans, or worms to worry about.

▸ There's less to learn, so it's faster to use and get things done.

▸ It has UNIX "under the hood" that can be accessed by the program Terminal for those who get real technical, geek-wise.

▸ It's gorgeous and environmentally friendly.

▸ It can run Windows (Linux or other operating systems) if necessary, using Boot Camp or virtualization software.

▸ It provides iLife software and comes ready to use.

▸ It has a tribe. Just ask any PC Switcher what they think of a Mac after they switched.

As the saying goes, "Once you go Mac, you'll never turn back!"

For your business, you're going to need some applications on your Mac to get started. Here is a list of some things you'll need, although most of what you have on your Mac will handle planning your business.

Which Mac you get will be determined by the type of business you're going to run. Whether it's going to be a technician-like business, such as audio-video editing that needs a Mac Pro for raw power, or a creative business such as a writer or consultant who needs an iMac or a MacBook. This book was written with the hardware that can run the Leopard Mac operating system (OS). You can run smaller businesses on older Macs. If that is the case, then check out a few websites to find other options, such as lowendmac.com. You can also Google for "low-cost Macs" and see what Google ads show up in the right column of the results page.

Mac minimum requirements: You'll need a Mac desktop or laptop with Leopard OS, iLife '09, and iWork '09 to do the work of an entrepreneur. You can use an older Mac running Tiger OS to run iLife and iWork '09. Macs running Leopard have been out since Fall 2008. The Snow Leopard was released Aug 28th, 2009 and offers mostly "under the hood" tweaks to offer improvements in your Mac experience. Mac OS Lion was released July 20, 2011 and offers iOS similarities to the iPad on the Mac. The OS X Mountain Lion was released July 25, 2012.

Tip. Mac speed. In most cases the only reason to get a faster Mac is because you need the speed to get things done, i.e., as a graphic artist or videographer. Or, you're impatient.

Mac recommended requirements: Software that is essential to run a business: accounting, graphics, database, communications, and utility software. Other things to consider for your business are: printer, fax (or fax service), email, scanner, iPhone, external storage (hard drive, flash drive), keyboard, monitor, mouse, USB microphone, digital or video camera, Universal Power Supply (UPS), or various types of cables to connect peripherals to your Mac.

Total Cost of Information Technology (IT)

Nearly every entrepreneur who is not in the computer business or who is not a geek at heart misses some of the essential aspects of the Information Technologies (IT). Running a business with a Mac, and its associated costs for a business, means seeing the full picture of using IT. There are four parts for buying IT and support for your business, Mac computer and the supporting hardware and software cast members to your business play. See Table 1 for a general outline of this principle.

A more detailed total cost of ownership of IT is best described in four areas:

▸ **Hardware.** Buying your Mac and the associated hardware, such as a printer, is normally what most users only see, but it's the rest of the following list that is not counted toward budgeting for businesses. Just like buying a car, driving off the lot is one thing, keeping it running is essential to keeping your business running.

▸ **Software and licensing.** While there are some free, shareware, and other licensing software versions, the most common is to buy one license per computer. In the case of server software, a per-seat cost or unlimited seats may be available to you, the business owner. Software *updates* are considered free and occur often; the price of software *upgrades* needs to be figured into the budget at about the 1½- to 2-year mark.

▶ **Installation and configuration.** This cost should be figured when you first buy, but also if a disaster occurs and you have to spend half a day or more reinstalling the Mac OS, associated applications, and your data.

▶ **Maintenance, disasters, and security: "budgeting for breakage."** When it comes to buying hardware or software solutions, their life cycle is between two to five years. This end of life around the three- to five-year point, as well as future purchases must be budgeted for in both capital expenditures and office expenses, including ink and toner cartridges for your printers. Regarding potential breakage, you should budget for the original purchase price.

Budgeting for your business computer needs

There are some areas that you need to budget for your business and your Mac. Here is a basic list of things to consider and plan for your business and your Mac:

▶ **Infrastructure,** such as AC power, HVAC costs (a cooled, dust free closet for your server's heat), space for a server room and/or wiring closet space, hosting or other services such as an ISP or website, and wired and wireless networking of your office, or on-the-road traveling with your laptop.

▶ **Hardware** lasts average users about three to four years and includes various internal parts such as video cards, DVD and hard drives, and motherboards. External hardware, such as printers, scanners, external hard drives, digital cameras, routers, and switches can last longer. Also include hardware costs such as network (Cat 6 or better to support Gigabit ethernet), USB, Firewire, Lightning, and power cables.

▶ **Software** includes free *updates* to your current software and low-cost upgrades that come out every one to three years.

IT "Big Picture" cost illustration	Cost
Hardware (first purchase)	$1600
Software (first purchase)	$300
Installation and Configuration (time and labor to install and reinstall OS + applications + files + backup files)	$200
3-4 years of ongoing maintenance, security, disaster recoveries, and upgrades (hardware replacements, software upgrades, downtime, etc.)	$1000
Total Cost of Ownership	$3100

Table 1: IT Costs Illustration

The longer you delay getting software *upgrades,* the more difficult it is to continue to use your files or get your information out if vendors discontinue maintaining the product. Also, check for other types of software licensing as there are multiple ways to procure less expensive software for your Mac.

▸ **Services and maintenance** that you hire others to perform for your computer equipment should be included in this if you reinstall the Mac OS or other applications. Doing this yourself takes time away from making money for your business.

▸ **Training and/or learning time** is usually needed for getting those major projects done. If you don't have the money, you have to spend the time to learn how to do things yourself if there are no other work outlets.

▸ **Consumables** that need to be replaced as they're used up such as paper, a blank DVD for storage, and toner or ink cartridges.

Where to buy Mac stuff

When it comes to your business and buying Mac hardware and software, you can go overboard. A business owner should never allow the cost of getting a Mac to outrun their business needs.

Once you have determined your business requirements for your Mac, you need to determine where to buy your Mac and the associated hardware and software. Some of the businesses that provide Mac stuff are: apple.com, macconnection.com, macsales.com, and macmall.com, just to name a few. Make sure that you ask if there are any available business discounts.

There are several ways to get less expensive products for your Mac. Here's a good list to start from:

1. **Clearance of older models.** Apple frequently announces and releases new products and models on Tuesdays to have inventory available for the weekends. Older models are automatically price reduced, so check out all available Mac sellers for any quick discounts. Check out the Apple store (store.apple.com) for clearance or older models that Apple sells on their online store. Also, talk with Apple's Small Business sales section or Apple Retail Business Partner to see if there are any available discounts. You can also check amazon.com for third-party sales of Macs and Mac accessories, especially just before new Macs are due to come out. The computer industry normally refreshes its hardware line around three times a year, in January/February (after the Christmas holiday), May/June ("Back to School" sales for teachers, college kids and those in the education industry), and September/October (just before the Christmas holiday) timeframes. Scattered throughout the year are other releases both announced (significant products) and unannounced (such as "speed bumps" of the specs of Mac hardware or upgrades to Mac software). **Hint:** No Apple employees, including retail employees, will ever know when a new release will happen.

Tip on Mac buying. When shopping for Macs from third-party resellers do not shop on price alone, but look at both the *model numbers* together with the *prices of the items* you are comparing because a cheaper price could indicate a different model rather than a better price. Check out the software MacTracker that keeps a list of all Macs ever made and their specs, including model numbers and essential information about each Mac produced (this excludes custom-ordered Macs).

---

2. **Refurbished.** First check out the Apple online store's (store.apple.com) Clearance and Refurbished section to see if there are any deals that are fit for you and your business. Third-party resellers may have refurbished units or open box items that might be something to look at.

3. **Geek websites.** If you do not need any computer help with deciding what you need, i.e., you're more on the geek side of the Mac, then try newegg.com, dealmac.com, and zipzoomfly.com for some of the best prices. Be aware that low-priced companies offer slim to no technical support, so you need to know what you are doing and getting.

4. **Used.** You can buy used Macs from ads in Mac magazines such as MacWorld. You can also Google for used Macs through online companies such as ebay.com or craigslist.com, or a check your local Mac reseller. If you buy used, and the Mac is less than three years old, see if the three-year AppleCare comes with it and can give a measure of "security" during the last amount of time left on the term. You can also check macprices.net for current and mac2sell.com for used Mac prices.

If you are switching from Windows to a Mac, there are a few things you need to know.

WARNING: When switching to a Mac, there can be complex and intricate problems involved. There may be a few Windows hardware and software solutions that may not work as expected. The switch can also become costly because of fear. EXAMPLE: using Microsoft's Exchange Server may have "connections" for Mac solutions but it may not be the most effective and efficient for getting things done. Hire a computer consultant who understands Windows and Mac solutions to help determine your needs. A mixed environment may be workable, because a complex mixed environment may be too costly to integrate. For example, emailing iWork PDF files may not get through Exchange server connections. Send through Microsoft Word on a Windows computer and double-check if your customer got your file.

Here are the steps to determine if you can use a Mac to run your business.

1. **Note how you work and which applications you use.** Your business projects or tasks determine the type of software and hardware you need to buy. Note your current Windows applications and hardware, then determine the type of application it is. For example, Microsoft Word is a word processor; Adobe Photoshop is a photo manipulation program. Now that you know the type of software, you can see if there are Mac solutions for you.

2. **Find Mac hardware and software solutions similar to Windows.** In the case of your hardware, if it has been bought in the last three to five years, it should not be a problem in most cases to use with a Mac, and you may only need the required software drivers. If the hardware or software is older than five years, there may be an occasional issue. For your business tasks, there are a many ways of getting your work done on a Mac and very few cases when you can't.

   a. **Cross platform applications.** These are products from the same vendor such as Adobe Photoshop or Filemaker Pro. Both run natively on Mac and Windows and files can be swapped between the different platforms.

   b. **Similar applications.** A Honda Accord or Toyota Camry are both very similar cars, but there are differences between them. The same goes for Windows and Mac applications. While most people may use Microsoft

Outlook, which handles email, calendar, and a contact list, Apple's Mail, Address Book and Calendar will handle most entrepreneurial needs. For instance, Act! 2010 for Windows is a contact management product; Daylite from MarketCircle on the Mac will perform similar functions.

c. **Web applications.** Windows web browsers such as Internet Explorer, Firefox, or Opera are used to access your business information on the internet. The key here is to make sure the website has been designed and tested for Apple's Safari browser, otherwise you may have to use another browser to work with those websites.

d. **Running Windows on a Mac.** If you cannot find the answers in any of the above solutions, then you can buy an Original Equipment Manufacturer (OEM) copy of a Windows OS (not the copy that came with your Windows PC) to run Windows on your Mac. Once you have a copy, there are two approaches to running Windows.

   i. **Part-time Windows: Boot Camp.** Part-time means you'd run your specific Windows applications, such as Quickbooks, once a day for a short while or once a week for a few hours and then reboot into your Mac OS. It's like driving a car; you can't drive two cars at the same time. To run Windows part-time you would use Apple's Boot Camp that comes free with each Mac. Running Windows with Boot Camp runs "on the metal," so you get the full benefits and speed of running on the Mac hardware. (Tip. You can run Windows on 1 GB of RAM, but 2 GB is better; also allow for hard disk space.)

   ii. **Full-time Windows: Virtualization software.** In full-time mode, you run your Windows application most, if not all, of the day for your business needs. If this is the case, you will have to use virtualization software such as VMWare's Fusion or Parallels Desktop. In virtualization mode the Window and Mac OS will run at the same time and a bit slower because of the complex layering of hardware, operating systems, virtualization software and applications. (Tip. You can run virtualization software on 2 GB of RAM, but 4 GB or more is better, and you should have at least 10 GB or more of hard disk space.)

3. **Recommendations for running Windows on a Mac.** There are certain reasons running Windows on a Mac can be troublesome. In descending order, below, are the recommended approaches to connecting to the internet (email, web, and social media software) and to reduce the number of Windows problems on your Mac. Starting with the most trouble-free approach:

   a. **Never connect to the Internet with Windows**. You decrease the chances of getting a virus, unless you load up an infected DVD/CD you received from someone. If you have to connect to the internet, then follow some of the steps below.

   b. **Connect only to update Windows or your applications.** When you update Windows and its applications, you limit the chance of being infected.

   c. **Connect to the Internet and only to trusted Internet sites.** Trusted sites are those sites that you're sure are virus free, such as your bank or other vendor sites. You probably still need virus protection.

   d. **Connect to the Internet and email.** You will need to get virus protection, if you are running full-blown Windows. If you connect to the Internet and someone sends you a Windows infected file through an application, it will infect the Windows side of your Mac, but rarely, if ever, your Mac side.

4. **Windows and Mac file formats.** Each program you use has its own file format. Microsoft's Word (PC versions 1995-2004 = .doc, 2007/2010 = .docx) or Excel, iWork's Pages or Numbers, have their own file formats. Switching to another program is sometimes like switching languages; you have to

translate the file format to the program it recognizes. Check out Wikipedia's "List of file formats" for more details.

Tip. If you have to run mostly Windows for your business as an independent contractor, you can run Windows "on the metal" during the day and reboot it into the Mac at home. This is the best of both worlds.

Chapter Three

Step 3: Business Research to Model

Learn to do common things uncommonly well; we must always keep in mind that anything that helps fill the dinner pail is valuable. -- George Washington Carver

Story: "Aha! That's it!"

Arriving at her local independent coffee shop one chilly fall morning, Erica sat down at an empty table with her favorite French vanilla latte. Erica settled into her thoughts and realized her feeling of excitement at her new job had descended into boredom. The job's first appeal left her feeling she might want to do it the rest of her life, but now she was having second thoughts. The job just didn't "feel right." Her parents sensed this: "Why don't you go back to college and get your degree, then you can really have a career." She felt somewhat obligated to go back to finish her college degree – her parents insisted since she was the only one in her family who had any college – but the idea of striking out on her own carried with it more excitement than returning to school. She wasn't against education or college, it was the learning that was most enjoyable, but if she sought out specialized knowledge (law, medicine, engineering, etc.) or worked for someone else she might need a degree. Working for herself, she just needed to learn and acquire more knowledge.

Erica sipped her coffee as she recalled growing up and the things that brought her the most excitement and joy, as a girl, and what she most disliked when she was young. Questions she asked herself were: What did she do that she could never tire of? What did her well-intentioned mother, father, and friends entice her to do that she disliked or felt strange and uncomfortable doing? What had made her cry as a five-year-old? Most importantly, she wondered which activities inspired her the most.

"Oh!" she inhaled with elation. So she wouldn't lose her thoughts, she grabbed a pen from her purse and began taking notes on her white paper napkin. With the excitement of a 6-year-old in PJs on a predawn Christmas morning, she wrote down all of her thoughts. Raising the napkin off the table and in a somewhat hushed tone Erica said, "Yes!"

She had rediscovered what she loved to do. Her *spontaneous, top-of-the-mind* reactions to situations revealed that her *dominant talents* were dealing with the excitement and pace of startups and her love of writing. Finally she wrote in large, dark letters: "Start a startup consultancy and market, sell, and monetize it with a newsletter!"

A business idea was born. As a newborn entrepreneur too excited to stop, Erica grabbed her Mac laptop and began expanding on the ideas and information on her note scribbled napkin. She had solved the *what*, the talent which drives *her*, now it was about finding out *why*, this drives her *business*.

Weeks later – with a mixture of "You can do it," "I have a friend that's an entrepreneur, maybe they can give you some good advice," "I had a friend who started a business and lost a ton of money and ended up having to get a job," and "You'll never make a go of it" – she forged ahead in fits and starts with her business *why* and design. Erica researched and recorded information on her idea's potential and tracked her various contacts using her Mac's Address Book and a Bento database. She used iWork Pages to keep notes and organize her product and service specifications. She used Numbers spreadsheets to put together a checklist of things to do, notes of what it takes to produce her product, and the costs associated with producing her product.

As her idea was finally taking shape, she was thrilled at the notion that her newsletter just might work. Casting off the weights and anchors that long ago had been submerged by past failures and false expectations. Her idea surfaced quickly and her excitement kept it afloat at the surface of her life.

Nearing completion of her first product idea she realized that coming up with a winning and sellable product is the spark, but to fan the flame – to create and build a business around it – takes business knowledge. Erica found she needed to learn quickly what it takes to create a startup, blending both a product and running a business together.

Undaunted and filled with a renewed passion, she moved from the idea phase, or determining if the idea could really work, to the business phase. She needed to see what the earning potential was with her idea. Could she make more than just scratching out a living for herself?

She had many discussions with other entrepreneurs who told her she was doing more than the other 95 percent of would-be entrepreneurs: she was executing her idea, or putting in the necessary work to make it happen. Local entrepreneurs told her, "Many others quit when the going gets too tough; if it's worth it you just can't stop." Using the same gusto she had in forming her first idea, she conducted business research with some of her potential ideal customers and input hard numbers to her Mac's business plan templates.

Meanwhile, her well-meaning parents told her, "You had better be safe than sorry and get a real job." Her close friends said, "If you get a college degree no one can take it away from you, even if you must go into debt to go to college." When she researched the costs of returning to college she saw that university prices had risen to the degree that attending college was beyond her ability to pay for it.

What was Erica going to do?

Motive: Define what your life will be like

In starting a business you'll research your business idea, your *why* you are doing it, and then crunch the numbers to see what level of business can be achieved. Failing to at least understand what it takes to run a business will surely land you in "Brokesville" or in bankruptcy court if you use other people's money. You have to take reasonable steps to figure out the financial numbers of running your own business. What will be your market share? Where are your customers coming from? What will be your profit? Having a good grasp of your potential business through market research will increase your chances of success.

Some of the first questions you need to ask yourself are: Who are you? What do you love to do? What is going to be your end game? Where do you want to be in one, five, ten years? Do you want to make just a steady income? How about growing your business to make a good/great/fantastic income? Have you ever thought about being wealthy? Did you ever consider wanting to completely change the business game rules, such as inventing the next Facebook or Twitter, or the next iPad or Google?

> *If you don't design your own life plan, chances are you'll fall into someone else's plan. And guess what they have planned for you? Not much. - Jim Rohn*

Determine your end game, think far ahead and see your business vision enough to pursue it and provide you with a compelling drive and passion to be an *entrepreneur*, not a *wantapreneur*. Compelling visions get you through some difficult times ahead. Here's a scope of your life; do you want to:

‣ Invent a product?

‣ Invent a product and start a business?

‣ Invent, start, and run a business?

‣ Invent, start, run, and build a business?

‣ Invent, start, run, build, and sell a small or big business?

Why are these questions being asked? Because it's really about understanding your personal, long-term goals. If you're an inventor and not an entrepreneur, you'll get frustrated or stop altogether before you get to the next step of starting a business.

If you love the start of a new business and don't want to grow it past a certain level, you won't. This longer-term view means that to start a business is just one milestone in a series of milestones toward your life's long-term personal goals.

Just writing a book is one thing, but a book can turn into speaking engagements, training, interviews, etc. So ask more questions of yourself and of your potential business. Do the same for translating your business into other areas once the first product is out the door. One of the tricks to starting a business is that you define the next milestone after you have reached your first one. After you have started a business, now what? Run the business. Then what? Continue to ask yourself, "What's next?"

Sometimes asking these questions leads you to stretch your current thinking. Be aware that sometimes the entrepreneur just wants to startup a business, nothing more. Or, the inventor just wants to invent. Starting a business takes more. Are you willing to follow through?

That is the business side of your life. Contemplate the prospects of being very successful or a total failure, either of which could happen. Either way, what would you do next? Is your business your life, or only a part of it? What is your life *outside* of your business? You have an identity outside your role as an entrepreneur: son, father, mother, friend, little league coach, volunteer, activist, granddaughter.

If you get so focused on "just your one thing," once you reach it you may find out it may not be what you had hoped for, so make sure that you have your larger life goals outlined to keep you moving. Life and your business should be a journey with multiple stops on the way. Consider it much like the earth's horizon, always there but you just can't quite get there from here.

10 Checkpoints to Startup Success

Here is a short list of things that you need to have in place to be successful as an entrepreneur. The more you can check off, the more successful you'll be.

☐ **1. Are you passionate about it?** Money only goes so far in motivation, you have to have long term passion so you can weather the dark day storms.

☐ **2. Do you know your customers?** Do you understand their problems enough to solve their issues?

☐ **3. Do you know your market?** What other competitors, vendors, and customers do you compete with?

☐ **4. Is it a unique idea?** Does it change the market enough to attract enough customers?

☐ **5. Is your market large enough to make a living?** Having just one customer is OK, but it better be a big sale.

☐ **6. Is it simple to start?** No matter what the idea, it always starts simple enough and then grows, just as planting a seed turns into something bigger.

☐ **7. Can you explain it easily?** If you can't explain it simply, you lose a customer's interest quickly.

☐ **8. Do you have one revenue stream?** Do you have one solution at one price for one ideal customer, now?

☐ **9. Is your product easy to sell?** A one step sale. The more steps it takes to sell and you begin to lose customers.

☐ **10. Are you sharing with others?** Forget hiding behind an NDA; get out from behind your desk and front door and into your customer's space.

Mantra: Find a pain/pleasure point = profit

Businesses solve discomforts, pains, and problems in addition to providing pleasure with solutions that are convenient, cost-effective, or timely for people. Where there are small pains there are potentially small solutions. Where there is a BIG pain/pleasure for one person, or small one that affects many people, there is the potential for a BIG business. The most important part of starting a business is determining what customer problem you are solving or what unmet need you are meeting. Starting your quest with an accurate problem statement from your customer's perspective is essential to keeping on track. Einstein is quoted as saying he would spend "fifty-five minutes defining the problem and only five minutes finding the solution" if he had one hour to save the world. Will your solution make things better? Will it take away someone's pain by creating something new? Customer pains come in many forms. Your business should find the *source* of the pain and treat the problem, and not the symptoms. A mile-long extension cord does not solve a short battery life in a laptop. Your product should solve the problem in a way that's better than other solutions.

> A problem well-stated is a problem half-solved. - John Dewey

"Why would I want to take care of two computers?" In 1993 many portable computer makers were struggling. Palm Pilot's designer was demonstrating an early, larger version and the most frequent comment was, "If you could make it smaller and allow me to take my contacts with me that'd be great." Listening to potential customers increases your success (true story). [68]

What kind of business do you want to own: wholesale or retail, service or creative, franchise or something that has not been thought up yet? Research for key pieces of information to help narrow the field. After weighing your various options with good and accurate information, go with your gut or intuition if everything else is equal.

That's why it's important to listen to your customer's problem in detail. You can help find a solution to their problem. Don't "get married" to your idea and miss the potential for a "for better or worse" solution to get your business off the ground. The simpler your "Big Idea" is, the more scalable it is for the market. What is most important is that you fall in love with the purpose of your business, and not your product. Be flexible because the product may change. Your business purpose may not.

---

[68] YouTube: The Palm Pilot Story

Watch and listen for pleasure and pain points

Watch and listen for opportunities/pleasure and pain points with your ideal customer doing market research to define your business solution. It's your customer's experience with your solution that makes the difference. In the beginning you can have a spark of inspiration and want to pursue it, but you have to do market research and find an untapped or underserved market. It could even be "scratching your own itch" of a problem you have.

"Do I have to be an expert?" Author Matthew Bennett[69] took three years to write the book, *Maternal Journal: Your Personal Pregnancy Guide.* The idea came to him while at lunch with a doctor who was explaining the difficulty dealing with the various health problems of first-time mothers and the goal of giving better healthcare to them. While Matthew listened – the most important step for *any* entrepreneur – he got an idea. He then spent time researching and putting the book together. Today, he's sold millions of copies of all of his books.

> *Fall in love with the **purpose (why)** of your business, not the **idea (what)** of your business.*

When Matthew conceived, researched, and then wrote his book he did not have any kids, was not married, and was not a doctor (true story).

What is your market? Is it first-time homebuyers? Real estate agents or brokers? Is it first-time mothers? Define who your customer is based on their need for a solution to a similar problem.

Bennett's book was for first-time mothers. To think bigger and broader for your business, consider the "end-to-end" aspect of your business idea: How do you get more of your product to your customer once your market is established? While most people think of amazon.com as the only place to sell books, Bennett sold considerably more copies through doctor associations, trade journals and OGBYN supplier channels.

---

[69] http://www.btdt.com

Tip. You don't have to initially *be* an expert to solve a problem. By putting together the best solutions and answers that solve a problem and your customer's needs you *become* an expert.

Talk to decision-makers in purchasing, retail sales, wholesale and distribution, and people in other distribution channels. Also think of demographics, such as gender, age, income level, occupation, education level, race or ethnicity, religious affiliation, culture, marital status, status of a person's health (blind, hard of hearing, autistic, cerebral palsy, elderly, amputee, Parkinson's disease, various diseases such as Lupus, etc. and include the various disease support issues involved), number of children in the household, home ownership, recreational activities, and location to your business, i.e., the ocean versus the mountains or the United States versus Africa or Asia.

> When I am working on a problem, I never think about beauty. I think only of how to solve the problem. But when I have finished, if the solution is not beautiful, I know it is wrong.
> - R Buckminster Fuller

You'll need to decide what they will do with your product. You'll also need to be aware that what you may design your product for may not be what your customers use it for. Keep your eyes peeled for new opportunities to change your product and look for more products or channels that might be revealed.

"Left field can become center stage." Watch for unintended new market opportunities. Nalgene[70] was a polyethylene laboratory equipment company supplying laboratories with plastic lab equipment. There were "rumors" about hikers. Nalgene's President Marsh Hyman saw hikers on a scouting trip using his company's plastic bottle products to solve their container problems. Hyman jumped at the chance and they expanded their business into the untapped outdoor market.

---

[70] nalgene-outdoor.com/

Google created Sketchup[71] as a beginning 3D modeling software. After its release, the Google team began getting many calls from parents with autistic kids. The parents said the software gave their kids the opportunity to express their creativity and potentially develop a life skill. Google's product became a completely unintended benefit to an otherwise unknown and unplanned customer. Apple decided a Mac with a word processor, spreadsheet, and a database was right for their customers. Wrong! Customers flocked to its desktop publishing solutions that eventually catapulted Mac sales[72] (all true stories).

> Accidents, obstacles, or failures can be **positive** detours on your trail to success and meaning.

Lastly, think size of your market (number of billionaires/Mac computer owners/autistic children) and availability of the product for your customer (i.e., selling the original Mona Lisa or making and selling copies of it). You must also consider the amount of supply for more than just your region or state if you're expecting to sell your product nationally and internationally. Don't water down a product and make it less unique. Adapt and change the product or create different products for different regions, cultures, demographics, or customers.

Strategy Search: Finding your first $1,000,000 idea

That One Thing. In the comedy movie *City Slickers*, the western cowboy character Curly dispenses some wisdom to the city slicker Mitch with the question, "Do you know what the secret of life is?" Of course, Mitch replies, "No, what?"

"One thing. Just one thing. You stick to that and everything else don't mean ?$%#"

"That's great, but..., what's the one thing?"

"That's what you have to figure out."

---

[71] sketchup.google.com/spectrum.html

[72] *Enchantment* by Guy Kawasaki, pg 84

A startup business is no different: Finding that one thing.

Everyone has at least one $1,000,000.00 idea in their head, incubating, growing, just waiting to get out of their head and into the market. Sad to say, most people don't take action on it.

A strategy search is finding a mantra, vision, or purpose for your company, like looking at the horizon: it is always visible, but you never quite arrive. Just like flying an airplane, from a vision you devise a flight plan with various stops or milestones. When you come across a storm or other obstacle, you go around it. This keeps your flight smooth and avoids wasting, consuming, and/or putting your valuable resources, money, and you at risk: a journey for life.

Finding your $1,000,000.00 idea:

1. *Ideas are insights.* Ideas come anytime and from anywhere. A breakthrough idea is rarely a single "That's It!" event, but normally a series of smaller, insightful moments happening before and after the big "Moment." How does an idea begin? It starts with a) looking at problems, b) being mentally and visually open to new ideas and opportunities c) incubating or working on the idea over time, and d) putting the idea in front of your target market to validate the acceptance of your idea. *It's about your overall business purpose, not necessarily your idea; the money follows later.*

> *Everyone should carefully observe which way his heart draws him, and then choose that way with all his strength. - Hasidic Proverb*

2. *Check out the competition.* Search for others that are doing what you're looking to do, whether it's a product or service. What makes your idea different? What does it solve that other solutions do not?

3. *Search for an idea that is profitable.* You may have multiple ideas, many that pop into your head. Just one good idea that will make you a few hundred or thousands of dollars is a start. If you're making money, you've got a good idea. Now, think bigger by searching for your first $1,000,000.00 idea. It means finding what people are "hungry" for, an underserved market or new market that has never been tapped. How do

you find it? Observe what problems or issues people encounter every day that they complain about; review best sellers on the internet (Craig's list, a company's quarterly financial reports, Amazon, social media posts, eBay); look at places that have frequent requests for solutions/ideas/answers; browse Q&A or FAQ sites for frequent questions that might indicate the potential hint of a problem to solve.

4. *Find $1,000,000.00 worth of customers.* Find a price point and then the number of customers to buy it. For example, at a price point of $100.00 for a Mac application you'll need 10,000 customers who are willing to shell out their money to buy it. A $4.00 cup of coffee needs 250,000 customers. Do you have the right number of customers to make a living? Use Google Analytics, Keywords, Trends, and Insights for insightful numbers. Use census.gov, your local Chambers of Commerce, direct marketing information, or other means to search for what your customers are looking for. You are looking for a "school of fish" to hook, the bigger the school, the bigger your business; you don't want a business idea that is on the "endangered species list."

5. *Evaluate your customer's total value.* While most think of a customer making one purchase, consider a customer's Total Cost of Ownership, i.e., the lifetime of a product or service for a customer. It's not a one-time buy $4.00 cup of coffee or an $12.99 book, but multiple cups of coffee or a book series. Buying a car is a major expense; how much does it cost to maintain it over the life of the car? A computer lasts 3-5 years, consider how it is maintained and when would a customer upgrade to newer models? Then there are additional products and services around your first idea.

6. *Prove your idea!* Let the testing begin. You need to validate your idea and this is the most difficult part. You need to get out and get in front of customers to see if your product solves their problem and if they'll buy. One simple question that helps: Tell them you'll give it to them for free and ask them if they'd take it? If they say no, back to the drawing board to fix your idea. If yes, you have a valuable product/service. Next ask them if they'd pay an exorbitant price for

your product (say $1,000.00 for a $5.00 product). If they vocally balk at the price, then ask them what they *would* pay for it? Their answer gives you the ball park of your pricing. Another idea is put a simple ad on Craig's List and see if you have any takers. It's free, so nothing ventured, nothing gained.

7. *Find your idea's sales repeatability.* Can you repeat the sale of the product or service with multiple customers or sales, such as multiple cups of coffee, variations of your product (espresso or Vietnamese coffee, MacBook or an iMac), or getting more new customers? It's not only: What Sells Now? But also: What Sells Next?

8. *Find your marketing.* As it has been reported in Apple's Cupertino campus, they have a saying posted for all to see about Apple solutions, "~~Simplify~~, ~~simplify~~, simplify." This means to simplify your marketing, just like Apple's "1000 songs in your pocket" for the iPod. Keep it simple.

9. *Drive, drive, drive.* Don't stop doing.

Models: Define what works best for you

Model or pattern your business after another to cut the amount of research and development time and effort it takes to become successful. Modeling is not the same thing as copying. Copying may not give you an understanding of how a business works. Modeling gives you a basis from which to start and allows you to adjust for different factors such as place, environment, industry, and most of all, yourself. Besides, you want to make your business your own.

> *Your people model is the **"soft element"** of your business and covers shared values, skills, style, and your staff, hired workers, and mentors and is the most difficult to apply.*

Define your mentors: Values and people model

Your people model means getting help for your business. You cannot do it alone, nor should you. There are just too many things that affect your business. Find experts in the areas you need help with; there are only so many hours in a day.

You'll need a host of people to turn to for help. You personally will have to have a set of core values and then associate with those with similar values. Here are some examples:

Core Values or Beliefs - You need to decide what is important to you running your company and how you will work with others. Your values and beliefs will help guide you.

Your People Team - These are people willing to help you and follow your company's ideals. They are:

▸ **Mastermind Group** - A small group of committed people meeting consistently to *strategize* the group's business for sustainability and growth.

▸ **Expert Advisors** - Individuals who can help you with *tactical advantages* in your business, such as a CPA, lawyer, accountant, bookkeeper, graphic artist, web host, mentor, coach, assistant or virtual assistant, computer technical support, and other industry professionals. Consultants may be too costly in the beginning for the job you need. Besides, you need to learn more about how things are done and set up processes to make sure you protect how your business is run.

▸ **Specialist Advisors** - These people help with *technical issues*: a Mac expert; a graphic artist to make your graphics or logos; an office worker; a book editor; or the system administrator or programmer to automate your workflow. Generally you don't want to overlook these as they can help with keeping details from causing major issues in future decisions.

▸ **Community (of Conversations)** - Here is where you connect with others and are interacting with a group of individuals around a subject matter or a location.

Some of the answers you should seek are: Can your business scale? Can you get the right people with the right skills? What industry do you want to pursue?

Define your money model: Product, service, or ...?

In most cases as an entrepreneur, there is no personalized map or blueprint to find your one thing, because it's personal. Your map will be different from anyone else's because you're exploring. That does not mean you can't learn from others to make your own path to greatness.

Using the four Ps in the first pages of Chapter 2 is a start, but you can also see a current product for sale in a different way. In the book *Cracking the Millionaire Code,* author Mark Victor Hansen describes 21 different ways you can view a product or service. For example, take any idea and see how you can: add to it, subtract from it, multiply it, exponential it, divide it, residual it, combine it, slow it down, genderize it, or recycle it to come up with something different.

After you have that one idea, you next need to look at four basic questions:

▸ Can what I am dreaming of be done?

▸ Can this product or service be sold?

▸ Can I make a profit?

▸ Is there room in the market for growing this business?

> *Big-government types can't comprehend that one of the beauties of capitalism is that it turns scarcity into abundance.*
> *- Steve Forbes*

What will be your streams of making money? Having only one income stream, such as a job, puts you at risk if this one source fails or is negatively affected. Your hours or income can be cut if you don't lose your job outright. Having multiple sources of income can prevent you from being hurt by changes in your main job and can allow you to stand a better chance of getting ahead. How?

Trading time for money? Not! The definition of trading time for money is you work to perform a specific task and then get paid for it. Nearly everyone does it. Trading time for money usually means working at a Walmart, selling a painting that you have made, writing an article to sell, performing a medical procedure, writing a contract, making a meal, or even mowing a lawn. The key to getting *out* of the "trading time for money" trap is to monetize your knowledge and expertise into other products so you can sell 24/7, while you're sleeping.

Having many product lines gives you more leverage and diversity of income for when a product, supplier, vendor or your health fails. If you start a business you might not succeed out of the starting gate. You might have to change your product until it becomes successful. Then once that becomes successful you add another product, then another one until all of them attain success. Now, if the market changes you'll have time and breathing room to change with the market because you won't have all of your income in one basket.

Next Thing. How do you view your product or service? A giveaway pen might be $0.59, a book might be $29.95, or your expert consulting fees may be $2,000 or more per hour plus royalties if you are that good at what you do. While a book normally gives your customer information, a concierge service is taking the idea and getting them to pay you for executing it for them. It comes down to a few different levels of business perspectives all based on your knowledge and experience. Below, with potentially mixed levels of profit, are the six ways:

> *Why would you study it when you could be doing it? - Mark Zuckerberg*

1. **Products - I'll sell you**. This is the standard wholesale, retail or reseller business. This could be selling crafts, candles, lumber, an informational website with memberships, paperweights, books, e-books, a book of Photoshop techniques, software as a service (SAAS), podcasts or videocasts, or presentation CDs or DVDs. It could mean opening up a brick and mortar store or an online store to sell others' products. It can also be a different process, such as the iTunes store versus buying CDs. Will you sell a one-time product to a customer, such as a pool for a home, or go for repeat business such as consumables like food or gas?

2. **Concierge services - I'll do it for you.** Here, the customer pays you to do it for them because they either don't have the time or the knowledge. A graphic artist can design a logo, a copywriter can create advertising copy, or a sales person can get a commission selling your product. If you attended college to become a doctor you can perform a medical procedure; an architect can design a blueprint for a building; a musician can write, sing and sell a song. If you sell a pool, you could also sell services to clean pools.

3. **Consulting - I'll help you.** You design the opportunity for a *one-on-one training* session. You can also offer a *tele-seminar* where multiple people are listening in on a discussion over the telephone or the web. You could have a *one-on-one consulting* session with some customers listening in. Lastly, you could host a private *tele-consulting* session where you would work with a single client charging more per hour.

4. **Speaking - I'll tell you.** This is where you engage your customers at speaking engagements or events by informing and educating them about what they can do with your expert information. At most speaking engagements your customers may take notes and you may give handouts for them on your subject. You can sell more of your product or service "at the back of the room" after your speech.

5. **Seminars and workshops - I'll show you.** When you lead seminars and workshops, your workbooks allow people to take notes and walk away from your event with an action plan with your information. It could be a HOW-TO seminar such as making a craft, a sewing workshop, or classes on a how to learn iWork. A workshop is more hands-on than merely speaking to an audience.

6. **Combination - I'll offer it all for you.** You may be doing a little of all the above. Some customers just want the information that you give so they can do it themselves. Others want you to do it for them and you can charge more per hour to them. However, the question is: How much is your time worth? Each of us has the same amount of hours

during the day, so consider how to maximize your time and efforts, to monetize yours or others' knowledge.

Three from one. When it comes to creating multiple products and services, one of the simplest things to do is to record video of your speaking engagements. Afterward you can check what you said and your customers' reaction, and then you can use iMovie and iDVD to create a DVD product to sell. You can also maximize the monetization of your time by making three products out of one of your speaking engagements: 1) a video, 2) an audio that is pulled from the video for your customer to listen to on their iPod, and 3) a book that is pulled from the transcript of the video.

Tip. When defining your products and services, think beginner, intermediate, and expert level of your customers. Experts may just want a small amount of information and they can do the rest, while beginners need hand-holding and more details to learn what you do. Charge accordingly.

Define your business model

Do you intend to work with a select number of clients? Do you intend to grow locally, regionally, nationally, or even internationally?

What business do you want to own? Which customers are you going to help? Where do they meet? Hockey moms may meet at ice rinks, but they also meet at sports stores.

What and where are your customers? The nine models are:

1. **Business to Consumer (B2C)** - Retail, home cleaning, lawn care, food preparation, retail to consumer.

2. **Business to Business (B2B)** - Bookkeeping, business support, consulting, virtual assistant, retail to business.

3. **Business to Government (B2G)** - Federal, state, and local governments, retail to government.

4. **Business to Philanthropies (B2P)** - Non-profits and 501(c)3 organizations, retail to non-profits.

5. **Buying a Business** - Franchise or business for sale.

6. **Joint Venture (JV)** - Working alongside various industries and partners to design, manufacture, distribute, and/or sell complementary products and services (tires and tire cleaner).

7. **Licensing** - License your product or service for others to use within their business model.

8. **Consulting** - Improving products, services or processes.

9. **Combination** - Combing elements of all the above, bundling to sell more of each.

> *Your business model focuses on strategy, structure, and systems and are the **"hard elements"** of a business, but the easiest to apply.*

Your business model is the structure of how you intend to make money. Even though you normally would follow just one model above, depending on your product, you can cross over to other models. For instance, if you have written a book about foreclosures you can sell that to a retail book store. But you can also find non-profits that help people work through their financial issues. Your book could be a resource.

Tip: Listen to your customers. Customers may use a product differently than the way it was intended. Keep your eyes and ears open for business and product opportunities from customers or other people's comments. A set of "fresh eyes and ears" from janitors to CEOs to soccer moms on your product or service may yield more product or business opportunities.

Money: Start good money habits

Your parents, family, friends, and teachers influence your views and habits about money, and those views vary across the financial map, both positive and negative. It is only how people view or feel about money that makes the difference. To earn money you need to learn about money, including finance, accounting, taxes, and bookkeeping.

In a slow economy or a recession there is less money to go around to small businesses. A tight economy does not mean that you can't start your own business. It is not uncommon to start-up a business during a slow economy. If you were to succeed during good times, you might never know what your business will do during bad times. On the other hand if your business survives during an economic downturn, you have an advantage over others as the economy rebounds. Better to fail now just starting out with fewer dollars at stake and do something "on the cheap." When things are good and you blow through good money for the "want" of a business, it can be harder to take the loss. If you do start a business during "inclement economic weather" and are successful, then you'll be even more successful when times get better. You will have survived the dark hours of your business.

> *Don't tell me where your priorities are. Show me where you spend your money and I'll tell you what they are.*
> *- James W. Frick*

Describe your financial situation. You need to know where you are financially. This means that you have to take stock of your personal finances. Create a Numbers spreadsheet of your net worth. List your assets (cash and checking, savings account, real estate or home, cars, bonds, securities, insurance cash values, etc.). List your liabilities (current monthly bills, credit cards and charge accounts, mortgage, car loans, finance company loans, personal debts, other debts). Subtracting liabilities from assets is your net worth. The iWork '09 Numbers program has a spreadsheet template called "Net Worth" that you can fill out to get a good idea what you are worth.

Remember, it means going through everything, including all of your furniture, clothes, etc., to find out your net worth. Not what you paid for the items, but what you would get if you were to sell them. Why catalog everything that you own? You may want to sell something to provide capital and keep your business going and knowing the value of everything helps. You may or may not be surprised at the value of what you own, but knowing also gives you an idea of the replacement value for insurance purposes.

Budget personal spending, then budget business spending. One of the essential parts of building a successful business is being able to pay your bills with your business income. Then, as your business grows you can begin to set aside enough and to prepare for retirement. As a business owner you need to set up a budget and then find a category for every dollar that you spend. Most importantly, you need to have good

> *Beware of little expenses. A small leak will sink a great ship. - Benjamin Franklin*

personal financial habits to start and run a successful business. The purpose of a budget is to know where you are spending your money to keep your spending and costs in line with your revenue and income. Here are some essential steps for starting good personal and business financial habits:

1. **Set up your accounting system.** Set up a system of chart of accounts, or buckets, to track where your money is and goes.

2. **Plan your spending and savings.** Your money should be allocated: 10% paying yourself for retirement, 10% to long term savings and spending, 50% to necessities, 10% to charities, 10% to education, 10% to play. Rich people invest first, then spend their money; poor people spend it first, then invest.

3. **Categorize every dollar and cent spent.** This includes rent, food, office supplies, advertising, and business expenses for tax purposes. Each penny will need to categorized.

4. **Pay each bill when it arrives.** Larger companies are now charging late fees which can affect your credit score, so it is best to pay it before it's due.

5. **Monitor spending and adjust budgets.** Go over your spending each month and adjust according to your personal, business and financial goals. Check for up or down trends

and research why they are happening. Find out why you were under or over your budget each month, this means watching both your customer and vendor bills for price increases with new or increasing fees and charges.

Determine business startup costs. Figure out where you need to be in gathering all the necessary elements to build your business. The smaller or simpler the business, the easier it is to research. You have to consider all of your startup costs: legal fees, location, inventory, equipment, labor, employee benefits and taxes, utility services, transportation, regulatory compliance, and of course paying local, state, and federal taxes. Also decide whether your product or service is a one-time, frequent, or ongoing revenue. Nearly every startup underestimates its costs, so double or even triple your startup capital to be ready for unforeseen issues.

> *Just because something doesn't do what you planned it to do doesn't mean it's useless.*
> *- Thomas Edison*

Funding: Money doesn't grow on trees!

Most people think that running a business needs a complete abandonment of your current working situation even when it is really not in your best interest to leave. Sometimes this happens by no choice of your own, other times you can't wait to take advantage of the opportunity and you take the leap into the unknown.

Think through how you will manage your finances while you chase your dream. Will you take on a second job? Dig into your savings? Will you seek financing? Consider some of these places to "fund" your business (in descending order of importance):

1. **Sales of a product** - This is the best and only way of being successful and is the most successful approach to building a business. Sell something and do your best to keep your costs low until you have enough money saved up to finance more growth. If your product does not sell, most of the other suggested funding avenues below may not help. It is best not

to try these other routes below because your product or service hasn't demonstrated a track record of success. However, here are four ways of finding more funding through your sales:

a. Find new customers.

b. Convince customers to buy more often.

> *I hate quotations. Tell me what you know.*
> *- Ralph Waldo Emerson*

c. Convince customers to buy premium priced items or higher volume.

d. Increase marketing and brand loyalty.

2. **"Bartering" for services** - Share resources with friends and family. As they're helping you, you also help their business and you learn from each other in an exchange of labor. Exchanging free labor to gain experience is one way to increase the value you bring to the market.

3. Crowdsourcing - Check out kickstarter.com, indiegogo.com, and microplace.com (a PayPal company) to allow the average Joe a chance at funding a startup idea. If you want to give back to the community, take a look at kiva.org for helping third world people, donorschoose.org for teachers in schools, and crowdrise.com for your causes.

4. **"Marketing" or "Sponsorships" for your services** - This is where larger businesses buy your product and donate it to others, especially to a help a non-profit and their customers. For instance, if you have written a book about how to save money at the grocery store, a large business might buy your book and give it to non-profits to give away to low-income clients. Businesses get the tax write-offs and the non-profit can get your product for free.

5. **Self-funded** - You can pay your own way using your own cash and savings. This also means finding free ways of getting things done or not doing them at all! The less you spend up

front, the more you'll keep for the downturns or for future expansion.

6. **Gifts versus loans** - A gift is a show of faith in you, but a loan is an expense. If you receive a loan, make sure interest is charged because the loan is tax-deductible, a gift is not.

7. **Home equity line of credit** - Don't go overboard on this if you feel like you're going to hurt your chances of recovering your assets if your business goes south.

8. **SBA Microloan** - This is a good bet if you need less than $35,000 and can swing the interest rates.

9. **Angel investors or venture capital** - If you are looking for larger capital amounts for going national or international, these investors supply amounts greater than $500,000 - $10M in funding for scalable startups.

10. **Bank loan** - You will need collateral for this funding source and it's one of the more difficult types to procure.

Keep in mind that when it comes to money, it's not only about paying for producing your product; you also have to consider the amount of time it takes to get paid by your customer. It could take weeks or months before you get what is owed you. Plan on this "floating" of payments when looking at financing your business.

"You're on the right road." The website 37signals.com has done entrepreneurship right and unconventionally in many ways (as well as others at 37signals.com/bootstrapped). They've grown successful companies with no debt and no funding. Now that's a company roadmap to emulate (true story).

Action plan: Write down your action steps!

First things first: Get your ideas and thoughts out of your head and onto paper or white boards so you can "see them." Businesses have succeeded and failed with or without a business plan. There are no guarantees. But writing things down gives a sanity check for you and those who connect with you.

This section discusses business planning and modeling basics. It is best to consult more authoritative and specific business plan books, or seek out professionals.

"Customer Experience Details." Steve Jobs was focused on details. For the design of Apple products, the customer experience was paramount, sometimes too much. In an Apple "Can We Talk" online logo discussion it was revealed that "Opening a laptop from the wrong end is a self-correcting problem that only lasts for a few seconds. However, the public viewing the upside down logo is a problem that lasts indefinitely."[73] Apple righted the laptop logo because of product placement (true story).

Jobs hired Paul Rand to do a world-class logo and, as a bonus, a calling card for Jobs. Both Jobs and Rand had a heated and lengthy argument of the placement of the period after the "P" in Steven P. Jobs. The argument was over digital technology and having the period nudged under the curve of the letter P versus old school lead type with the period to the right of the letter. Jobs won and used the digital version (true story).[74]

To Business Plan or Not to Business Plan?

You may have heard the saying, "When the only tool you have is a hammer, it is tempting to treat everything as if it were a nail." Abraham Maslow's quote, known as Maslow's hierarchy of needs, explains an overuse of a familiar tool to solve all the problems that one meets. A hammer can't and shouldn't be used as a screwdriver or a chisel. It is the same for business plans. Google, Apple, Starbucks, and PayPal, according to the book *Getting to Plan B* by John Mullins, all started with a business plan. All the plans changed when the results were not being achieved as expected. Your business and plan will change to fit the market's needs and wants.

---

[73] http://blog.joemoreno.com/2012/05/upside-down-apple-logo.html

[74] *Steve Jobs* by Walter Isaacson, pg 574

Mullins reiterates in his book some great business advice for budding entrepreneurs; that advice was originally published in 1937 during the Great Depression in Napoleon Hill's *Think and Grow Rich*:

> *If the first plan you adopt does not work successfully, replace it with a new plan; if this new plan fails to work, replace it still with still another, and so on, until you find a plan which does work. Right here is the point at which the majority of men meet with failure, because of their lack of persistence in* **creating new plans to take the place of those which fail** *(author's emphasis).*

A current debate is whether a business plan is a waste of time and effort. Depends. Completing a business plan is not the main goal for any budding entrepreneur; it's the entrepreneur's *exercise in planning, knowing their business numbers, and finding insights into their idea and business model that fits the customer's needs that are the most important skills to learn.* The history of business plans is that the necessity came from larger corporations and banks that wanted to document the requirements for any new business that was going to be pursued.

> *Doing business research gives a sanity check to your business idea. - Laz Chernik*

However, yesterday's *business planning* de facto prominence among "old school" corporations and educational institutions is quickly being replaced with the rapid ascendance of *business modeling*, the constant searching for a repeatable and scalable business model. Modeling (following Col. John Boyd's OODA loop) means most successful startup founders:

▸ *Observe* something isn't working in a current business model,

▸ *Orient* themselves to the newly discovered facts,

▸ *Decide/Pivot* (change in) a major part (vs details) of their business model, then,

▸ *Act* decisively to execute the change.

Blending business planning (knowing startup numbers) and modeling (changing more rapidly to unfolding events than an opponent) a business "gets inside" a competitor's decision cycle and gains the advantage in a business environment with their customers, i.e., skill versus strength, quickness versus slow to change.

In some cases you may start with a basic idea then progress over time as your idea and business grow. Most investors are interested in how you arrived at your facts, not how great

> *Operating in Chaos +*
> *Speed + Pivots =*
> *Success*
> *- Steve Blank*

your business plan looks. Many angel investors or venture capitalists have seen thousands of business plans and can tell which ones have "canned" information.

Ideas are a dime a dozen, proven inventions are worth bucks, but it's action, executing on your idea, that will make the difference between failure, success, and having a large income.

Future of Startups: Business Model Canvas

Business Model Canvas. Good startup entrepreneurs know that it's first *all about your business numbers and results*, not flowery marketing words. The business model canvas is what every entrepreneur needs to fill out with their business and customer data. What content is contained in each section in the Business Model Canvas? The Chart 3 of the Business Model Canvas outlines the placement of each element.[75]

Value Propositions: What value do we deliver to the customer? Which one of our customer's problems are we helping to solve? What bundles of products and services are we offering to each Customer Segment? Which customer needs are we satisfying?

Characteristics: Newness, Performance, Customization, "Getting the job done," Design, Brand/Status, Price, Cost Reduction, Risk Reduction, Accessibility, Convenience/Usability.

---

[75] http://www.businessmodelgeneration.com

Key Partners	Key Activities	Value Propositions	Customer Relationships	Customer Segments
	Key Resources		Channels	
Cost Structure			Revenue Streams	

Chart 3: Business Model Canvas

Customer Relationships: What type of relationship does each of our Customer Segments expect us to establish and maintain with them? Which ones have we established? How are they integrated with the rest of our business model? How costly are they?

Examples: Personal Assistance, Dedicated Personal Assistance, Self-Service, Automated Services, Communities, Co-creation.

Channels: Through which Channels do our Customer Segments want to be reached? How are we reaching them now? How are our Channels integrated? Which ones work best? Which ones are most cost-efficient? How are we integrating them with customer routines?

Channel phases:

Awareness - How do we raise awareness about our company's products and services?

Evaluation - How do we help customers evaluate our organization's Value Proposition?

Purchase - How do we allow customers to purchase specific products and services?

Delivery - How do we deliver a Value Proposition to customers?

After sales - How do we provide post-purchase customer support?

Customer Segments: For whom are we creating value? Who are our most important customers?

Types of markets: Mass Market, Niche Market, Segmented, Diversified, Multi-sided Platform

Key Activities: What Key Activities do our Value Propositions require? Our Distribution Channels? Customer Relationships Revenue streams?

Categories: Production, Problem Solving, Platform/Network

Key Resources: What Key Resources do our Value Propositions require? Our Distribution Channels? Customer Relationships? Revenue Streams?

Types of resources: Physical, Intellectual (brand patents, copyrights, data), Human, Financial

Key Partners: Who are our Key Partners? Who are our Key Suppliers? Which Key Resources are we acquiring from Partners? Which Key Activities do Partners perform?

Motivations for partnerships: Optimization and economy, Reduction of risk and uncertainty, Acquisition of particular resources and activities

Revenue Streams: For what value are our customers really willing to pay? For what do they currently pay? How are they currently paying? How would they prefer to pay? How much does each Revenue Stream contribute to overall revenues?

Types: Asset sale, Usage fee, Subscription Fees Lending/ Renting/Leasing Licensing, Brokerage fees Advertising

Fixed pricing - List Price, Product feature dependent, Customer segment dependent, Volume dependent

Dynamic pricing - Negotiation (bargaining), Yield Management, Real-time-Market

Cost Structure: What are the most important costs inherent in our business model? Which Key Resources are most expensive? Which Key Activities are most expensive?

Is your business more: Cost Driven (leanest cost structure, low price value proposition, maximum automation, extensive outsourcing), Value Driven (focused on value creation, premium value proposition)?

Sample characteristics: Fixed Costs (salaries, rents, utilities), Variable costs, Economies of scale, Economies of scope

"The Million Dollar Idea." In one *I Love Lucy* episode, named *The Millionaire Idea,* Lucy and Ethel go into business together selling Lucy's Aunt Martha's salad dressing. Problem is, they did not calculate how much they'd profit from sales. Ricky calculates it for them and figures out after all of their work they'd be making only pennies. So much for "getting rich" if you don't know your numbers. Knowing your numbers prevents wasting valuable time, money, and reputation.

Essential spreadsheet tips for business planning and modeling: Spend more time with the spreadsheet side of your business model rather than the marketing side. Learn to calculate in your head the profit and value potential of your numbers. Getting the "numbers right" for your business modeling is important. You should split a spreadsheet into three areas in a large worksheet: data, calculations, and display or summary.

▸ *Data* is where you can literally type or key in the information and make sure that there are no typos or import data exported from another spreadsheet or database. If you do not have much data, you can highlight or colorize the cells containing just the data and blend it with the next areas.

▸ *Calculation* areas allow you to take the input from the data area and begin number crunching the data to get the results. You may have to do some calculations, so design the spreadsheet so you can check your calculations, i.e., step through each calculation. It's about getting the resulting answers to your data questions, not about how it looks. That's for the next area to discuss.

▸ *Summary/Display* area is where you rearrange the results to fit your message or the business plans's or model's "look and feel." The summary cell can refer to a results cell, but can display the information completely differently, especially if you are including charts or are mixing various sources of data results to arrive at your message.

Chapter Four

Step 4: Business Model to Actions Steps

Keep away from people who try to belittle your ambitions.
Small people always do that, but the really great ones make
you feel that you too, can become great. -- Mark Twain

Story: "Blazing a new business trail"

Erica had done her business research and set her business
Go/No-Go date, a date a decision needs to be made, but she was
in a quandary. Pressure from her parents and friends was pushing
her to a tipping point in her life: the choice of whether to pursue
her business, go back and finish her degree, or work for someone
else. Erica's own self talk of "I can't do this" and "You'll never
be good enough" stalked her thoughts and didn't make it any
easier for her. A friend suggested, "Why don't you visit your local
small business development centers or talk with other local
entrepreneurs and get the gist of what they go through?" Erica
took the advice and her many discussions with other
entrepreneurs helped put mental restraining orders on her
doubts, allowing her to continue on.

Erica considered her dilemma: spend money and time going
to college, or spend the same amount of money and time and
start her own business. College gave her the time to test out her
idea in the comfort of school, but great school grades do not
necessarily equate with success in the marketplace, and many

schools do not offer entrepreneurship courses. As one local college recruiter said to her, "A college education provides the necessary accumulation of specialized knowledge for lawyers, doctors, engineers, and a host of other careers including the skills for life-long learning."

Erica also knew that college certificates and degrees provide only enough specialized knowledge about a career, but not enough about running a business or earning a living as a freelance artist or business. She also knew that attending college may not be, is not, or — for circumstances beyond a person's control — cannot be for everyone.

What is more important, Erica knew that situations like hers should not stop anyone from pursuing their dreams and using their talents. As an entrepreneur, she could get some of the specialized knowledge she needed from regular meetings with fellow entrepreneurs in a Mastermind group, other business connections she would make, and from lessons learned from the "School of Hard Knocks." A local entrepreneur who had sold her product to a Fortune 500 company told Erica, "If you were to branch out and sell something to a Fortune 500 company, it would not only be great exposure for your business, but getting their professional feedback to get into their systems over time is like earning an MBA in their industry."

Saying "goodbye for now" to college, Erica decided to follow the entrepreneurial path of Steve Jobs, Bill Gates, and other business heroes. Instead of getting graded by school, her grades would be measured by sales and making a profit.

Erica learned from history classes, business autobiographies, and talking with other entrepreneurs like James, a newly started custom furniture designer. She learned that planning for her business' opening day is no different from what John Jacob Astor[76] did in the early 1800s when he became America's first multimillionaire. No matter what level of income you want to achieve, whether a few thousand or millions of dollars, seeing an opportunity to make money always takes an investment in time and money.

---

[76] http://en.wikipedia.org/wiki/John_Jacob_Astor

Astor planned and financed trips over the Oregon Trail after reading about the Lewis and Clark expedition results. While Lewis and Clark's government-financed expedition (by Thomas Jefferson) "for the purposes of commerce" did not come back empty handed[77], the endeavor failed in its primary goal: to find an easy route to the Pacific Coast. Astor heard what Lewis and Clark found and, seizing the potential business opportunity, financed expeditions to set up a fur-trading enterprise at the mouth of the Columbia River. It was during an Astorian group's return trip to the East Coast that they discovered the only easy navigable route, the 20 mile wide South Pass in Wyoming.[78] Through this route, supply ladened wagons weighing an average of 2000 pounds could cross the Continental Divide headed for the Pacific Coast.

The idea of "jumping off cities" of the Oregon Trail – those cities in which settlers congregated to wait for the right time in the spring to head west – was similar to Erica determining a good time window to start her business. James said, "You need to take your business model and translate your model from paper and spreadsheet numbers into actual processes, a real design for how your business can work in real-time. Then you need to set a date to begin selling." Taking James' advice, Erica decided on a date – there's no perfect "Grand Opening!" date – with that leap of faith that begins with each new journey.

Over many weeks Erica's new friend James, fellow entrepreneurs, serial entrepreneurs (those who had only one business or had successive businesses), and parallel entrepreneurs (those running multiple businesses at the same time), all made a familiar comment. "You've done all the right things to increase your success with your first business planning, better than most. Just keep moving toward your goals and see through your obstacles."

However, while getting her business off the ground, Erica began hitting snags. "I'm frustrated," she told James. "My planning hasn't led to what I'd hoped, sometimes not even close!"

---

[77] http://www.library.csi.cuny.edu/dept/history/lavender/jefflett.html

[78] http://en.wikipedia.org/wiki/Oregon_Trail

"Don't worry," James said, "It happens. Put a date to make a decision on, gather as much information about the obstacle, make the decision, then move on and learn from it."

After leaving the jumping off cities, many of the settlers along the Oregon Trail dumped off their unneeded or unwanted stuff. Similarly, Erica began dumping her product overstock and ill-conceived business solutions on Craig's list at a loss. At least someone could find a use for her business throw offs[79], and she'd get *some* money back; the Oregon settlers lost it all.

In her entrepreneurship journey, Erica discovered "vegetation overgrowth" of hostile, entrenched, and entangled government bureaucracies. The hot, dull and boring flatlands of "gnats" of paperwork and endless "flies" of small errands. And of course, new "Indian" client nations of customers and entrepreneurs with which to trade and learn from were the many startup discoveries as a business trailblazer. Erica kept a journal of her business journey so that she could write more about it in her newsletter. Others would be interested in her story and it would inspire them to do the same, just as Astor had been inspired by Lewis and Clark.

Erica's excitement at achieving an entrepreneurial goal was growing, and so were the cheers from others around her. Building a business from scratch taught Erica and her colleagues to always explore forward thinking. The cuts, bruises and scars of backcountry entrepreneurship would be considered badges of honor to all who are business or industry pioneers. Erica and her team posted a new sign on their startup business wagon: "Open for Business or Bust!"

Business startup summary

With a plan in place, it's time to start step by step. There is a four-step process nearly all businesses follow:

‣ Marketing - "Attract Me"

---

[79] http://www.isu.edu/~trinmich/Allabout.html

▸ Sales - "Educate Me"

▸ Operations - "Sell Me"

▸ Customer Service - "Serve Me"

Each stage refers to the customer's viewpoint of your business and how you are engaging them. You start by getting your customer interested in your product (marketing). Then you make a compelling argument for them to buy it (sales). You have to make a great product, get it to your customer and get paid for it (operations). Once it is sold, you make sure they like it and would be willing to do business with you again (customer service).

Business modeling and fishing: What's common?

Finding a business model is like fishing:

▸ You have to know the "fish" that you are fishing for, whether it's salmon, tuna, or trout. (**Who** is your *ideal customer/tribe?*)

▸ You have to know the eating habits of your "fish." (**What** does your *ideal product or service* solve? What is your crowd "hungry" for?)

▸ You have to know where the right "fishing spots" are. (**Where** are your customers? Where are the *ideal locations* they visit, hang out, and connect with others of their tribe?)

▸ You have to have the right "bait." (**Why** would your customer choose your product over others? What's your *ideal message* to your customer? What makes your product different or makes it stand out?)

▸ You have to have the right techniques to lure your "fish" toward your bait. (**How** do your customers make buying decisions about your product? What *ideal techniques* hook them? What makes them tick about how they choose your product?)

▸ You have to know the right time to "cast" your line. (**When** is the *ideal time* to promote your product to your customer?

How often do you have to talk to your customer to get them to consider and then buy your product?)

The essential point about marketing is to find a market "sweet spot." A product released too early gives competition time to catch up, released too late and your market may move on. In addition, it's taking and *putting the information into a sequence* for a project plan.

Branding, marketing and products

As an entrepreneur, where do you start?

Start with an idea. Most people won't even get beyond forming an idea and if they do have an idea, they don't follow through. There are thousands of great ideas, but ideas are worthless if no one acts upon them. You can be different; take some type of action on that idea. A well-executed idea, no matter how bad it might seem, could make you tens of thousands if not millions of dollars. Nearly every entrepreneur has at least one million-dollar idea in them, so why not work it out and take a chance on your dream?

Where do you start first, the product or the marketing?

Ideally, product development and marketing are done concurrently. As you figure out what problems your product solves, you develop your marketing to appeal to your customer.

The reasons for doing product development and branding/marketing at the same time are:

▸ To decide if your product is "on target" after you have begun working to produce it.

▸ To cut down on steps to get your product into your customers' hands faster.

▸ To place Version One in your customer's hands and be ready to produce Version Two from plenty of feedback.

▸ To provide a way for you to start "pre-selling" your product before it launches in order to gauge interest.

▸ To have instant website marketing copy ready to go.

▸ To have basic information ready for press releases announcing your product.

Marketing and sales. They are critical functions of building a business. A discussion with a business friend illustrated this idea. I said to him, "Marketing is about getting new customers and sales is taking care of those you have. Why then do you say, 'sales and marketing' and not 'marketing and sales?'" He answered, "I've known some companies where sales drives the company and they feed their sales information into their marketing department while others have great marketing which drives sales."

It doesn't matter which is first. Either way they are both important to the success of your business.

Plan and manage time and projects

Two questions in starting any business are: How much do I have to spend and how much time do I have to put into it?

Money and Time perspectives. Costs are a normal course of building a business. Most often overlooked, however, is how much time you'll have to put in. It's a matter of defining the size and scope of a project and knowing how to get the job done.

Project versus process times. Total project time is equal to the total time of all the steps it takes to finish the project. For example, the project of publishing a book. The major steps include writing, editing, printing, and shipping. The project could take a year and each step will take varying lengths of time.

Defining and sequencing the steps of the project. Defining each step of the process and the proper sequence can save valuable time and money. You don't build the first floor of a house before you put in the foundation; the same goes for business projects.

For instance, indexing a book should come after editing, otherwise indexing will have to be done again, costing you time and money. Some things have to be done in sequence, others can be done in parallel, such as developing a book cover while writing or editing. Everything has to be completed by the publish date.

Marketing can be done weeks or even months before release to presell the book.

Establish an "Open for Business," "Release," or "For Sale" date. You may need to set a date for some reasons: You're leasing space to open your business. You're trying to catch a holiday rush. A vendor or customer has a date that the project needs to be completed. See about creating soft and hard dates below.

Set a customer's date, then back up the bus. Base your launch date from a customer's point of view. For instance, for a Christmas launch, you want to have the book ready to go under the tree before November 25. Most customers would love to have it by December 11, about two weeks before the holiday date. To plan accordingly you need the book released in September, or at least by October, to get a big bang from the Christmas rush. Plan your marketing and press releases to garner interest and to increase sales.

Below is an example of a simple project plan. In a spreadsheet, such as iWork's Numbers, create five columns (See Table 2 below):

Column 1: Define the necessary project steps and the correct sequence of each step to complete.

Column 2: Your start date is figured after the other columns are filled out with information.

Column 3: Estimate the amount of time needed to complete each step. (Keep in mind an end-to-end project, including product development, production, distribution, and promotion.)

Column 4: Provide cost estimates for each step.

Column 5: The Date Due column is when the customer wants it or you can deliver it.

How to figure a project Start Date: work backwards. In Column 1 list the correct sequence of process or project steps. In Column 3 calculate how long in days (or minutes, week, months, years) it will take for each step. In Column 4 figure out costs. In Column 5 establish the Date Due. From the Date Due in Column 5 (11/14) you subtract the number of days (7) in Column 3 to get the Start Date (11/07) of the step (Column 5 minus Column 3 = Column 2). Repeat that process until you reach step one and your

1	2	3	4	5
Step	Start Date	Days To Complete	Cost	Date Due
1. Write a book	03/20	180		09/16
2. Book editing	09/16	21	$1,000.00	10/07
3. Design book cover	10/07	14	$500.00	10/21
4. Index book	10/21	4	$300.00	10/25
5. Final Title decided	10/25	1		10/26
6. Produce book(s)	10/26	7	$20.00	11/02
7. Inventory book	11/02	5		11/07
8. Ship a book	11/07	7	$7.00	11/14
9. Customer's date				11/14
Project Totals		239	$1,827.00	

Table 2: Project Management of book publishing

actual Start Date. For larger or more complex projects, the more important these planning steps become. NOTE: In some cases you can do some steps at the same time, thus reducing the project time.

This is a simple way to get started. Project management software, for larger projects that involve more details and resources, can help keep you on track. You can use this method in marketing, manufacturing, operations or any other type of project.

Find your ideal customers

As you research constantly for the type of customer you're looking for, your fish, you need to know the channels or "fishing spots" to sell your product to those customers.

If your ideal customers are the affluent, those with money and who are willing to pay for certain services, where do they visit the most? Business people? Do they visit specific places such as hotels and motels for conferences and regional meetings? Retail business people? How about shopping malls? Golfers? For sure golf courses, but how about sporting good stores? Greeks or Koreans? Are there parts of town that host these cultures? Teenagers? Writers? College students? Where are each of these types of customers and what places do they frequent, whether it's online, a physical location, or the various types of media such as magazines or TV shows? Once you have a good idea where your *customers are* this will narrow down which *sales channels* to use and understanding those channels to sell your product or service.

Pick and create your products

Creating your product or service means that you start from scratch. Or, it can also mean that you add value to someone else's by adding features, different pricing, or better service or delivery.

There are many hindrances to getting a product to market. On one end is working to produce the "perfect product." The other end is releasing a poor product so that someone else copies it and brings a better product to market after you. You want to find the right timing window to release your product or service into the market-place when the market is ready for it. Market research will go a long way in determining the best timing for you.

> *No individual has any right to come into the world and go out of it without leaving something behind.*
> *- George Washington Carver*

If some of the current social networks such as LinkedIn, Twitter, or Facebook had existed in the late 1990s, what do you think the reaction would have been? It would have fizzled out for sure. These in-products today would have been too early for the market for various reasons, change being the significant part of the equation.

When you're ready to take your product to market, you want to have a "good enough" product for the right niche. The reason for a good enough product is because a perfect product is never truly perfect. Waiting for perfection may take longer or cost more, giving your competition a heads up. Having a good enough product allows you to get it out the door, then, let the market give you feedback on what's important to them and improve it from there.

The response is important to your business longevity. Listen to your customers' comments and criticisms and adjust accordingly. Not all customer criticisms need immediate action. Sometimes a single criticism can make or break your product. Other times many of them are poor suggestions and need to be discarded into the annals of "dead ideas."

Channels to market to create demand

A channel is a means of distribution to get your product to your customer, either directly, such as your own website, or indirectly, through an intermediary like Amazon. Operating in every channel can be expensive and not all marketing channels will work, so triage and prioritize your channels.

Marketing is about creating demand for your products and services. Word of mouth is a great way to market. You cannot do enough to make sure that people will talk positively about your product to their family and friends. There are many ways to get your message out.

Advertising in trade journals, websites, emails, social networks, and magazines are ways to engage the market. You can involve a small group in what's known in the software industry as a "beta" release. A "beta" release means the product is nearly complete, but you want customer comments on final details. It's the way Apple releases some of their products to developers. Some authors pre-announce or "pre-sell" up-and-coming books to see what kind of response they'll get so their printers can ramp up or limit production.

However, the critical issue is being able to market your products and services to generate demand to sell your products. Having a difficult time marketing your products makes it that much harder to create the sales that you need to earn a living. Some businesses start with creating the "perfect" product before they ever begin to market what they intend to sell. Part of this can be "paranoia" to keep any competitors away from your idea and has a certain amount of legitimacy to it. Other businesses delay their release because they just don't know how or they don't understand the timing of both their message and their product.

Some of the various "fishing spots" or channels on which to advertise your product include, online, print media, radio, TV, trade shows, conferences, article writing, or affiliate marketing advertising.

Produce or procure your product

This is where the rubber meets the road.

You may have to line up engineers, vendors, chemists, marketing, copywriters, distributors, nutritionists, publishers, graphic artists, editors, or whoever you need to make your product. You have to test to make sure you meet your and your customers' expectations. Getting to the final good-enough specs of your product will be the most important part of your business.

Pricing and Profitability

"Free" to "Lowest Price" to "Premium"

Pricing your product to sell takes place between two extremes: "Free" and "Premium." Free means you give things away, such as a sample of what you provide. Most businesses start at "Lowest Price" and go from there. The "Lowest Price" is your industry's break-even point plus a percentage over for profit. In the burger industry, there are McDonald's, Wendy's, In and Out, Good Times, Carl's Juniors, Fat Burger, and Ruby Tuesdays as well as smaller mom-and-pop types of burger joints. Some are similar, others are close, others are "Premium" and are considered "out of this world," where pricing is not a problem. In between "Lowest Price" and "Premium Price" is "Better Value" pricing. "Better Value" is not so much a "super size me" which is an up sell, but a much better value than "competing on price" viewpoint.

Focusing on "lowest price" means beating competitors for cheaper customers by reducing your operating costs and thus reducing your prices. You have to be great at cost reduction to go cheap. However, if you add more value you'll always risk loss.

Regarding pricing, you can do it all. For instance, if you create and sell an $800 print of a graphic, you can sell the same graphic on a coffee cup, T-shirt, etc., and that's another way of selling your product to customers that is less expensive. Be aware that your market wants some things "their way" and you may need to change your approaches and prices to sell more of what they want. Question is, do you want to build a business to make money or not?

Add value, resist price discounts

There is an interesting game that describes the difference between the value of an item and its price. It's called the Economic and Business Trading Game in chapter one. Refer to the example of a test game, or try it out yourself.

"It takes years." There's a famous story of a woman seeing Picasso sketching in a Paris café. She asks him to sketch her, and he agrees. Five minutes later, he presents her with the sketch — and asks for five

> *Price objections are value problems.*
> *- Dan Kennedy*

hundred francs. She says, "But it only took you five minutes!" "No, madam — it took me thirty years."

"Every artist was first an amateur," Ralph Waldo Emerson said. It's about experience, not about the price. It's also about protecting your brand. The woman could have taken that sketch and sold it to someone at a profit. With Picasso putting such a high price tag on her painting, its higher value might make her think twice about selling it (good story, don't know if it is real).

Tip. Markets are based on supply and demand. Your product is only worth what people are willing to pay for it. There is no reason you can't raise or lower your prices based on that principle and there is no reason you can't charge different prices to different markets. Think colas and how much it costs for a 12 oz.

123

can that's already cold in a vending machine versus a 1 liter bottle in the grocery store: same product, different sizes. Also think FEDEX and U.S. Post Office pricing structures: It's about supply (your time) and demand (your customers wanting your time).

People will give you all sorts of reasons why you need to discount your product and services. You should rarely or never discount! Why? Because the perceived value of your product becomes diluted with continual price discounts. It also depends on the vendor or customer you are dealing with. Amazon discounts: if you have a large order, then you'll get a discount. If a customer squirms for just one item at your price then they really can't afford it, or, they have excuses why they don't want to pay for it.

"House for Sale." One of the easiest ways of seeing economic pricing in action is watching the selling price of a house. If the house is desirable, people look. If the house is desirable but overpriced you'll get people to look, but no buyers. If you get an offer or two then you're in the right price range. Multiple offers create a bidding competition that will raise the price to near the market's view of the right price. If it's priced too low, there will be an offer frenzy and an ensuing bidding war on the property. For those who may not understand, different markets (city, rural, regional, and states all) also have different housing prices (true story).

Getting into a price war with a competitor is not always a good thing. You should resist the "run to the bottom" in pricing as an entrepreneur with inexpensive products because the time it takes to produce the product may not be worth the time to sell it.

Deciding to pay for something is more likely a state of mind and not a resistance to pay a certain price. If people truly want what you are offering they'll hustle and find ways to buy it. It's about a win/win situation for both you and your customer, your hard work and their hard-earned money.

Launch and sell your product

When it comes to launching your product, two things will affect your plan: a launch date and budget. You need to put a stake in the ground regarding both. As an entrepreneur, it's about learning how to do both, being "on time, on target." This is one of the chief business skills of any leader and one needs to cultivate this leadership skill.

"Hard" and "Soft" Launch Date. Launching your product or service really comes down to having two dates, a soft and a hard date. For example, you do not announce a *soft date* in the retail environment, but open for business to see if and how your various processes handle your business traffic and issues. A *hard date* is your "Grand Opening" date once various systems have been tested to make sure there is a smooth operation for your customer. There still might be issues with your processes, but you'll avoid total disaster if you planned and worked it right.

Once you have lined up your own or someone else's products and services, it's now about making sales. With your marketing efforts to create interest and "buzz" around your product(s) complete, it is now time to sell it. You'll need to map out a launch plan to time everything so that all the critical factors have been met and you have a successful product launch.

Get out there and repeatedly educate, entice, and entertain your customers, through a variety of delivery methods (such as through email, direct mail, video, email, faxes) with your marketing message.

Your business: Working On/In/For It!

The steps above assume that you have set up your business and are running it on a daily basis. However, one of the critical aspects of running a business is to improve your business processes. It's necessary to improve the delivery of your products and services, but also to lower your costs to improve your profitability. Great companies are always looking at improving how their business work, to reduce costs and increase profitability. The perspectives and definitions are:

1. **CEO thinking = Working ON your business.** This starts by creating and defining how your business will work by: creating systems, processes and procedures; developing people to handle the business; and working with both your vendors and customers on designing business systems and processes. If you don't work ON your business you'll end up working FOR your business. Here is how working ON your business is defined: doing the right *things* the right *way* at the right *time*!

2. **Business Owner thinking = Working IN your business.** This means you are following the steps to get things done that you have defined in the working ON phase of your business. Even while you are working IN your business, you're never quite done working ON your business. You will always want to find both money and time savings so that you can earn or save more time and money. This means also delegating or outsourcing tasks to others.

3. **High Pay Job thinking = Working FOR your business.** This means you just have another job, hopefully higher paying, but you do not change how your business is run over time. If you can't let others take over and build in some accountability to your system it becomes just another job. If you do not change with the market, the customers' expectations, or the suppliers and your business takes you over, you're working FOR your business. No matter how long you are "in the trenches," you still need to keep the 10,000-foot level view of your business.

While nearly every entrepreneur becomes "obsessed" by working their business, better entrepreneurs rarely work FOR their business because they stay "on top" of their business and have figured out how to improve their business over time. It's a matter of perspective, focus, and attitude. Good businesses come from good habits, which come from good discipline, which comes from good decisions. A good decision is never to be "controlled" by your company; you control it and your life. You start a business, not to create another higher paying, stressful job for yourself, but to gain freedom with your life while contributing and serving your customers and your community.

Know yourself. When you know what your strengths and weaknesses are, you can delegate a task (though not the responsibility) to others and oversee it until it is completed. Not all weaknesses are bad because you can improve some of them yourself over time, such as bad habits.

Set priorities: High versus Low Priorities. Working ON your business means that you set good priorities so that you manage your time and your physical energy well. That includes those people you work with and their time and energy, as well. Time is a constant and everyone has the same amount of it allocated to do with as they please. It's what you do with that time that makes the difference between the successful person, the not so successful, and the failure. You have to define how you intend to work your business.

> *A business that makes nothing but money is a poor business.*
> *- Henry Ford*

Setting priorities is about working on high-value priorities versus low priorities and finding ways of offloading the lower priorities to someone else, like a temporary hire, virtual assistant, or even an intern.

Take action on priorities now! When it comes to your business the simpler the better. Overcomplicating your business with unnecessary details robs you of precious time and energy.

Your next products

Now that the money is beginning to roll into your bank account, you should celebrate for all the hard work that you have done in getting your product out the door. This celebration should be short-lived, as now the real work begins because you need to watch the market, both customers' and competitors' responses to what you are doing, so that you can keep ahead of the crowd and competition.

Whatever you do, do not let your first product or service languish. Once the market finds out that you have a hot seller, the market will look to take advantage of you and try to cash in on your success. Watch the market's reaction to what you are doing. This includes both your customers and vendors, as they might make a knockoff of what you are providing. While you can provide some protection from knockoffs legally through copyright, trademarks, and patents, the best preparation is to have more versions in the wings ready to be released to keep ahead of competition, or a combination of both strategies.

One of the critical factors in running a business is watching for any changes in the market that relate to your business. Once your first product is out, you need to work on Version Two of your product or another product that adds to your product line, like good, better, or best lines. The speed at which you can create the next version or partner product will keep your competition behind you. Apple initially created the Apple I, then the II, IIe, III (failure), the Lisa (failure), Mac (some failures), iPod, iPhone, and its most recent product addition, the iPad.

When you first start building a business, you don't know if it's going to be a success or not, so producing your first product is just to test the market to see if your idea truly solves a problem. Keep in close contact with your business lawyer to protect your business intellectual property and assets.

Action plan: Create an action plan of goals

After you have written your business plan, taking business steps is next. Keep in mind that you are now starting to do project management for your business, so you'll need to start writing down and tracking all the various tasks that will make you successful.

Don't put that business plan on the shelf to gather dust; you'll need to refer to it during your project management phase to see where you are. Your business plan is a "living document" that needs to grow, expand, and change as you do. But while markets change, principles of good business do not.

You can initially use pen and paper to track your tasks for your tax or legal records. Or using your Mac, create and print project or process templates to take notes on. Next is to go completely digital and let your Mac manage your business, projects, and tasks. Calendar/Mail can handle basic tasks and events. Numbers can be used to track larger projects, as can the personal database Bento. For larger projects, you can find the solutions in the next chapter under Project Planning Software.

Project plans do not have to be an either/or situation, but could be both a mixture of paper and digital solutions to manage your various project plans. Just ensure that you have printouts or backups of your digital files for your records.

One of the more significant factors in starting a business is how big it will be. If you are a freelance writer then your needs will be far fewer than opening up a retail store, or multiple stores that go nationwide.

Here is how to take action on what you have written in your business plan. The larger the goals of your business plan, the more detailed your goals may need to be.

1. **Specific goals.** Write down your top three to five critical, specific, and reachable goals. Don't think about it, get them out of your head and on to your Mac or white board (ideapaint.com's, whiteyboard.com, or chalk board paint solutions) so you can visualize and organize what you intend to do about and around them. Why so few goals? Because there will be smaller and more detailed tasks associated with these larger goals that will fill up your time and energy. Your goals need to be SMART: specific, significant, stretching; measurable, meaningful, motivational; agreed upon, attainable, achievable, acceptable, action-oriented; realistic, relevant, reasonable, rewarding, results-oriented; time-based, timely, tangible, trackable.

Tip. Pick the right goal, "Is this for personal, business, or a little of both?" If you have a fruit company, great results come from setting the right goals. If you have both consumer and business customers, don't emphasize one over the other as a goal. Setting a goal of selling more to businesses will skew your results and customer data accuracy. The more accurate goal is to get 100 percent of your customer's information, whether they're business or consumer, and let *the customer and their data* tell you how you're doing. While you as the CEO may think a numerical goal is good, the reality is you'll miss out on what your consumer or business customers are trying to tell you about your sales numbers (true story).

---

2. **Find/Set a deadline!** Here you, a customer, a vendor, an industry, or a time period, set a stake in the ground dictating an action deadline. Why? Because the longer you have the slower you'll take action. Remember the SMART "R" in "Specific Goals:" you want to be realistic about the deadline. This also means that any changes to the first deadline may have to be negotiated again. "A goal is a dream with a deadline." - Napoleon Hill

3. **Make a goal task list.** Take your goal and break it down into smaller and smaller pieces, detailed enough to show significant issues, but not so small that you track too many details.

4. **Sequence and prioritize the task list.** Take the above list and sequence things as appropriate, i.e., you may find it difficult to sell anything until you have leads/web traffic, so getting that information comes before qualified leads which come before sales. Check for task dependencies, i.e. you can't go fishing without bait. After you have identified the task dependencies, rank each task and find tasks can be completed separately and in tandem with others.

5. **Take action on priority No. 1.** Now take action on your #1 task. Remember that some tasks do not involve you but others so that getting to your goal you can do some tasks in parallel. Getting leads/web traffic is first, then qualifying them, etc. on down the line.

6. **Adjust task sequences, priorities, processes, and goals.** As you move through your task list you'll adjust every task as things move forward. Prepare for Murphy raising his head and the need for you to overcome these obstacles by pressing

forward to achieve your goals. Also as you begin taking actions you'll learn more about the process and the necessary changes that need to take place. The time it takes to finish a task can affect goals and priorities.

7. **Stabilize, standardize and systematize your business processes.** After you begin marking off your goals, you need to implement standardized, repeatable business processes to become effective and then efficient. *Effective* means getting things done according to you and your customers' level of expectations; *efficient* means getting things done smarter and quicker to cut your costs and increase profits -- or, even finding uses for waste byproducts. **"John D. Rockefeller: 300 oil products and one drop of solder."** During the early days of the oil industry, John D. Rockefeller knew that success would come from working on improving business processes and reducing costs and wastes, i.e., being efficient. Rockefeller refined crude oil to get kerosine, and rather than throw away its waste byproducts like a majority of his competitors did, he hired a research team and created over 300 products from it[80]: paint, varnish, dozens of lubricating oils, etc. Rockefeller's business was so good at making kerosine cheaply that whale oil, coal oil, and for a while, electricity, lost out in the race to light American homes,

> Courage is being scared to death...and saddling up anyway.
> - John Wayne

factories, and streets. By discovering products in waste byproducts, he made even more profits, so Rockefeller truly did turn trash into treasure. In other example of efficiency, Rockefeller asked an expert about how many drops of solder they used on a machine soldering caps to five-gallon tin cans of kerosine. "Forty," the man replied. Rockefeller asked him to reduce the number, without leaking, but in the end 39 was the right number to use without leaks. This one drop saved $2,500 the first year, but the kerosine export business

---

[80] *John D. Rockefeller and the Oil Industry,* <u>thefreemanonline.org</u>

increased each year thereafter, so Rockefeller's savings were even greater (true story[81]).

If you need a summary of what to work on, see the section "Move the Needle 10,000-foot Business View" in Chapter Nine It is a general layout of most all business processes; you need to adjust it to your requirements and needs.

---

[81] *Titan The Life of John D. Rockefeller,* page 180

Chapter Five

Step 5: Your Business & Mac Software

It is better to have one person working WITH you than three people working FOR you. -- Dwight D. Eisenhower

Story: "Pay enough to get the job done"

Erica had gotten to know and trust James. He told her, "I worked for my father for years when he was in construction and woodworking, and I recently started up a different type of woodworking business on the side." Erica, wanting to gain experience for her consulting business asked, "Can we swap our services? I'll help you get your business up and running on a Mac if you'll help me fix some of my antique furniture." James saw the benefit of bartering and agreed to the deal. It was more about free labor and gaining a reputation than materials.

James had a little more business experience than Erica, and he told her about his business – he needed supplies such as wood, nails, glue, woodworking tools, a truck, and a computer to help him run the business. To build a piece of furniture, James would need a design plan, buy the necessary wood and other materials, cut the wood according to the plan, find the correct nail or fasteners, and put the wood together. To run his furniture company he needed a Mac, but as James said, "I run rings around other woodworkers, but I'm computer and Mac illiterate."

Erica said the steps to building furniture are similar to those for buying his Mac software. "Defining your business and how it works narrows the search for the types of software you'll need," she told him "The software you buy then determines the right Mac to run your business software on."

The significance of what she told James was revealed when she caught the entrepreneurial bug about "running a business" during her college marketing class. The class project was to create and sell a business newsletter: her project subject was about startups. Erica had written a number of the newsletter stories, and one was so good her class professor read it to the class. After reading the story she commented, "While you wrote a great story, it does not have the required 350 words in length. Why?" Erica responded, "I fulfilled the requirement to tell an effective story even though I used only 241 words. I sell ads in my newsletter, using fewer words means consuming less space that I could use for selling more advertising, thus making more profit for my newsletter." While the professor could argue over the paper's requirements, Erica's comment was spot on if she was running her own business.

One day at their favorite coffee shop Erica explained to James that, "Not all of your business processes will need a Mac; we need to take a look at all aspects of your business." They looked at marketing, sales, accounting, taxes, mailings, scheduling, and a host of other business processes.

Erica admitted that some computer consultants can get caught up with seeing only Mac solutions to business problems when sometimes the best business solution to a problem doesn't involve a Mac at all. A great example was James' use of a shadow board, outlining where each tool goes to keep tools accounted for, versus creating a Mac database. Defining all of his tasks into manual (analog), digital, or a combination of both would help determine if James needs to buy any software Erica recommends for his Mac and business.

James was beginning to like Erica; they were close in age. James was impressed with her knowledge of the Mac's capabilities and her simple explanations of the Mac's ease of use. James commented during one of their morning coffee meetings,

"So is it really true then, once you go Mac you never go back?" Erica laughed, "Yes, it is." She was pleased that James was finally catching on to the Mac's great utility for a small business.

Because James is a small business owner, his core business competency for woodworking means he'll likely not need the most complex and expensive pieces of software available. Erica warned him that most salespeople will try to up-sell almost anything he might be considering, so he smartly decided to keep his costs low until a business need arose for software that had more bells and whistles.

Erica and James spent many a morning together helping each other build their respective businesses. All of James' family lived in town so Erica met each one of them; his grandparents were a hoot to be around. James showed much respect for his grandfather, who had lived during the Great Depression and passed on this advice, "Pay enough to get the job done, and no more."

Enough said for James.

Your business defines your Mac

If you're a writer, you need to learn the skills of writing and then buy the various writing tools to help you write. Just like a carpenter uses tools to build a house or deck or new kitchen table, every person needs their various tools to perform their job, profession, hobby, or craft.

A writer having once acquired the writing skills can now use tools such as iWork Pages that will make the process of writing easier. A great tool does not make a great artisan; a great tool makes the production of performing the craft easier. A dull blade versus a sharp one makes the job of cutting down a tree more difficult.

> *An invention has to make sense in the world it finishes in, not in the world it started.*
> *- Tim O'Reilly*

So a writer will buy tools like software for collecting information, writing text, managing business finances, and other applications that may be needed. If you're a lawyer, you need software to write legal briefs and to track your billing expenses. If you're a carpet cleaner you need software to schedule your work, to market your business, and to manage your business finances. If you're establishing a retail store you'll need a Point Of Sale (POS) system to track sales and maybe an eCommerce system for online sales.

For each type of business and its associated processes, you have to decide how much you are doing things analog (paper and pencil, dishes, posters, shelves, or other implements) or digital (keeping information and files on your Mac). The basic principle is really simple. Your type of business defines the software that you will use, which defines the Mac hardware you'll need.

Tip. Your business needs define your software needs which define the Mac to run it. Too often people do it in reverse, buying the hardware first and then the software.

Designing systems for businesses and Macs

Most of us are familiar with the need to create a business plan. Most are not aware of other documents and processes that can help move you forward: a business system plan regarding how to run a business, a project plan for significant amounts of resources, and an action plan to get it all done. Even though each plan may not need to be completely detailed, writing them down can aid in keeping you on track with dates, times, and associated sequences of steps with the effort that is being put forth. The purpose of various plans is to track how your business is running. It is no different from taking a trip and knowing your destination when driving across the country. You can get lost driving around if you don't have a destination, know your starting point, and devise the route you're going to take. Getting lost traveling, without a destination and a plan or course of

> A good business system is a number of interconnected analog and digital processes collecting critical and accurate information on which to base good business decisions.

action, is exactly like getting lost in business; you have to know your sales goals, profits, and how to grow a business and know where you are starting from financially.

Additionally, creating good systems based on your plans helps you make good business decisions based on good information. Getting bad or incomplete information or making decisions on assumptions can lead to problems down the road. Begin to design and document your critical business functions. You should be able to describe a system and its sub-processes in enough detail in your reports, filings for taxes, and other documentation to decide how any decision you make affects your business.

In-house computer systems

You control in-house systems. You buy the hardware and software solutions, in this case a Mac, install them, and keep track of the software updates yourself.

You can use simple systems that come with your Mac, such as Address Book and Calendar. These aren't normally thought of as true CRM (Customer Relationship Management) systems, but they can be a great start for a small business as it grows. There are also less expensive third-party products such as Marketcircle's CRM package Daylite, a one-time buy with periodic updates.

> *Starting a business is not about creating another full-time job but increasing your choices for your life.*
> *-anonymous*

However, there are other software solutions available, which can help cut your costs. For example, if you need a customer relationship management solution, you can choose Salesforce. You can also choose an open-source solution, such as SugarCRM, which you can download for free and manage yourself or pay for a hosted solution.

Some advantages to using in-house systems:

▸ **DIY (Do It Yourself)** - This system is less expensive up front, but you bear the full responsibility of both time and money of keeping it running.

▸ **In-House use/Outsourced maintenance** - You may still want to run the system yourself, but hire someone else to handle the upgrades and maintenance. The Apple Consultants Network (consultants.apple.com) can help. Outsourcing allows you to concentrate on what you do best. You still drive the car (your business) but someone else takes care of the maintenance.

Hired or outsourced computer systems

Outsourcing means that you pay a third-party company to handle operations, such as an email list or your website. Some reasons for outsourcing include: lack of time or desire to master those skills and expense.

When it comes to outsourcing your data needs such as a company hosting your website or a CRM software package, the idea of handing over control to someone else can be frightening. If you do your homework and ask for references, you can find people who can become very helpful to your organization.

Good, better, best, or custom solutions

When it comes to hardware and software to run your business there are good, better, and best solutions, not only in features and benefits, but also in costs. The tools to do your work depend on the size of the job or your budget. For instance, when it comes to tracking your customers' contact information, you may have many reasons to choose a good, better, or best solution for your business. Keep in mind that the larger, more expensive solutions mean that to get the information out can be more time-consuming and costly because each solution has more capability, features, and benefits and handles various aspects of a business differently. For example:

> *Success is never final, failure is never fatal.*
> *- Winston Churchill*

▸ **Good** - Address Book and Calendar can keep track of the basics of your customers and you may not need much more.

It can also be a great starting point for your business, but keep in mind that you will have to "export" your data from one application to another, so choose wisely which application you will use in the future.

▸ **Better** - If you need to move beyond Calendar and Address Book to something with more capability, you'll need something like MarketCircle's Daylite, which is a CRM package and scales to under 50 employees. Again, putting data into an application means you may have to take it out again.

▸ **Best** - If you need even more storage capability, then you might take a look at a custom database or SugarCRM.com's solution to scale to larger numbers of customers. A one-size-fits-all solution can cost you more because it has features which you may never use.

▸ **Combination** - In some cases finding the one, right solution may not be the best approach or be readily available, but combining solutions will fit your business. Tasks such as accounting and tracking customers could be solved by combining a few simple programs, or a simple plus a more complex program to act as one.

▸ **Customization** - This is the most expensive and time-consuming prospect for your business. You

> *As you begin changing your thinking, start immediately to change your behavior. Begin to act the part of the person you would like to become. Take action on your behavior. Too many people want to feel, then take action. This never works. - John C. Maxwell*

should develop customized solutions *only if* you have a good grasp of business and software processes and are willing to devote time and money to the problem. If you do customize solutions, seriously consider how to recoup some of your investments by selling your solution to other businesses. It may water down your ideas but it will cost you less to develop since you're spreading the development cost among others.

Set up your business, office, and Mac

You'll need to set up your office with more than just a Mac and a printer, it also needs other items from a process standpoint. You'll need paper, desk, pens and pencils, storage bins and boxes (like bankers boxes).

Manage your business

You'll need to set up your office with more than just a Mac and a printer; the system will also need other items from a process standpoint. You'll need paper, desk, pens and pencils, storage bins and boxes (like bankers boxes).

Manage your business

Plan, Do, Check, Act (PDCA). There is a specific, iterative approach to organizing your business and computer processes and it follows a few steps that run in a problem-solving cycle.

You *plan* what you intend to do, *do* it, *check* it to see if you're achieving the results you are expecting, then *act* and accept the change or revert to your earlier way of doing things if the change does not meet the expectations. Once you have finished the Act stage, you now begin the cycle again with planning what you are doing.

You'll need to do this PDCA cycle through your *business plans* to see how close you are at reaching your business goals in your industry, *financial plans* to see if expenses and income are on track, *operation plans* to see about the capability of your various business and computer processes, *improvement areas* essential in continuing to grow (incremental, short or small improvements, or innovative, a big step or leap in improvements), or *other areas* that come to mind.

In some cases you might go right back and reassess the same things you just went through. The frequency of going through each area will depend on the situation that you are in, in some cases more often than others (see Table 3).

Steps	Example
Plan out how you intend to get things done with your business. The bigger the obstacle, the longer the time that may be needed to come up with a solution. Don't plan for perfection; do plan for problems.	1. Pick one business process to improve using Pareto (80/20 rule) analysis (product delivery: 80% of vendor problems caused by 20% of vendors). 2. Measure improvements (percentage of late shipments). 3. Benchmark industry best practices (FEDEX shipping).
Do your plan, act on it. Don't shut things down at the first sign of problems, unless it's that essential, such as safety, etc.. Stabilize each process so that you can accurately determine the causes of problems.	Incremental (small) improvements or completely reengineer (large, leaps in improvements) the process by starting from scratch on a totally new process.
Check your results and the gap between your plan and your results. If you're close, press on. If you're way off, hit the next step quickly.	Track and monitor the results; watch for trends.
Act to either keep the plan that you have made, or change things as appropriate based on the results.	1. If the results are good, continue to watch. 2. If results are bad, research why. 3. Repeat as necessary.

Table 3: Plan, Do, Check, Act Improvement Steps

Processing your stuff. David Allen, in his book *Getting Things Done,* covers a good approach to managing all of an entrepreneur's activities and tasks. While all of it may not be for everyone, you can still glean some good ideas for yourself to make you more productive. Gathering stuff, taking action on stuff, categorize stuff, see the stuff in the big picture, and then acting on your stuff.

You also need to physically set up your Mac, office, desk, and filing system to manage all the items above. Keeping your things simple will allow you to be more productive in the long run. You've heard the saying: Keep It Simple, Salesperson. The simpler, the better. The less that you are touching and working with, the less chance for errors and mistakes and the more time you'll have to do the more critical items.

Software that comes with your Mac

Once you buy your Mac, take some time to get familiar with it. Open a few programs and see what they do. Where are your programs on your Mac?

Applications folder. Here's a short list of software that you might find useful in your business *(Lion/Snow Leopard)*:

▸ *AirDrop (Lion only)* - Share files wirelessly with no WiFi network needed.

▸ *Address Book* - Keep your contact list here. Mail and some third-party billing or relationship management suites use this application. You can also print information for note taking to be input in your favorite day planner.

▸ *Automator* - Create programs that automate frequent, repeatable computer tasks.

▸ *Auto Save (Lion only)* - You no longer use Command-S.

▸ *Dictionary* - A dictionary and thesaurus used by some Mac programs such as Mail and Safari and third-party applications.

▸ *Font Book* - Helps keep track of your computer's fonts and allows you to see what they look like.

▸ *Front Row (N/A in Lion)* - Use Apple's Remote to access your computer's photos, videos, podcasts, and TV shows into a presentation-like experience.

▸ *GarageBand* - A program for music and audio podcasts.

▸ *Calendar* - An entry-level calendar and to-do list. You can share it with others, subscribe to other calendars from the web, such as holidays and sports schedules, or print out a weekly calendar for your family

▸ *iChat* - An instant messaging, audio chatting, and video conferencing application, which all can be recorded for future reference. You can use multiple services such as AIM, Jabber, and Google Talk.

▸ *iDVD* - Allows you to create custom DVDs of your pictures, music, and movies.

▸ *Image Capture* - A program that allows you to transfer images from your digital camera or scanner to your Mac without the need for drivers.

▸ *iMovie* - A program for creating movies from video clips, photos, or music, or even podcast material such as audio overdubs that you can save to DVDs, CDs or the web.

▸ *iPhoto* - Manage your photos and do minor touch ups using this program. You can create books, calendars, and cards using your own photos.

▸ *iSync* - Provides an interface for you to sync your computer with various devices such as an iPhone, Palm hand-held, or Blackberry.

> *No matter how carefully you plan your goals, they will never be more than pipe dreams unless you pursue them with gusto.*
> - W. Clement Stone

▸ *iTunes* - Manage and play music, TV shows, videos, podcasts, and more. You can sync your media with your iPhone and iPod.

▸ *iWeb* - Create web pages and websites.

▸ *Launchpad (Lion only)* - Instant access to your apps.

▸ *Mail* - An email client integrated with Calendar/Address Book.

▸ *Mission Control/Dashboard+Spaces+Exposé* - Mission Control combines: Dashboard (an area that allows for running widgets, little programs that run in the background), Exposé (a feature that makes it easy to find your various windows and applications that you have running, great for keeping your workspace organized) and Spaces (creates virtual desktops).

▸ *Photo Booth* - Capture pictures and video right from your computer's built-in camera.

▸ *Preview* - A PDF viewer in which you can add comments, alter, and convert various files from one format to another.

▸ *Quicktime Player* - Plays Quicktime audio and video files and records screen capture.

▸ *Time Machine* - Backup software.

▸ *Versions (Lion only)* - Charts the history of each working document or file and displaying old and new side by side.

Utilities folder. There are more applications that let you monitor your Mac's health or activity. Some of these are:

▸ *Activity Monitor* - The activity monitor acts as your Mac's dashboard of computer activities that monitors CPU, memory, network, disk activity, and disk usage. It's a handy tool if your Mac gets slow.

▸ *AirPort Utility* - This utility allows you to set up an AirPort wireless network and reset or reconfigure settings.

▸ *Audio MIDI Setup* - Adjusts the computer's audio input and output configuration settings and manages MIDI devices.

▸ *Bluetooth File Exchange* - This is used to exchange files to or from a Bluetooth-enabled device.

▸ *Boot Camp* - Allows you to configure a Mac to install and run a Windows operating system.

▸ *ColorSync Utility* - This is used to manage color profiles and filters used in Apple's PDF printing workflow, or applying filters to PDF documents.

▸ *Console* - Allows programmers to see the various logs of messages sent by applications and your computer system.

▸ *DigitalColor Meter* - This utility can measure the color of any pixel on your screen and translate the color value into standards like RPG, YPbPr, CIE or Tristimulus.

▸ *Directory* - Allows you to connect to various directories within your organization to share information.

▸ *Disk Utility* - Fixes file permissions and creates HD partitions.

▸ *FaceTime* - Enables video calls using various cameras.

▸ *Grab* - A utility that can capture a selection, window, screen, and timed screen on your Mac desktop.

▸ *Grapher* - A mathematical graphing calculator.

▸ *Migration Assistant* - Migrates information from one Mac computer to another, including configurations and programs.

▸ *Network Utility* - This is an interface that provides information and helps you troubleshoot your network.

▸ *Terminal* - The UNIX Command Line Interface (CLI) that provides access to the Mac's UNIX tools and programs. Powerful, detailed, and very specific if you know what you are doing. Not for the faint of heart.

▸ *X11* - This utility allows you to run UNIX applications that run under the X11 UNIX windowing environment. Check out the macforge.com website sponsored by MacTech magazine for Free and Open Source Software (FOSS or OSS).

Mac software: Licenses, types and issues

Software for any computer, including a Mac, is key for you to perform the tasks necessary to power your business.

Software licensing. Check each vendor's software requirements before you buy. Be aware of licensing issues, including site and dual licenses, standard and professional or premium versions of the software, upgrade paths, compatibility requirements and warranties. If you're using a PC, Adobe and others may allow you to switch from PC to Mac versions of your software without buying a new license. Check product websites for up-to-date licensing agreements, program versions, and for any changes that may affect your decision. Keep an inventory of your software to refer to when making decisions.

Types of software. When it comes to software solutions there are different approaches:

1. **Single/Multiple copy** - This software allows you to install it on one or more Macs, depending on the license requirements.

2. **Server-based** - Server-based solutions come in a few different forms (see Lion Server). They are:

   a. **Hosted: Shared to Dedicated** - You pay a regular service fee. Shared means you have low-bandwidth server needs and share the same computer server hardware with many others. Dedicated means companies place software on an ISP's or your own server for your business.

   b. **In-House** - For more control, you can bring the hardware/software solution in-house. You have more control over what you can do, but you also have to manage it yourself or pay someone to manage it for you.

   c. **Client/Server** - Here is where you normally install a client version of the software on your Mac and you need a server to access the information, much like Lotus Notes or FileMaker Pro Server. You'll need an office network or a business broadband internet connection to be able to access the information.

3. **Web-based 1.0/2.0/3.0(?)** - You use Safari, Firefox or another web browser to access information or use the software on hosting servers. The difference between 1.0 and 2.0 web applications is the increased functionality of the software. It may not matter whether you use a Windows or Mac O/S; the functionality should be the same if the software developer has followed World Wide Web Consortium (w3.org) standards.

4. **Single or Integrated Functions**

   a. **Single/simple function** - Calendar has a limited calendar and to-do list for a business and most solo entrepreneurs can get by using it.

   b. **Integrated functions** - Here many functions are in one package. It may have a to-do list, calendar, contact list, and project management functions in one package.

Something to consider with integrated applications is that if you decide to change, it may be more difficult and time-consuming to get your data from there into something else. While not totally "locked in" to the solution, there are barriers to exiting if you want to use something else later.

Entry-level software is normally a single copy, however, as you grow, you're likely to need integrated applications. Getting cross-platform applications can be helpful, but if you've hired others who use PCs, web-based may be your best choice to avoid incompatibility with your Mac and PC choice.

Issues surrounding Mac software. As a Mac user, if you are by yourself and will rarely work with others across a network, there is generally little to worry about. Collaborating with others outside your business adds some complexity.

▸ **File Formats, see the choices under a program's "Save As..." menu.** Different programs have different file formats and not all are compatible. Word uses .doc or the most recent .docx file formats. iWork Pages uses .pages. Adobe's Photoshop uses .psd. Generally, when you are trying to share files with others, you must have a program that can read these file formats. Check which file formats the program can save to (under File > Save As... or File > Export menu). Ask your business associates what file type to send to them to avoid conflicts. On occasion, it may require a two-step process working with an intermediary program in between to convert the file to a different format.

> *You don't **sell** your product to your customer, your customer **buys** your solution to their problem.*

▸ **Working with Windows.** Working with Windows can be a little troublesome. Generally files handed to others on a CD/ DVD or flash drive that has a copy of the file on it have few problems. It is when it is sent through Windows Server email that you may have issues. Apple's Mail program has an attachment setting, "Send Windows-friendly attachments," that helps reduce this little issue. But send a Pages-formatted file to a Word user and the file won't work. In this case you will need to File > Export the file for Microsoft Word users to edit it.

Tip. When sending Mac files to Windows users such as resumes or work proposals, do *not* assume that the files make it through. Ask the person that you are working with to double-check to see if the files made it through their system *and* they can read them. Generally, it is in working with larger, Fortune 500 companies that use Windows Servers that this becomes the biggest problem for Mac users.

Home Office/Office: Solo Entrepreneurs

Many entrepreneurs who start a business begin by moving into a "spare space" in their home to keep their costs down. This home office becomes a work "nest" to build their business. Here are some items to create this new space that should be considered business expenses, as well:

Space: Corner of a room, spare bedroom, or a designated space in the basement.

Furniture: Desk, chairs, a file cabinet, shelving for placing business materials or products, books, and reference materials.

Equipment: Mac, printer, external hard drive, scanner, lamps, DSL or Cable internet connection, surge protectors/UPS (Uninterruptible Power Supply) large enough to plug in your cable/DSL modem, and router for power outages, or fax machine (see eFax.com as one example).

Supplies: Paper, pens and pencils, file folders, file holders for current projects, bankers boxes for storage to replace a file cabinet, and other office essentials.

A Mac is no different, especially when it comes to a Mac Pro tower that can take up large amounts of space. Keep them off the floor so as not to allow them to become your under-the-desk vacuum cleaner. Dust causes your Mac to run hotter than is best for it.

Startup Spaces: Virtual Offices, Co-working, etc.

As any economy changes, so does the neighborhood, state or national business environment. This includes the space for a businesses to start up, grow, and work in. While most people consider starting a business on their kitchen table, times are changing how businesses are starting up. While the kitchen table is still the "preferred" way, shared offices and other spaces are providing incubator spaces for startups.

In between a home office and dedicated office space, a number of options are available for startups. Here are a few reasons why not having a regular office can be a good thing. The subject is virtual offices.

Good reasons for virtual offices, co-working, etc.:

▸ You're a start up and you need to conserve your cash and test the business waters before you take the plunge and sign a long-term lease for office or retail space.

▸ People may not care if you're a virtual office or not.

▸ Your business lends itself to working from home; you have a "virtual" storefront or you travel extensively.

▸ Your business team is technically savvy enough to operate in an environment of various locations and virtual offices.

▸ Your business requires flexibility as your needs change or grow over time.

▸ Home, health, or family requirements may force you to work away from an office.

Bad reasons for virtual offices:

▸ Your industry, both vendors and customers, do not respect home-based or virtual businesses because it may not appear professional enough.

- Social aspects: those that require large amounts of face to face communications, team building and customer needs.

- "Exporting" of sensitive financial, technical, and customer information and data with foreign workers.

- Opportunity for abuse from employees.

- Legal issues such as regulations, zoning, and immigration issues prevent it.

- Tax, payroll, and insurance related deductions may not provide enough benefits.

- You have higher Information Security requirements of your business information.

Here are a number of views on being a mobile professional:

- **Co-working - "Officepoolers."** Co-working is similar to carpooling in that you share a resource since you're all in the same situation. This is where you are in between having a home office and a traditional office and not quite a road warrior where you are constantly on the go. A co-worker is one with whom you share office space, expenses, and daycare or other "social" parts of any business. Rather than only being on the road, you now put down roots so that you have a place to socialize with others of like interests.

- **Mobile Professionals - "Road Warriors."** A mobile professional is one who is constantly on the road, such as a traveling salesperson, a national or even international consultant, or a CEO who travels extensively. Whatever your title, the mobile professional is one who is mostly on the road. Mobile professionals have some differing needs than both the Remote and Virtual Professional. Lightness and portability are the name of the game.

- **Remote Professionals - "Telecommuters."** Remote professionals are those who work both in an office or work environment and from home, and mainly stay inside of these two work environments. A remote professional may be a lawyer who occupies a desk at an office, who spends time in court, who keeps notes on a computer in the car, and who sometimes works from home doing administrative work.

▸ **Virtual Professionals - "Shadow Pros."** If you are a Virtual Professional, such as a consultant or part of a team of mobile professionals, then you'll more than likely have a laptop and travel to offsite locations. This scenario has become more prevalent than in past years and this trend is expected to continue to grow in numbers and locations. This means the distance and availability of online services will allow your movement to be shorter, saving you time and money.

When running your own consulting business or starting virtually until you have the resources to have your own office location, you have to be well organized and disciplined in order to be productive on the road.

You will be either a Virtual, Remote, or Mobile Professional such as a single consultant or you will be a Virtual Office or Team where you will have other teams members in dispersed locations with a need to collaborate. In each case, the Internet becomes the glue that holds you to your customer or you to the rest of your team, vendors and suppliers.

> *Business Success Formula: Discover a starving crowd and sell them what they're hungry for.*

While each of them have a common thread of being mobile, what matters is how long they are on the road as well as how they interact with others on a regular basis.

All of them may use the mobile tools such as laptops and online storage; they will differ on other tools and tricks of the mobile trade:

▸ Telecommuting, coffee shop, co-working, virtual offices and teams, and office/executive suites to suffice as you grow, but require some Mac issues to consider:

Document storage and sharing - Emailing documents back and forth can work, but storing documents online using Google Docs primarily as a general writing and document creation tool, can be a document saver in a virtual environment. You can also group edit and share/store your working documents online using off-site storage sites as a virtual backup. You'll always have the most recent document backup online using these services.

Teleconferencing/teleseminars - Audio-only group meetings for chatting, social networking, teaching content, or collaboration with team members or with customers.

Web Conferencing/webinars - Conference with others using tools such as video, audio, whiteboards, and document sharing.

See the section *Integrated Mac/iOS and Web 2.0* below for more information about collaborating with others using technologies.

The issue with distributed offices is that as you begin to grow beyond five to ten people, you can "fracture" your various communications as people are added to your working environment.

Integrated Mac/iOS and Web 2.0 software solutions

Integrated software solutions offer a one-stop-shop solution for what your business may need. There are two solutions for every business: a combination of the Mac and iOS solutions and the Mac/iOS and web/internet solutions. Both allow one to share data across platforms, however the Web 2.0 solution requires the data to be hosted on another platform, in most cases a website, and could be shared with others.

Mac and iOS apps. When the iPhone and later the iPad were released, the trend became having a Mac app that syncs your data with your iOS apps. Generally, if there is a Mac app such as a calendar, To Do, or data app, there is a corresponding iOS app that allows the synching of data between your Mac and iOS app. A solopreneur will most likely be synching the data. In the case of apps with greater functionality, the apps can share data with others in your business, such as an administrative assistant.

Web 2.0. With the Web 2.0, SAAS (Software As A Service) allows you to use your web browser to connect to the software. You'll need to check your business needs and each vendor's offerings for a fit with your business. Here are some reasons for and against using Web 2.0 solutions for your business:

▸ **Pros**

- It's universally available from any browser and any platform such as Windows, Mac, or Linux.

- Data storage is off-site, not on your computer. Some allow for storage on your own computer.

- Application improves with the service.

- Support and maintenance are outsourced to the application provider. You no longer need to keep updates or track licenses for what you own.

▸ **Cons**

- Broadband internet access is essential and places that you visit may not have it, especially rural areas.

- Security and privacy of your data is vulnerable. For example, if you're in the health-care field, under HIPAA you don't want to give away your customer list to another company.

- Exporting data can be time-consuming and costly.

- Ongoing costs of a subscription can add up.

The degree to which you get increasingly complex can mean higher and higher costs to you and your business. Here are some online Web 2.0 solutions for you to consider that are low-cost for startups:

▸ Zoho.com has email, Office-like applications, CRM, invoicing, projects, reports, contacts, and a lot more that are a good fit for distributed small businesses.

▸ 37signals.com has projects, contacts, communications, organization, and much more.

▸ **Google Apps for Business** (google.com) gives you an Office suite, contacts, email, maps, and a lot more.

As we progress into ever-advancing network and software technologies and applications, the business solutions will also increase in price and complexity. What is essential is how you get your data out of these systems, if you so choose, to move elsewhere. Larger solutions offer more complexity and vendor "lock in" (it's more time-consuming or difficult to get your data out of their system). Even though Web 2.0 solutions can be good, make sure that you can download all of your files or data if your internet connection goes down so that you can continue to work your business.

Marketing: Mac tools to attract customers

This section is very important because without getting your company's message out to your customers, you'll have few sales and little to show for all of your hard work. You need to be contacting your customers either directly or indirectly through the various channels that are available.

Apple provides inexpensive software solutions to help you with your marketing tasks. As with all software, check out the limitations of each product to see if it can handle your desired tasks and can scale with your needs.

Audio, video, web: iLife '11

iLife comes free with many Mac models. It provides some useful programs to help create marketing material for your business. These tools are GarageBand, iWeb, iMovie, iPhoto, and iDVD. Here are some ideas on how to use them:

Storytelling: Create a 30-second film for your marketing. When it comes to your audio and video marketing, the basics are the same: it's about scriptwriting your story. The *Save the Cat* book series, Mac software, and cheat sheets by Blake Snyder (blakesnyder.com) discuss screenwriting your story about your business in easy steps to follow. You can combine Apple's iLife and iWork software tools to develop your compelling message.

GarageBand. You create audio using GarageBand that can be used in other programs or as stand-alone files. While music is the first thing that comes to mind when you think of GarageBand, you can also use it to produce:

▸ an introduction to your own commercials.

▸ a podcast, online audio manual, seminar, or instructional audio.

▸ a voiceover to be placed in iMovie or Keynote.

▸ a commercial for your local radio station or for your own establishment that can be downloaded to an iPod or posted to YouTube with timed images.

▸ a custom ringtone for your customers based on your brand.

▸ an audio book or lecture series for those who have difficulty with text or video, or who want to listen during trips or commutes.

▸ an interview recording for downloading later using iChat between two Macs.

iPhoto. This program is useful for managing your photo library and minor photo editing. With iPhoto you can:

▸ manage all of your marketing photos for your newsletter, product line, and those homes for sale for your real estate business and find them easily using keywords, dates, and face recognition.

▸ create a picture book to give to your client showing before, during, and after shots of a $1 million dollar house that is being built.

> *Sales are contingent upon the attitude of the salesman - not the attitude of the prospect.*
> *- W. Clement Stone*

▸ create a marketing calendar to include Calendar events of your special events or holiday sales. A restaurant could include discount days or when classic menu items are offered. A real estate agent can showcase open houses or special showings.

▸ create a picture book of your craft shop's high-end inventory to ship to customers.

▸ create personalized thank-you cards, invitations, and postcards. Example, a real estate agent creates personalized moving cards for a client to send to friends and relatives.

iMovie. Creating your own video is easy to use for:

▸ a travel business website.

▸ demonstrating do-it-yourself construction projects that people buy as kits from your business.

▸ seminars for customers who cannot attend.

▸ tours of homes, businesses, or lines of products.

▸ application instructions.

▸ editing a Photo Booth video for a video blog about your business to post on the internet.

iDVD. You can create CD/DVDs to give to your customers that include documents, audio, and video material to explain your product or service. You can:

▸ send an audio of your book.

▸ send a multimedia presentation or demonstration of your product.

▸ send testimonials of satisfied customers.

▸ send a compilation of all the material you've created in iLife.

▸ send free information and product as a sample of your work.

iWeb. Build your own website, post information, and interact with your clients. This would be great for small firms just starting out, but if you intend to grow your web presence, then consider your growth needs before using iWeb.

Print and presentation: iWork '09

iWork is a suite of programs made up of Pages, Numbers, and Keynote -- applications to create any number of marketing products for your customers.

Pages. This program provides both writing and page layout functionality within documents you create. You can:

▸ design flyers, newsletters, brochures, menus, posters, cards and invitations, certificates, sales letters, and faxes.

▸ build reusable templates for others and their businesses that speed up their business tasks.

▸ write a book or Ebook to help others in their life and use a Print On Demand (POD) publisher to get your message out.

▸ save your documents as PDFs to email to your customers or post on your website for them to download.

Numbers. Numbers is a canvas-like spreadsheet which allows for greater creativity than other spreadsheets. You can make:

▸ a catalog of your products and services with specifications, a comparison of your products or a competitor's, or a planner for your product launch.

▸ a campaign tracker for your marketing campaigns.

▸ a project manager or checklist with graphics depicting stages and milestones.

Two fonts walk into a bar. The bartender sees them and yells, "Get out of here, we don't serve your type!"

▸ a storybook or graphic illustration of a project to include cost and associated steps to completion.

Keynote. With iWork's presentation software you can be more creative. You can:

▸ explain simply what you do and how you do it.

▸ show homes with audio and video for a real estate business.

▸ add an audio recording to your presentation that seminar participants can take with them or download from your website.

▸ export your presentation to a QuickTime movie to be loaded onto an iPod.

Sales: Mac tools to manage contacts

Running a business, you need to keep track of all the things necessary to make a living and grow your business. You can stay on top of things with your Mac using the To-Do list, Calendar, and Address Book for your contact list of customers and vendors. Using your Mac makes some things just that much simpler.

Contact management

Keeping a contact list is essential to building your business. Most applications that share contact information use the vCard industry standard (version 3.0 and 2.1).

▸ *Address Book* (free with each Mac, apple.com) keeps track of most contact information and allows contacts to be put into multiple groups.

▸ *Daylite* ($189, marketcircle.com) is a robust application that includes calendar, contacts, projects, To-Do, etc.

▸ *SOHO Organizer* (free, chronosnet.com) adds a bit more functionality than Address Book.

▸ *Highrise* ($24/month, highrisehq.com) is an offsite web service of contact management software.

▸ *Zoho* (visit the website, zoho.com) is a contact management system with other applications.

Tip. To get your contact information from Address Book into a format a spreadsheet or database can read, you'll have to export the data and convert the selected Address Book vCard information into a tab delimited, or a Comma Separated Value

(CSV) file using programming scripts such as **Export Address Book** 1.5.1 from versiontracker.com.

To-Do / Information Organizer

Getting things done is important; tracking what you are doing is also important, especially having to prove to a tax or IRS auditor or a lawyer by documenting what you have done over the course of the year.

▸ *Calendar* (free, apple.com) has a basic to-do list.

▸ *Pagico* ($50, pagico.com) is a task planner and personal database.

▸ *BusyCal* ($29.99, busymac.com) is a third-party organizer that goes beyond **Calendar**.

▸ *Things* ($49.99, culturedcode.com) is a simple task manager that has received good reviews.

▸ *Omnifocus* ($99, omnigroup.com) delivers personal productivity tools in the GTD (Getting Things Done) method on a bigger scale.

▸ *Yojimbo* ($39, barebones.com) is a "collect all" software application.

▸ *Nova Mind* ($49 and up, novamind.com) is mind-mapping software that collects your thoughts and ideas.

Calendar

Making a list of your meetings is fine, but viewing it in calendar form makes it much easier to see your daily events.

▸ *Calendar* is Apple's basic calendar that you can publish, subscribe, print, and share with others.

▸ *Google Calendar* (free, google.com) can sync with Calendar.

▸ *Timebridge* (free, timebridge.com) helps with sharing, connecting with others, and connecting with Mac and Windows.

▸ *Mozilla Lightning* (free, mozilla.org) brings the Sunbird calendar as an add-on with Thunderbird mail client.

▸ *Fantastical* ($19.99, flexibits.com) provides a much improved way of looking at your calendar, including keep the calendar in your menu on your Mac and iPhone.

▸ *Calendar* (free, qbix.com) provides and improved interface from Apple's Calendar from the menu bar.

Tip. Calendar uses the iCalendar format and Address Book uses vCard format; both are standards. It's when application makers do not follow industry standards that you'll need scripts to convert or "translate" information between applications.

As another solution, you can sync your *Calendar* information with other applications or servers so that the information is shared and "secure" against single points of failure such as a hard drive crashing. Here are some of those tools:

▸ *Calendar* from Snow Leopard to Mountain Lion lets you sync with CalDAV and other calendar servers through Calendar Preferences > Accounts.

▸ *BusyCal 2* ($29.99, busycal.com) is a full featured calendar allows sharing of Calendar data on a network and sync with iCloud, Google Calendar, and other CalDAV servers.

▸ *Calabunga* ($3.95/month, calabunga.com) allows you to import and export to Calendar.

Sales tracking/Point Of Sale (POS)

There are two things to be aware of when dealing with sales. The first is tracking only the sales amount, such as the selling price of a house. The second is tracking both your sales commission and your expenses. If you are looking for just basic number crunching, there are many solutions that can handle most sales tracking. In a retail environment, POS systems are normally more integrated to keep a handle on what you have to sell. Ensure you research your intended software if you can use your iPhone/iPad to take POS payments.

Merchant Services. Research companies regarding the pricing, transaction features, hardware compatibility, and the licensing agreements doing POS transactions using your iPhone/iPad. Some companies *forbid certain industries or merchant types to use their systems.* You don't want them to shut down your account for violating their agreements, putting your business at risk. In addition, look for the volume break-even point between the price per transaction (%) and a monthly fee plus transaction fee ($ + %).

> *If your actions inspire others to dream more, learn more, do more and become more, you are a leader.*
> *- John Quincy Adams*

▸ **Basic**: You could use *iWork's Numbers* (apple.com) or *Microsoft Excel* to track basic sales numbers. You could also use *Bento* (filemaker.com), a database application to track your sales and create a simple, customized, integrated application. You can use other applications such as *Checkbook* or *Checkbook Pro* (splasm.com) or even *iBank* (iggsoftware.com) to manage basic business finance and accounting. It really depends on the number of transactions and sales you make.

▸ **Intermediate**: One of the better solutions is *Daylite* by MarketCircle.com with its Billing software add-on. You can also take a look at Filemaker's *Bento* or *FileMaker Pro* (filemaker.com), plus the Business Productivity Kit for Filemaker Pro which can handle thousands of contacts and associated information.

▸ **Advanced**: Advanced solutions require larger numbers of transactions. Suggestions: SugarCRM.com, Infusionsoft.com, or Salesforce.com. Some advanced marketing and sales solutions are available for you to manage tens or even hundreds of thousands of contacts. These solutions normally charge a monthly fee.

▸ **Point of Sale (POS)**: Take a look at *Checkout* by checkoutapp.com, *POS/IM* at posim.com, *MacPOSX* at macposx.com, *Lightspeed* by xsilva.com, *ShopKeepPOS* at shopkeep.com, or *Shopify* at shopify.com.

▸ **Mobile Payments:** Take credit card/PayPal payments using merchant services on your iPhone/iPad and a card reader. iPhone POS app *FlagshipROAMPay* at roamdata.com, *Leaders* at leadersmerchantservices.com, *GoPayment* from intuit.com, *Merchant One* at merchantone.com, *Merchantware Mobile* at merchantwarehouse.com, *Square* at Squareup.com, *Chase Paymentech* from chase.com, or *Credit Card Terminal* from innerfence.com. See more details in the footnote.[82]

Also look into tracking sales numbers by themselves or integrate the transaction details with your accounting software, thus reducing time spent inputting the numbers.

Operations: Mac tools to run a business

Operations are the system and processes that you define to run your company. Organizing your business and Mac means organizing yourself based on your way of getting things done.

This involves:

▸ defining only the necessary and critical items such as business cards, paper, pens, reference materials, books, promotion and media kits, envelopes, labels, stamps, documents, and file folders to hold on to, and to use.

▸ defining where each item will go: daily items, readily available items, and items that need to be archived. Each needs to be labeled, categorized, and organized for each area.

---

[82] http://iphone-card-reader-review.toptenreviews.com

With your Mac and a good backup solution, you can keep clutter at bay by digitizing as much as you can.

How do you get organized?

▸ Sort things so that related items are stored together.

▸ Decide how long you will keep records, then clear out things based on business needs.

▸ Find a home for everything that is important to you and your business and make sure things are labeled.

▸ Containerize things and label them to make it easy to have one place for similar items.

▸ Keep up with your system to be productive, lean, and mean.

You can scan hard-copy pieces of paper into your Mac so that you have multiple copies: one digital in your Mac, and one analog that will be filed away.

As your business grows, keep remembering the Plan, Do, Check, Act approach to constantly improve your business processes to make and save money.

Accounting/Finance: Tracking your Money

Even though most people consider accountants to be "bean counters" and accounting as nothing more than putting each of those beans into their respective buckets, there is a reason accounting is important.

Why is accounting like a jar of jellybeans? Accounting is like having a jar full of various colored jellybeans. You still need to know the exact number of each one of those colored jellybeans. Each bean represents a categorized, transaction dollar spent by you and your business. Then each color represents the type of account that you place the jellybeans in, such as expenses, insurance, taxes, etc. Where most people get into trouble with accounting is being color blind and placing an orange jellybean

> The way to get started is to stop talking and start doing.
> - Walt Disney

(buying a Mac or an office expense) into a yellow bucket (advertising).

Budgeting. You'll have to track the money you are spending to see if you are making money or not. Most financial programs around $100 or less are designed for just that purpose and can do a good job at managing and providing information about your financial trends over time. They can also import your information into tax packages. To do some numerical analysis of your finances you can import that information into Apple's *iWork '09 Numbers* spreadsheet program. For example, you can import your online banking QFX files (Intuit's file format for its products) into *Numbers* checkbook template and you can do numerical or quantitative analysis of your finances.

Accounting packages manage your finances and are great at giving you the info you need. However, they do not do a very good job of managing your business operations. That requires separate skills and tools.

Tip. If you enter information into a Numbers or Excel spreadsheet-created invoice, you can get it to your customer quickly. However, if you want to find end-of-year tax information or "drill down" to research a specific answer, it is best to have an accounting package that can slice and dice your expense, revenue, and deduction information. It takes a bit longer to set up and keep up, but the end-of-year benefit makes it well worth it.

Here are some suggestions that could do a good job financially for your business:

1. **Personal Finance/Accounting packages:** Your business may not require a large finance or accounting app if you have low transaction volume, such as a lawyer or CPA might have. Here are some packages available for the Mac:

   a. *Checkbook* ($14.99, splasm.com) is a basic checkbook register that can perform most beginning business needs.

b. *MoneyWiz* ($19.99, silverwiz.com) is an entry level personal finance application.

c. *Moneywell* ($49.99, nothirst.com) is personal finance software with powerful "envelope" budgeting.

d. *Quicken Essentials for Mac* ($49.99, intuit.com) can be used by most beginning entrepreneurs.

e. *Moneydance* ($49, moneydance.com) runs on Mac, Windows, and Linux.

f. *LiquidLedger* ($59, liquidledger.com) is another workable accounting system for a startup business.

g. *iBank* ($59.99, iggsoftware.com) is for money management than can handle your everyday accounting.

h. *AccountEdge Basic Mac* ($99, firstedgeapp.com) is a good business accounting program with plenty of growth potential.

i. *MoneyWorks* ($99, cognito.co.nz) is an entry level product by this company and has a few others that might fit your needs, and it works on Windows as well.

j. *Xero* ($19/mont to start, xero.com) online accounting.

2. **Invoicing/Time Tracking:** When it comes to invoicing your clients, here are some that will help you. Some are stand-alone applications, others are web-based and may require an internet connection to access your data.

a. *On the Job* ($39.95, stuntsoftware.com) is a time and expense tracking software.

b. *Harvest* ($12/month to start, getharvest.com) is an online invoicing solution.

c. *Billings* ($39.99, billingsapp.com) works with Daylite from Marketcircle.com.

d. *Freshbooks* ($19.95/month to start, freshbooks.com) is a time and invoicing online service for your clients with third-party add-on software plugins.

e. *Blinksale* ($15/month, blinksale.com) is an online invoicing of your clients.

f. *Timenet Law* ($249.99, applesource.biz) is a Mac version of Timeslips for lawyers.

g. *Studiometry* ($249.95, oranged.net) is a full-featured time tracking, invoice, and client management package on both Mac and Windows.

h. *Zoho* (visit the website, zoho.com) has multiple applications to use for your business.

This list is not exhaustive. As a quick solution to get your business up and running, you can use iWork's Pages or Numbers to create quick invoices that you can print out or save as a PDF. If you need to invoice your customers and you do enough volume that at the end of the year you find yourself struggling to find all of your tax info, then choose one of the accounting applications listed.

Office suites

In most cases, Apple's iWork ($19/application, apple.com) suite of applications can handle nearly all normal business documentation. As long as you are on a basic to intermediate level of creating documents, you can export Pages, Numbers, and Keynote documents to Word, Excel, and Powerpoint files. The more complicated documents you create, the more problems you will have translating the files from one file format to another such as iWork Pages to Microsoft Word or iWork Numbers to Microsoft Excel.

1. *iWork* ($19.99/app, apple.com) is Apple's office suite that has a word processor and desktop publishing program in Pages, a spreadsheet called Numbers, and presentation software named Keynote.

2. *MarinerPak* ($79, marinersoftware.com) has a word processor and a spreadsheet program. The company has a host of other Mac programs that are fit for writers and various office tasks.

3. *Office for Mac 2011* ($219, microsoft.com) comes with Word, Excel, and Powerpoint. Also check out Office 365, an online version for $99/year with added applications.

4. *NeoOffice* (free, neooffice.org) is like Open Office, but uses a Mac user interface.

5. *Apache OpenOffice* (free, openoffice.org) comes with Writer, Calc, Impress, Draw, and Base that run on Windows, Mac, Linux, and Solaris.

Project planning and databases

1. **Project Planning**: For those larger projects, it can sometimes be hairy to manage all the details, but that's what project planning software is for.

   a. *Things* ($49.99, culturedcode.com/things/) is a small to-do list that can create projects out of to-dos.

   b. *xPlan* ($79.99, xplanapp.com) is designed to keep track of tasks and calculate a project's cost.

   c. *iTaskX* (€80, itaskx.com) is another project management application that provides numerous views of your project.

   d. *Curio 8* ($99, zengobi.com) does a lot more than just a project management tool; it collects data, as well.

   e. *Omniplan* ($149.95, omnigroup.com) is a great project-planning application.

   f. *Merlin* ($199, projectwizards.net) offers a server version, as well, and can access projects from the iPhone and web.

   g. *FastTrack Schedule* ($349, aecsoftware.com) is a complete solution for all businesses.

   h. *Zoho* (visit website, zoho.com) has multiple applications.

2. **Databases**: Gathering more data about your customers into a customer list allows you to take care of them and your business better. Flat file databases such as a digital Rolodexes can handle a large number of records while a relational

database means you can relate various tables to slice and dice the data, mining it for new business opportunities.

a. *Bento* ($49, filemaker.com) is a generic database program that is handy for all startups to begin collecting data for your business.

b. *Panorama Sheets* ($39.99, provue.com) is a spreadsheet-like database program. More than a spreadsheet of data, fewer functions than a full relational database program.

c. *OpenBase SQL Solo* ($249, openbase.com) is a good and fast database environment to work with.

d. *Filemaker Pro* ($299, filemaker.com) is one of the best databases for small businesses on Mac and Windows.

e. *Panorama* ($299, provue.com) is a RAM-based database.

f. *4D* ($399, 4d.com) is a more detailed database.

g. *MySQL* (free, mysql.com) is an open source database used by most websites because of its speed.

h. *PostgreSQL* (free, postgresql.org) is another open source database that is like Oracle in size and scope.

Graphics and desktop publishing software

1. **Graphics**: Graphic programs can handle two types of images: draw/vector graphics and paint/image editing. Check with your graphics professionals to clarify which is best for your graphics situation. Here's a small list of both vector graphics/draw and image/paint programs:

a. *Draw* and vector programs create output in EPS, TIFF, SVG, JPG, PNG, PDF, and Postscript file formats for *print* using CMYK colors and 300 dpi.

i. *Inkscape* (free, inkscape.org) is an open source software vector graphics program.

ii. *iDraw* ($24.99, indeeo.com) is an inexpensive but powerful vector-based illustration program.

    iii. *Artboard* ($29.99, mapdiva.com) is a graphics application that will surely fit in your Mac toolbox.

    iv. *Sketch* ($49.99, www.bohemiancoding.com) is a good, simple vector drawing program.

    v. *Intaglio* ($89, purgatorydesign.com) makes good use of Apple's technologies.

    vi. *easydraw* ($95, eazydraw.com) is a less-expensive replacement for Illustrator.

    vii. *Omnigraffle* ($199.99, omnigroup.com) does a lot more than the average graphics application and keeps up with Microsoft Visio.

    viii. *Illustrator* ($699, adobe.com) is *the* professional illustration program.

b. **Paint** and image editing programs create output in bitmap/raster graphics that use BMP, GIF, JPG, PNG, and PDF for *online graphics* using RGB colors and 72 dpi.

    i. *GIMP* (free, gimp.org) is a free open source software Photoshop-like program.

> *Empty pockets never held anyone back. Only empty heads and empty hearts can do that.*
> - Norman Vincent Peale

    ii. *GraphicConverter* ($39.95, lemkesoft.com) is similar to Photoshop, but inexpensive and good enough for entrepreneurial use.

    iii. *Artrage* ($49.90, artrage.com) is a basic paint program, for the iPhone/iPad, as well.

    iv. *Acorn* ($49.99, flyingmeat.com) is a basic image editor that can be used by most anyone.

    v. *Pixelmator* ($59, pixelmator.com) is an image editor for the Mac. It's Photoshop-like, but without all the higher-priced bells and whistles.

    vi. *Photoshop Elements for the Mac* ($99, adobe.com) is the entry-level version of the professional version of Photoshop.

    vii. *Painter* **12** ($429, corel.com) is an extensive paint program for Mac and Windows.

    viii. *Photoshop* ($999, adobe.com) is *the* image editor for the Mac.

2. **Desktop Publishing** is about creating documents that are used for print, such as flyers, brochures, and even books. iWork Pages gives you a great start at creating print documents. Other applications, such as Scribus, have a larger learning curve, while professional programs such as InDesign and QuarkXpress are very robust but require the largest amount of effort to learn the details.

    a. *Scribus* (free, scribus.net) is an open source desktop publishing solution that runs on Windows, Mac, and Linux, and gives more control over the typesetting of your documents than Pages.

    b. *iStudio Publisher* ($17.99, istudiopublisher.com) is a graphic and desktop publisher application.

    c. *Pages* ($19.99, apple.com) is a part of Apple's office iWork productivity suite. It does a great job in page layout that is simple, quick, and quality work.

    d. *Swift Publisher* ($19.99, belightsoft.com) has many startup templates and clipart.

    e. *InDesign* ($699, adobe.com) is a part of Adobe's Creative Suite, and gives you the tools to produce print and other graphic designs for more detailed, higher-end publications.

    f. *QuarkXpress* ($799, quark.com) is an industry standard for enterprise and large publishers.

As one graphic artist said about open source software, "If one of these free applications has a tool that proprietary or purchased ones do not, I'll download it and use it." As an entrepreneur, you may not have the budget to get many applications and your requirements may be to just do a simple, one-time job. Some of these open source software titles can tide you over until you need a larger, more complex, or more expensive application.

Mac applications for your office

There are many tasks that a person in startup mode needs to do. In no particular order, here are some software solutions that can help you:

Mailings and Labels: These range from simple to more advanced.

> *Coming together is a beginning. Keeping together is progress. Working together is success.*
> *- Henry Ford*

▸ *Address Book* (free, apple.com) comes with every Mac, gives basic contact information, and creates mailing labels.

▸ *Labels and Addresses* ($49, belightsoft.com) creates a variety of mailing and shipping labels using Apple's Address Book as the address source. It gives very good control over the output.

▸ *Endicia* ($9.95/month to start, endicia.com) provides mailing and shipping software.

Backup and Utility software

When it comes to keeping your Mac running smoothly, there is one piece of software that's especially important. Utilities are small programs that are considered the tool box of usefulness to both your Mac and your business. Here are two areas that might help.

Backup Software. Time Machine is bundled with each Mac, but other solutions may add more features and benefits to your Mac.

▸ *Time Machine* (free, apple.com) backs up everything.

▸ *SuperDuper* ($27.95, shirt-pocket.com) is another backup solution.

▸ *Chronosync* ($40, econtechnologies.com) synchronizes, backs up, enables bootable backups, and archives.

▸ *Drobo* (starting $399 and up, drobo.com) is similar to Time Machine, but you buy both their hardware and software together and can add more hard drives at *any* time. It's especially great for companies with growing storage needs. A true no-brainer solution.

Online backups: Storing your data on a hard drive next to your desk? Also consider taking your data offsite, which can save just as many headaches. Compare prices.

▸ *iCloud* (free or check Apple's pricing) is Apple's online storage service and has other features such as IM, audio, and video chatting and recording capabilities.

▸ *Dropbox* (dropbox.com) allows larger email attachments (>5 MB sizes), as some email systems (Google, corporations) won't allow large files to be sent.

▸ *Carbonite* (unlimited backup for $54.95/year, carbonite.com) is another online backup solution.

▸ *iDrive* (2GB free online, idrive.com) charges $4.95/month for 150GB.

Essential utility software. Make sure to acquire all necessary plugins and utility software. While the below list is a generic list, find more specific software for your Mac for your needs if needed.

▸ *Flip4Mac* (telestream.net) lets you play Microsoft wave (.wmv) movie files in QuickTime player.

▸ *Flash Player* (adobe.com) plays web Flash applications.

▸ *Acrobat Reader* (adobe.com) works in certain circumstances where Apple's Preview may not.

Miscellaneous. Here are some favorite utilities for your Mac:

▸ *iStat Pro* (free, bjango.com) is a dashboard of the health of your Mac's CPU, hard drive, memory, temperatures, fans, etc.

▸ *DiskWarrior* ($99.95, alsoft.com) helps keep your hard drive running nicely.

▸ *Onyx* (free, titanium.free.fr) runs the Mac's UNIX maintenance scripts.

▸ *AppDelete* ($7.99, reggieashworth.com) deletes almost anything.

▸ *CleanApp* ($14.99, synium.de) finds all of your applications' wayward and hanger-on files and deletes them.

▸ *QuickSilver* (free, qsapp.com) provides a keyboard shortcut software that speeds up getting things done.

▸ *Data Rescue 3* ($99 personal use, prosofteng.com) recovers data from your hard drive.

▸ *Carbon Copy Cloner* ($39.95, bombich.com) is a utility that helps keep your data safe.

▸ *Cocktail* ($14, maintain.se/cocktail/index.php) helps with Mac maintenance and other Mac under-the-hood processes.

▸ *Adium* (free, adium.im) is a third-party IM application connecting to 17 different IM technologies.

▸ *Skype* (free, skype.com) provides computer to computer or computer to land line or cell phone calling.

▸ *VLC* (free, http://www.videolan.org) is a format-friendly multimedia player.

▸ *MPEG Streamclip* (free, squared5.com) allows you to work with CODECs of multimedia.

▸ *OmniDiskSweeper* (free, omnigroup.com) helps keep your Mac free of stray programs and frees up disk space.

▸ *Burn* (free, burn-osx.sourceforge.net) provides advanced features to burn onto a DVD/CD.

Automate business workflows with your Mac

Automating your business begins with thinking about your business and computer processes and then thinking about how to improve your results to save time and money.

Most people think that automating your Mac means taking an analog process and moving it to a computer. This is true, but it also means automating your processes once data is entered into your Mac.

There are five ways of being more productive and automating with your Mac, with the first being the easiest and the fifth requiring a programmer for complex and large projects. The five ways are:

1. **Folder Actions** - Actions that you assign to a folder that do a task and are repeatable. You access folder actions by right clicking or CNTL+mouse click and select "Folder Action Setup" from the contextual menu on a folder. Some actions to automate:

   a. Keep your desktop cleaned off of all files; this keeps your Mac running at its fastest.

   b. Duplicate or convert image files.

   c. Automatically upload files to your website.

2. **Smart Folders** - Smart folders are available for most Mac applications such as Mail (Mailbox > New Smart Mailbox) and Address Book (File > New Smart Group). Smart folders are also available through third-party applications that allow for tracking changes in your data, and updates the Smart folder automatically. Examples of what Smart Folders can do are:

   a. **Mail**: Using Mail rules, sort incoming emails into folders and then track the number of "Flagged items," "Unread emails," or "Last 7 days of emails" as a smart folder.

   b. **Address Book**: Track changes in your Address Book when you add, change, or delete contact information.

c. **iPhoto**: Track changes in next month's newsletter photos using keywords, such as "Nov" + "2010" (multiple, separate keywords) or an architect "residential" or "commercial" building.

d. **Third-party applications:** Track changes in client status or 30/60/90 day accounting problems. Track changes in keywords in iPhoto for a monthly newsletter.

3. **Spotlight Saved Searches** - If you often search for the same files, you can save the search and launch it with one button.

4. **Automator or Applescript** - With a bit of work, these programming languages can make your repeatable tasks executable by your Mac very quickly. More information about this can be found at macosxautomation.com or at apple.com/downloads/macosx/automator/ where you can get some free resources.

5. **Scripts** - To write scripts requires a programmer to use Python or Ruby On Rails to write complex and multistep tasks and is usually reserved for very large projects that are both business critical and labor intensive repeatable.

Tip. Not every business process and task will require a script to automate. Do some research first; it may not be worth the time and effort to automate a task. However, a single instance of slicing and dicing a very large database might.

Chapter Six

Step 6: Mac Hardware Tools

Production is not the application of tools to materials, but logic to work. -- Peter Drucker

Story: "Get neural with a Mac!"

To make her business known, Erica began attending local business meetings. At a number of them, she befriended Kathy. Kathy had suffered a brain injury from an accident. Brain injuries are similar to other brain issues such as ADD or autism when it comes to "therapy" that hopefully retrains or works with the brain's limitations. Kathy had decided to start an information business surrounding her brain issues and she sought to tailor the information to others in similar situations. "I've learned," she told Erica, "that because of my brain injury I have to do things differently. A Mac can help me with my brain issues, help me manage my work and life in a different way. Can you help me set up my Mac?"

"Sure," Erica told her. "I'd be glad to."

Erica began helping Kathy research her software needs. Computers quickly facilitate management of information and communication, and Kathy could pace herself with a Mac at her side. She could use the Mac to help control her life. Because her brain had difficulty processing some tasks, she could use the calendar, alarm, and a timer application to track how much time had elapsed or to remind her of meetings. She would also be able to use the Mac to help manage her newfound business. With Erica's help, it would be less overwhelming for Kathy to handle.

Erica had recently read about Cornelius Vanderbilt, one of the wealthiest business men in America, who made his wealth from sea and rail transportation. The one fact that stuck in Erica's mind was Vanderbilt's use and exploitation of his day's technology. During the 1850s, it was standard practice for steam-powered paddlewheel boats to use a side-lever engine, but Vanderbilt decided that the walking-beam steam engine would do a better job in his boat design. His combination ship hull and engine design efficiencies (both were lighter and cheaper) used one-third less coal and cut his round trip travel time compared with other ships, saving Vanderbilt valuable operating costs.[83] Erica knew the Mac's design was similar for all types of businesses; it would save time in the business operation long run, allowing business owners to compete favorably against their business rivals.

Erica asked Kathy, "Can I take notes on our discussions about getting you up and running so that I can add our experiences to a future business newsletter?"

"Sure," said Kathy.

Fortunately, Erica shared with Kathy some sources that sold Macs: an Apple Store, an online reseller, a local reseller, or even previous users if she needed one used. Kathy knew some of early adopters who wanted to sell their slightly used Macs so they could purchase the latest and greatest ones.

The first step was deciding between the desktop or laptop models. Erica helped her consider her needs and the differences in the models:

▸ Did she want "portability" or "power"? Laptops offer mobility in and around the house and on the road, while desktops offer larger hard drives and screen real estate. If the

---

[83] *The First Tycoon: The Epic Life of Cornelius Vanderbilt,* pg 200

need arose, Kathy could attach a keyboard, monitor, and a wired or wireless mouse to a laptop, achieving similar results.

▸ Did she have any large storage needs for significant *numbers* of or *size* of audio or video files? If her file and storage needs were mostly for movies, photos, and podcasts, she might have larger storage and CPU needs. Otherwise, her storage needs were average and any of the various Mac internal storage configurations would be suitable.

▸ Was she a true "road warrior" and on the road constantly, with weight being a serious issue? Or a "telecommuter" just needing something to take back and forth between home and work? If she traveled frequently, her laptop, coupled with her luggage, would increase her total carry-on weight and the MacBook Air would be the better choice. If she had light travel back and forth from work to home, a heavier MacBook or MacBook Pro would be fine.

Kathy eliminated the CPU and storage powerhouse Mac Pro option because it was way over budget and beyond her computer needs. The Mac Mini was a simple computer for someone like her dad or an Administrative Assistant, but it was just not for her. The iMac was an All-In-One idea, but Kathy finally verbalized her thoughts, "I've listened to the information you have given me, Erica, and I have decided I like the portability of a laptop and not being chained to a desktop."

Taking a look at Apple mobile solutions, Kathy saw that the MacBook Air was really light, but she decided she needed more than it offered in RAM, hardware ports, CPU, and graphics speed. The MacBook Pro satisfied those needs, but was over budget. "I think I'll take the MacBook for my first Mac," Kathy said.

"Good choice, Kathy" Erica nodded in agreement. "Have the salesperson get your new Mac together while I jot down some quick notes about what we did, before I forget."

Kathy smiled. "I know how that feels; I mean forgetting about things. Been there, done that, and have a neurologist to prove to me I forgot it." They both cracked up laughing.

A MacBook it is.

Kathy was set and with her new business software, CDs and DVDs, and with Erica's coaching—plus her Mac's brain assisting her brain—she was ready to go "neural" with productivity.

Selecting Mac hardware

Nearly every Mac from the Mac Mini to the Mac Pro can handle nearly all your daily business needs. It is when you move to larger numbers of files or sized files that more powerful Macs may be needed. Computers are like trucks, you have small pickup trucks, pickup trucks, SUVs, one and one half ton trucks, and 18 wheelers used for large loads and long distance hauling jobs. The same goes for the Mac. The work you need to get done will decide which Mac you'll get. Mac Mini's can be used for administrative assistants, data entry, etc. The Mac Pros will do the 18 wheeler level of work. Deciding on whether you get a desktop or a laptop comes down to trading the desktop use of "power" over the laptop use for "portability."

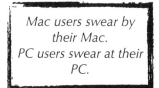

Mac users swear by their Mac.
PC users swear at their PC.

Laptops: *MacBook, MacBook Air, MacBook Pro*

Laptops have so improved that more people now buy laptops to replace desktops because of portability. Reasons to get a laptop include: getting more done because you have it with you, immediacy of access to information, WiFi connectivity and up-to-date information. Other advantages of laptops include: smaller size than desktops, lower power consumption, quiet, and an All-in-One design.

Laptop disadvantages involve their lack of significant computing power and upgradability. They also suffer more wear and tear and require both expensive parts and more physical security than a desktop.

MacBook Air. The 11.6-inch and 13.3-inch MacBook Air are used by those who do not need the heavy, powerful computer, but primarily need something on the road to do "administrivia" work such as accounting, email, or writing marketing copy. The Air line can perform some basic multimedia functions, but probably only as a rough draft or quick editing. Most CEOs who travel will transfer their data between the MacBook Air and their other Macs.

MacBook Pro. The 13.3-inch and 15.4-inch MacBooks are t able to perform all your normal business work, such as spreadsheets, writing marketing materials, or even being creative with podcasting and making music. Once you create the file, you can import it into faster Macs and use faster hardware and software.

Tip. If your laptop's screen goes blank, versus the video card going out, hook up an external monitor to serve as the laptop's screen until you are ready to get it fixed, especially if you're on a tight deadline.

Desktops: *Mac Mini, iMac, Mac Pro*

Mac Mini. The Mac Mini is a small desktop form factor that is great for doing light business or office work such as editing documents, financial data entry or analysis, or even surfing the internet doing market research. It is just about as powerful as an iMac and its form factor makes it great for low-budget startups. An added bonus for a startup business using a Mac Mini is that you can buy a less expensive, non-Apple monitor, keyboard, or mouse. The Mac Mini is ideal if you frequently swap out keyboards, mice, or monitors to keep your business rolling or have the need to move your computers around.

> *The secret of getting ahead is getting started. The secret of getting started is breaking your complex overwhelming tasks into smaller manageable tasks, and then starting on the first one.*
> - Mark Twain

iMac. The 21.5-inch and 27-inch iMacs are great for doing just about anything when you need a larger screen. The iMac's screen size and hard drive makes it perfect for the average computer startup that requires an all-in-one form factor.

Mac Pro. Your Mac Pro is intended to be the 18-wheeler truck for doing the heavy CPU workload, such as video and audio editing for large projects. It can also be used as a simple file server for multiple people in an office environment.

OS X Server: Mac Mini, Mac Pro, or Mac

If you plan to utilize a network or two or more people, consider purchasing the Mac OS Lion Server (apple.com/macosx/server/) with unlimited seat license. You have three main options with which to install it on any Mac with an Intel Core 2 Duo:

1. **Mac Mini** bought with OS X Server installed starts at $999 for an entry-level office environment for two or more Mac users, especially if one is a laptop and one a desktop and is generally used for businesses with up to 10 Macs.

2. **Mac Pro** with installed OS X Server is the next level, with the potential of having up to four hard drive bays for large storage space.

3. **OS X Server** software by itself can be purchased at the Mac App Store for $49.99 and you can install it on an in-house available Mac that runs an Intel Core 2 Duo and is able to run Lion.

OS X Server is for home-based businesses, small studios, retail shops, even virtual offices that can all benefit from its capabilities. You can put the server wherever there is a stable network or broadband connection (business class broadband for home, a hosting service for business servers, etc). Even though you may not need the server's services in the beginning, you can be ready for future business growth using Lion Server. Turn on only those services that you need right away, such as email and Address Book services, and leave the others alone until the need exists. Lion Server comes with the following:

- *Calendar Server 3* uses open calendar protocols to share calendars, schedule meetings, and coordinate events throughout your business, and it can grow with you.

- *Address Book Server 2* allows you to keep track of all of your contact information on your Mac as well as to access business contacts kept on the server.

- *Podcast Services* creates any number of podcasts for and about your business. This is a full end-to-end solution. Use it for training, lectures, presentations, and more.

> Ability is what you're capable of doing. Motivation determines what you do. Attitude determines how well you do it.
> - Lou Holtz

- *iChat Server 3* allows you to collaborate with others, conduct an audio conference, transfer files securely, and share a persistent chat room. With iChat Theater, you can broadcast a presentation, movie, or photo slide show to other iChat users.

- *Wiki Server 3* allows you to create an online "encyclopedia" of your business, using both internal and external files. You can collaborate and communicate with others. With a few clicks you can insert hyperlinks, link between pages, add images, attach files, and change formatting.

- *Web Hosting* provides you ease of use for configuring, hosting, and managing your personal or business websites.

- *Mail Service* is an open standards service that provides compatibility with your existing network infrastructure, as well as with email clients on the Mac, PC, and even iPhone. Junk mail filtering, virus detection, secure email, and push email are all features.

- *Mobile Access Server* enables a Mac laptop to access corporate websites, online business applications, email, calendars, and contacts, all without having to create a Virtual Private Network (VPN).

▸ *File Services* allows you to share files between Mac, Windows, UNIX/Linux and Internet (WebDAV) systems.

▸ *Client Management* and Workgroup Manager simplifies system administration by providing centralized directory-based management of users, groups, and computers across your organization.

▸ *Networking and VPN (Virtual Private Network)* is Apple's Server Assistant and Server Preferences allows you to easily configure your VPN just the way you want, safely and securely and with an AirPort Extreme Base Station (802.11n). As an Internet router the server software can automatically configure services such as iChat, Mail, Web, and VPN to be accessible on the Internet.

If you choose to install a Lion Server for your business and need help then contact the Apple Consultants Network (ACN, consultants.apple.com) in your local area for any one of the hundreds of certified Apple Consultants to help with custom configurations. Because of its UNIX architecture, you can pay an ACN consultant to service your Mac server remotely. You or your dedicated hosting services may have to push the on/off button if things get really bad, then the ACN can do the rest.

Got a new Mac? First things first

When it comes to running your Mac, there are some first steps that will help you get going in short order and allow you to worry less about things that are occurring on your Mac. You've probably already gone through many of its steps to get you running out of the box. However, there are some more suggestions you should consider when setting up your Mac.

> *A wise man will make more opportunities than he finds.*
> *- Sir Francis Bacon*

1. **Configure your Mac for security.** The Mac is secure to a certain extent, but there are other steps to make it more secure. They may not stop a professional, but they'll hinder

most thieves. Here are some of the essentials for your Mac. Check with a computer security expert for more advice.

a. **Disable automatic login.** Under System Preferences > Accounts > Login Options disable Automatic Login. If your Mac is stolen without this disabled someone can access all of your hard drive's information or any of your logged-in accounts on Safari.

b. **Turn on the Mac's firewall.** The firewall prevents outside users from gaining access to your Mac over the network. Even though your cable/DSL modem and wireless router has a firewall, most default router settings leave them unsecured. Make sure your modem, router, and your Mac's firewall (System Preference > Network > Advanced) are turned on.

c. **Create a Standard Account.** Turning on a new Mac allows you to boot straight into your Mac without a password. If your Mac were ever stolen, the thief would have complete access to all of your data such as emails, financial data, and Facebook and Twitter accounts, opening you up to identity theft. On your Mac, create a Standard Account versus using an Administrator Account for your normal day-to-day Mac use. This can also help with troubleshooting problems in the future.

d. **Turn on Screensaver and password-protect it.** Setting up a Screensaver password prevents someone from walking away with your computer while it is on and accessing your vital information. The amount of personal information on a stolen laptop is paramount to identity theft.

2. **Update your Mac OS.**

a. Go to Apple menu > Software Update. Verify your system requirements before installing the updates to determine your correct update version. Always download the updates from Apple's website.

b. Go to support.apple.com/downloads/ and download the most recent Mac OS updates. Choose the Update (Combo), which updates from 10.8 to 10.8.3 and combines all incremental releases into one complete package. If this is not available, then use Update; this is an incremental update going from 10.8.2 to 10.8.3.

3. **Download or buy and then install the other Mac software applications.** Microsoft Office 2008, iWork, Adobe Photoshop, etc., can be installed from disk or downloaded. The steps follow:

a. **Visit the App Store and install apps.** If you have a new Mac with Snow Leopard and Lion and for some new applications, may not be for previously purchased ones, skip to the next step.

b. **Download/insert the DVD with the application (.dmg) file.**

i. **Mount the install file.** Your Mac normally automatically decompresses and opens most .dmg files and follows this pattern: When a file is decompressed you will see a 3D white or iconic image on your desktop. Double clicking on this icon opens up the software window. In most software install cases, a window should already be open with the application icon and an Applications folder alias.

ii. **Install your Mac applications.** Two approaches:

1. **Drag and drop**. Normally drag the Mac application icon in the window onto your Applications folder (an application icon with an arrow pointing toward the Application folder is an alias to your folder). As a security precaution, you will be asked to enter your password. *If you're not installing an application, stop right here: SPAM Alert.*

2. **Double click**. Double clicking on the application icon runs an installer script, rarely done today.

c. **Perform third-party application updates.** Update your Mac application after you have installed them.

4. **Download and install any Mac maintenance software.** This software checks the health of your Mac. Activity Monitor comes free with your Mac. Place the Activity Monitor application icon in your dock to see essential Mac systems within the dock such as memory, hard disk, or CPU use. Also check out the Mac software section below for other solutions.

5. **Back up your Mac!** Once all of that work is done, it is now best to back up your Mac using Time Machine or other back up software. This "pristine" copy of your Mac's hard drive makes it easier and saves time when recovering from Mac maintenance issues.

> *Do not wait; the time will never be "just right." Start where you stand, and work with whatever tools you may have at your command, and better tools will be found as you go along.*
> *- George Herbert*

Tip. Keeping multiple copies of your data and Home or Documents folder is important because files, on occasion, can be corrupted. Keeping multiple versions of the same file makes business recovery much easier.

Now you have a basic Mac setup to handle just about anything that comes along. If you need more information, check out Apple's Support section (apple.com/support) for more information.

Printers: Ink, Laser, AIO (All-In-One)

There are two prominent types of printers: ink and laser. Their outputs are measured in dots per inch (dpi) and are expressed in 1200x1200 or 9600x2400 dpi -- the number of dots placed horizontally and vertically on a page. The higher the dpi, the more detailed the output. If you intend to print from your 3 megapixels (MP) point-and-shoot camera, it will produce a 6x4-inch print just fine, a 6 MP camera will print 8x10-inch, a 10 MP 8.5 by 13, and 12 MP will print 9.7 by 14.5 inch prints.

Ink. Most average low-cost ink printer's output quality range is from 4800x1200 to 9600x2400 dpi or higher and is intended for low volume and higher quality printouts such as personal photographs. The reasons for getting these low-volume output printers are: you want quick, convenient prints for short business deadlines or emergencies; you want control over the results.

Because of the higher quality output, most ink printers are used for photos, business flyers, and brochures. Some ink printers have both large and small black ink cartridges so you can print out many business letters or correspondence in black ink and still have enough black for your graphics output.

Make sure that you get specific ink printer paper as it absorbs the ink better than laser or copier paper because of its special coatings. Occasionally, you can get non-ink paper if you are in a tough spot, but it's not recommended. Problems can occur with the ink jet rollers and other mechanical pieces of your printer over time. Besides, the output looks better if you want to give a higher quality printout to a client.

Laser. Average laser printer output has a smaller range of dpi compared to ink printers. The dpi is between 600x600 up to 2400x600 output which should satisfy nearly every owner's general business printing. Laser printers are used for larger volume printing, in the range of thousands of pages per month. Laser printers are your best option to keep your printing costs lower, compared to ink printers. In addition, laser paper is specially formulated to take the heat used to melt the toner to the paper. Since ink paper has special coatings to absorb the ink, you can ruin a laser printer using ink formulated paper.

> Don't worry when you are not recognized, but strive to be worthy of recognition.
> - Abraham Lincoln

All-In-One (AIO) Ink or Laser Printers. AIO or multifunction printers have a scanner, printer, and copier (and fax in some cases) built in. This can be great for an average business owner to save desk real estate. Generally, lower cost AIOs have scanning software which uses the Mac's CPU to scan and produce the output. A higher priced AIO can cost around $1,000 but has higher scanning technologies built into the hardware and does a better job of producing scanned image output. If you intend to scan a lot or need higher-quality scanning, then consider the higher priced AIO scanners. Beware that AIOs with scanning software may not be up to the task of doing good scanning.

Set up all of your Mac printers

If you are like most businesses, you'll probably have multiple printers for different outputs. For instance, an ink printer can be used for special marketing material. A laser printer could be set aside for volume printing. A multifunction printer could be used as a fax and a scanner and for backup printing. Your printers also might have different connections, such as USB, wireless, or wired network connections. Each will have varied settings and configurations, so it is important that you set up your printers to show each change in physical settings. The more configurations, the more you have to differentiate them. The main settings include:

▸ *USB printer settings* - In this scenario, just go to the System Preferences > Printer & Fax and set it up normally. If you have no other printers or settings then stop from going any further.

▸ *USB Share printer settings* - In some cases you'll want to share your USB printer over a home or office network. In this case, you can share your printer through the System Preferences > Sharing > Printer Sharing settings. You'll have to network all of your Macs to do this, as well as have the printer's Mac turned on during printing if you don't have a connection to an AirPort Extreme with an available USB port.

▸ *Wired and wireless ethernet printer settings* - Both wireless and wired settings may need different configurations. You may be able to share your printer on your wireless network via the

USB port of a Time Capsule, AirPort Extreme, or AirPort Express base station.

Scanner Note: One of the little-known aspects of running a multifunction printer/fax/copier with a Mac is the fact that most multifunction printers/scanners need the scanner part to use the USB cable, not the network, to scan. If you decide to connect the printer to a router on your network, be aware that you have to be within 16 feet to switch the USB cable from the router to your scanner. Some scanner-sharing capability is available; refer to your manufacturer's manual for configurations.

Multiple printer configurations. Naming each of your printer configurations separately will go a long way toward troubleshooting and preventing most printer problems, especially when you are selecting one to print. The most troublesome question is, "I'm printing and nothing is coming out of the printer!" The purpose of naming each configuration setting differently is that you have *different hardware and software paths* through which you can send your file. Provide a hardware path and printer name for each separate configuration so that you know which one is which. For example, naming them "*USB* HP Deskjet D2660," or "*Shared* HP Deskjet D2660," or even "*Router* HP Deskjet D2660," you will reduce confusion, especially if you are constantly changing a printer's physical connections.

Tip. Go Green! Send PDFs to your customer or vendor as a PDF or secured PDF email, or allow them to download it from your website. You'll save yourself time and money and help protect the environment, especially with marketing documents.

Scanners, Cameras, and Camcorders

Scanners. Scanners come in three versions: AIO (All-In-One), flatbed, and an ADF (Automatic Document Feeder). All of these provide ways of getting various types of files, such as images, documents, or to Optical Character Recognition (OCR) documents, into your Mac instead of retyping the document.

The AIO has a printer, copier, and scanner in one unit and occasionally has a fax as a fourth function. Scanning using an AIO puts graphics or documents into your Mac for digital storage. Flatbed or stand-alone scanners are generally higher-end scanners and the multifunction or AIOs are generally used to scan documents into the Mac to be stored on a hard drive to save paper or send a PDF by email.

If you intend to use the scanner for general business, almost any scanner or AIO will handle your scanning needs. However, higher scanning quality would be used for copying graphics to your computer to be used in brochures or websites. Consult a graphic artist to find out the specifics of your graphics needs.

Images that are printed are defined by dpi (dots per inch) and scanned images are defined by ppi (pixels per inch), but these terms are interchangeable. A higher dpi/ppi means that an image can be blown up with little "pixilation" of the image, i.e. seeing small blocks of color. Typically, you will be scanning color photos for video or printer output. You would use a 75 to 200 dpi setting. You may want to use 200 dpi for printing on photo quality printers, and 100 to 150 dpi for video monitors. Most of the time, 300 dpi may be unnecessary, but book printing requires 300 dpi. The larger the dpi, the larger the size of the image, which can grow to 200+ MB or more per image.

Cameras and camcorders. Reasons for startups to use digital cameras and camcorders are varied. You may want pictures of your products, customers, vendors, business site, etc. For video, you may want customer testimonials, videos about your business, your business team, specific processes that you'd like to highlight, or even a marketing or training DVD/video of how to use your product.

Both Apple's iPhoto and iMovie help entrepreneurs with multimedia for their business, an important marketing element in today's business environment.

Digital cameras for general business use: any camera above 8 MP is fine for most business use and will print an 8x10-sized image with few problems. Most digital cameras today are at least 12 MP and are great for the average business.

You can buy a point-and-shoot camera or a much more feature-rich digital SLR (dSLR) camera for greater control over your results. The average point-and-shoot camera has a smaller digital sensor than a dSLR camera. Cost versus quality are the two big differences between the cameras. Image quality can vary among the point-and-shoot cameras while the quality of the dSLRs is generally equal. Talk with a professional before making a purchase decision.

Because point-and-shoot digital cameras have become so inexpensive and have automatic features, they can become a problem when dealing with action shots: during the time between the trigger being depressed and the shot being taken the "event" has often since passed, hence the reason for the dSLR cameras. You can always move from a high-quality dSLR RAW image down to the lower-quality point-and-shoot digital camera's JPEG, but not vise versa.

Video camcorders are moving toward HD quality, but not all small businesses need high quality for their everyday shots. There is one important aspect of taking video that requires attention: the method of storing the video on the cameras. Only two are recommended for startups: digital or flash memory, and mini DV (digital video) tape. Other camcorders need more steps to get video into iMovie. iMovie file formats that import directly are: DV, DV Widescreen, HDV 1080i (25 and 30 fps), HDV 720p (25 and 30 fps), MPEG 4 Simple Profile, and iSight.

A startup business needs to keep costs low. Point-and-shoot digital cameras can function both as a camera and as a low-cost camcorder, if shooting a video is needed. Most cameras and camcorders will work with a Mac, but check with a video professional and/or Apple's Support website (http://www.apple.com/support/) for compatible devices that will work with iPhoto and iMovie.

Chapter Seven

Step 7: Marketing Plan - Customer Funnel

*If the circus is coming to town and you paint a sign saying, "Circus Coming to the Fairground Saturday," that's **advertising**. If you put the sign on the back of an elephant and walk it into town, that's a **promotion**. If you write about the circus and give it out to others, that's a press release. If the elephant walks through the mayor's flower bed, that's **publicity**. If you get the mayor to laugh about it and/or someone else writes about it, that's **public relations**. If the town's citizens go the circus, you show them the many entertainment booths, explain how much fun they'll have spending money at the booths, answer their questions and ultimately, they spend a lot at the circus, that's **sales**. If the customers keep coming back from more, that's a **customer relationship**. Mixed comments from others.*

Story: "Market, market, market!"

Erica was told by a longtime entrepreneur, "You're familiar with the advice to focus on 'location, location, location' from all of your business circles and classes, but for all small businesses, the overall issue is about 'marketing, marketing, marketing' to get business." For example, the figure for authors is that 10 percent of your effort is in writing a book, the other 90 percent of your effort is in marketing. That's not much different for any other startup business that is heading out the business starting gate.

Erica and James both learned together how to use their Macs to be more productive and improve their marketing using iWork and iLife. James told Erica, "I can't believe that my Mac makes it so much easier to get my marketing done compared to other systems."

There are many factors that go into a marketing message that leads to positive customer response. As Erica began her startup business, she soon realized she was behind the marketing power curve. During a moment of clarity she said to James, "Oh no! My marketing message and campaign needs to begin at the same time I work on my product, not after I'm done with it, because I can get my marketing message out before my product release by weeks or even months."

"Yep, glad to see your eyes are open here. In school, you're taught a lesson and then given a test. In life, you're given a test that teaches you a lesson," James chuckled. Erica realized that customer comments and feedback can help shape the size and scope of her product to fit her ideal customer's needs. More accurately, customer comments save her valuable development cycle time and money. After deliberating about it some more Erica concluded, "I need to write this down; this *has* to go into an issue of my newsletter. It's too important not to."

Erica's market feedback helped her to customize and focus the design of her product to her customers, but she got some of her best advice from a long-time entrepreneur who told her, "You have to have such a good product that a product 'sells itself' to your clients. A good product needs great marketing to get mediocre sales. A great product means less marketing work for better sales, but a great product and a great marketing message mean great sales. A one, two product and marketing punch!"

Failures in her product and marketing only mildly troubled her. It was Erica's family and close friends' ignorance and impatience with Erica's seeming "lack of success" that was stressful. Erica told James, "It's bad enough to fight my competition, but family should at least be more supportive."

James paused, considered her comment, then said, "Sometimes families are well-meaning but shortsighted. They don't want to see you get hurt, end up financially strapped, have to explain to others your failures, or have their own fears or failures surface in a projection toward you. Take what they say with a grain of salt. While there might be some truth to what they say, they might not always have your complete story."

Erica told James she was running out of money. At first, Erica's family thought she was "going through a phase" and so were not critical with her, but after seeing she was serious about the business they began to change their tune. Erica read *The Millionaire Mind* by T. Harv Eker and saw what he meant by her family's *money blueprint* and how it shaped their view of earning a living and their frequent "get a job" comments to her.

James was able to help Erica because he had some experience with his dad in his small business. It was becoming clear to Erica that she had to choose between her parents' desire for her to get a job and receiving entrepreneurial coaching from James and his dad (much like Richard Kiyosaki's *Rich Dad, Poor Dad* book had described). Erica would dislike moving in with her parents because of the lack of money, but her current financial situation was a strain.

As James's grandfather Poppop told Erica, with a smile on his weather beaten face, "As the owner of your own business you get to choose which 80 hours a week you work." Erica laughed out loud and saw he understood the guts needed to push through something like a starting a new business. He continued, "Your family and friends may not love what they do, so it becomes work for them. One thing is for certain, even though you choose which 80-90 hours you work, when you love what you do it'll rarely feel like work."

"Thanks Poppop."

One thing Erica understood, after months of work, was that an entrepreneur's devotion to making a difference in people's lives was their inspiration. If her family could just hold out and wait until she'd moved forward, maybe, just maybe they'd see the benefits of her efforts. So she kept trudging up the hill of success determined to keep testing, trying, and improving and testing for results. An entrepreneur's satisfaction of seeing a happy customer who loves the product would inspire the work, marketing, and sales cycle. Sure, some money was there and more would come, but it only came with satisfying customers with products they loved.

To help her with her marketing, Erica wrote as a way of getting her problems and ideas out of her head. Writing was a way of emptying her brain so she could see and visualize what she was doing. Verbalizing what she wrote allowed her to make different connections with her issues. Each writing and verbalizing episode became future content for her newsletter.

It's all about the combination of the right solution communicated the right way to the right customer and market, market, market. Her business newsletter would help do this.

Branding and marketing defined

Branding is a promise. It is the totality of your business actions toward your customer -- what you are willing to do for them -- and is derived from who, what, where, when, why, and how you operate as a business. It includes the practice of creating a name, symbol, or design that identifies and differentiates your product from other products in an industry.

Marketing is a subset of branding that encompasses creating and communicating your company's message to your customer through various marketing channels. Essential to marketing is measuring and tracking what you are doing and looking for results from your marketing efforts. After your marketing has been sent out, it's a matter of checking the market's response and eventually making the sale.

Too often marketing, and for the most part advertising, is money thrown down the drain. For example, for every $1 you spend on marketing you need to bring in $1 or more in sales, otherwise you mainly market someone's art.

Otto Rohwedder sold his jewelry business to fund, invent, and make the first commercial slicing and wrapping bread machine in 1927. When Continental Baking Company introduced the first sliced bread -- Wonder Bread -- in 1930, sales took off (true story). It's not your invention or patents, but spreading your idea among your customers. Make the customer's experience with your product the best first; the brand and marketing plans need to follow. It's about the cycle of creation; one affects the other and back again.

Always be marketing

Always Be Marketing! Never stop, especially in slow times.

Materials "published" and product produced

You need to decide on a date to release your marketing materials to the various media outlets to coincide with the release of your products. The release also depends on your budget, the number of marketing materials you intend to produce, and how much time you have to publish them for your product release/launch. Both your marketing and product may take the same amount of time to design, so you may only get out some general materials at first, followed up with more and improved versions later.

> @LIDA360: RT @smallbiztwit: "I tell my friend about your brand not b/c I like your brand, but b/c I like my friends." via @edwardboches

You have to decide how much marketing you'll be doing as well as when they'll be released. All of your hard work is now at the mercy of the market and if you have done your marketing work right, you should be luring customers to contact you.

Mantra: Define and find your ideal customers

Define your ideal customer. One definition of successful marketing is getting customers to call your business ready to buy from you. Even though most people want to throw out a "fishing net" to find customers, in most cases it is a waste of marketing money and valuable time. In today's business market, most entrepreneurial companies will have niche products that they spend their marketing dollars on and, therefore, need to "fish where *their* fish are." It first requires determining which fish to catch; see the section "What do fishing and marketing have in common?" above to go over this idea again. The first question to answer is, "What kind of fish do I want to catch?" The answer will determine the direction to take for the other questions that need to be asked.

Find your ideal customer and how many are there. After answering which customer or "fish" you want, you have to ask: where are they? This requires finding where and when your customer "feeds" or looks to buy your type of product or service. If you intend to sell high-end ink pens, you won't want to "fish" at Target. You would not go to a lumber store to get hair products. So, where are your "fish"?

This also means that if your ideal market is teenagers and your product is urban, you'll get a better response from urban teenagers in trendy New York and California first and not teenagers in small town middle America. Make sure you get your message to the right customers in the right place, otherwise you're wasting your marketing efforts. You wouldn't go fishing for salmon in the Colorado Rocky Mountains, would you? You definitely won't go into a Colorado bait shop and ask where the local hot spot for salmon are, either.

Same goes for how many customers there are for your product? For instance, Apple sells about three million Macs each quarter, and not all of these sales are to businesses. You need a number of how many customers will potentially buy your product.

Find leads or solicit customer names for the number of customers you might have. Normally, when finding customers you also find a source to market to them. It comes down to two possible ways of getting customers:

▸ Putting your marketing materials out into certain channels that your customers visit, such as an industry magazine or newsletter ads, to get a response from those ideal customers.

▸ Creating or buying a list of potential customers to send your marketing materials.

It will take momentum to keep finding new customers. Here is a breakdown of the ascending difficulty of attracting customers, number one being the easiest:

1. **Current customers:** This is the most important part of your business, your first and current customers.

2. **Referrals:** Word of mouth is your next priority. Customers who love your product will tell others about it.

3. **Past customers:** Customers who have bought before but don't buy often. If you sell one product, here's a chance to sell more.

> ...the aim of marketing is to make selling superfluous. The aim of marketing is to know and understand the customer so well that the product or service fits him and sells itself.
> - Peter Drucker

4. **New customers:** Ones who have never bought from you. This is by far the most difficult because you'll spend the most time to lure them. If you are starting your own business, this is where you start looking for that first customer.

You get that first customer and then the next. It is also the job of each entrepreneur to keep that customer and work to keep them coming back to you. Once you begin attracting customers, you reverse the process above, concentrating on your current customer and then working backwards to find new customers. Once you have a customer, you don't want to lose them.

Medium & money: Channels and costs

Now it is on to researching the various market channels to see if the costs fit into your marketing budget. If it is a magazine ad, how much per full-page, half-page, or quarter-page? If it's radio time, how much per minute? How much is it for video?

If you have a website, you need to be aware of the amount of traffic you'll be drawing to your site. Do you have the necessary bandwidth to handle text, audio, and video files that your ideal customers may want to download from your site? **Note:** Some web hosts charge after you have reached a certain amount of traffic. You'll need to calculate these costs if you are showing videos versus text.

Marketing channels: There are many marketing channels to reach your customers, but you'll need to budget your time and resources to decide if your marketing goals are achievable. Here are a number avenues to get your marketing message out:

1. **Referrals** from family, friends, customers, and anyone doing business with you, such as your personal lawyer or accountant

2. **iPhone/Smartphone** advertising for mobile applications or create software that supports your product (i.e., see AAA or other iPhone/iTouch software)

3. **Office/Retail establishments** that cater to your type of product or could become a joint venture; visit a neighborhood establishment with which you could cross-sell your products

4. **Online or social media** such as niche websites, blogs, social networks (Facebook, LinkedIn, Twitter), Craig's List, eBay, YouTube, and others that would be interested in your product or service

5. **Print media** such as magazines, newspapers, guides, Yellow Pages, brochures, flyers, or direct mail; industry-specific print such trade journals or niche directories;

6. **Direct mail** to ideal customer mailing lists

7. **Broadcast media** such as cable, internet, satellite TV, or radio/internet radio

8. **Signage** such as billboards, flyers, vehicles, retail, or window signs

9. **Trade shows** *(tsnn.com)* your customers and other vendors visit

10. **Public relations** is about interviews in newspapers, radio, internet radio, magazines, and TV (helpareporter.com and reporterconnection.com)

11. **Affiliates** that help you market your products and services; you share some of your profits with those that sell your product to others

12. **Associations** (library.dialog.com/bluesheets/html/bl0114.html) that are industry-specific

13. **Conferences** that are hosted by major industry businesses or associations or a local quorum of experts

14. **Speaking engagements** where, as the subject expert, you offer advice at business meetings, Mastermind groups, various trade or volunteer associations, your local small-business development center, or your local high schools; point people to your website for more information or sell your product at the back of the room

Marketing costs. Researching the various marketing channels and finding out their associated costs will help you decide where to spend based on your marketing budget and where your customers visit. In some cases, you can get free marketing dollars from publicity such as interviews by magazines, radio, local newspapers, and TV shows. Free publicity is always good, so don't discount any chance to get your business name and marketing message out. For example, speaking for free may mean you can also sell your product to your audience members. Each channel requires a specific way of addressing your message. By doing your marketing research, you'll discover the methods and message you can tailor to the outlet. Just make sure that you improve and get your marketing message down cold.

> If I had eight hours to chop down a tree, I'd spend six sharpening my axe.
> - Abraham Lincoln

Message: Finding the customer "bait"

Your marketing time and money will go toward "catching" your customer. You'll need to understand what it will take to get them to respond to your marketing materials. There are only certain types of "bait" that fish like; this means that you need to define your marketing message. This includes the fact that some fish may not like any of your marketing message "baits" at all. Most do respond to some marketing messages. So how does one do this? Follow these steps to get raw material for your message.

1. **Know who your ideal customer is.** Describe in as much detail as possible the demographics of your customer base. Don't chase after a customer who is not defined, but do watch for those who might come along that you did not think about.

2. **Know your product completely.** List all the *features* and *benefits* of your product. If you have "been away" from your product, you may find that going back over your business plan may give new ideas about what your product has to offer.

3. **Select the benefits that fit your prospect.** Pull together all the specific information that will drive your customer to your product. List all your *feature*s and translate those into *benefits* for your customer: How does each feature benefit them?

4. **Highlight Reason #1.** Out of all the information above that you have written, you need to rank them and find which one stands out as the biggest reason your customer should buy your product. What's in it for them?

5. **Write your marketing copy.** Copywriting is one of the more important aspects of marketing; it's telling your customers what is great about your product or service. Getting the wrong words down can hamper your sales, so make sure that you make the right impression to your customer. Take the pieces of information from above and begin to answer these questions:

   5.1. State the problem your market faces, i.e., what problem does your product solve? Focus on and the then dramatize the problem.

   5.2. Who are you and why should they listen to you?

5.3.   What is your product and how does it solve their problem and other benefits. Your product needs to be the hero, the #1 reason, and proof of what your product can do.

5.4.   Why should they order now instead of later? Create a sense of urgency here: what do they get for their money?

5.5.   Finally, write a compelling headline/subject line.

Now that you have the basis of your marketing message, you need to decide which channel to use and adapt your marketing message to the media.

Media: print, audio, video, live

Selecting the media channel to send your marketing pieces to is your next step in marketing your products and services.

Print and Internet. Print includes direct mail sales letters, yellow pages, flyers, brochures, or other printed medium that you send to your ideal customers. A 4x6 postcard is the least expensive way of direct marketing to your customer list. You can use:

▸ iWork Pages or Numbers to create print copy.

▸ MS Office, NeoOffice, or other third-party applications.

Audio. When discussing marketing to an audio channel you can create an audio recording for a conference call or a podcast. How can you create an audio recording?

▸ *iChat* can start an audio chat; then select the iChat menu View > Record Chat and you can record audio files of your conversations with others for future playback.

▸ *GarageBand* records your own audio program/podcast to post on your website; you can also send the link to the iTunes Podcast section for greater reach (apple.com/itunes/podcasts/creatorfaq.html). Create your own music to be added to your marketing message.

▶ *iChat + GarageBand* can record a teleconference. Make sure all participants are on and allow you to record them. Start both programs up, start your audio chat, and then select View > Record Chat. The audio will be recorded in GarageBand as two separate recordings that can be edited in GarageBand.

Now your audio recording or conference call file can be used as a teleseminar where people call in to listen to the recording. It can also become a webinar with access to the recorded file on the internet.

Audio is one of the least-understood aspects of marketing and has the most impact for a startup marketing, especially in retail or office environments. This means not only the songs that are played but also the types of sounds in those environments. View Julian Treasure's talk on ted.com called *The 4 Ways Sounds Affect Us* to better understand the power of sound. Treasure says that open-plan offices have a 66-percent drop in productivity because of poor sound quality. The Four Golden Rules of commercial sound: make it congruent, make it right, make it valuable with your brand, and test and test again to get it right with both your customers and employees.

> No pessimist ever discovered the secret of the stars or sailed an uncharted land, or opened a new doorway for the human spirit.
> - Helen Keller

Video. Video channels have changed in recent years from TV and VCR tapes. An easy, inexpensive, and effective way to get this media out now is YouTube, Facebook, and other social networking outlets. Here are some tools you can use on the Mac:

▶ *iSight or video camera.* iSight is built into all iMacs and Mac laptops, or you can acquire a video camera to record your message.

▶ *iChat.* You can record a video chat that you can post online or burn to a CD/DVD. Sell it or give it away to your customers.

▶ *Photo Booth.* This is a simple program that allows you to record video using your iMac's or laptop's iSight camera.

▶ *iMovie.* Using iChat, Photo Booth, or a video camera you can edit video together, and add an audio recording from GarageBand and photos from iPhoto to create a movie.

Live. Yes, you can market live with your customers at book signings, seminars, or speaking engagements.

Market your product when you can and ask for the sale. If you're giving a seminar, tape it. Take the video, split out the audio, and transcribe the audio into text. You now have three methods (video, audio, and text) of communicating with your audience and customers.

Tip. If something is successful in the print industry, you can nearly always translate *the idea* directly into audio and video and vice versa. When contemplating a marketing piece in print, don't think of a "one-hit wonder" or just one piece, just once. Map out at least eight approaches, and about 15-30 steps total, for each campaign, around the same idea across the marketing spectrum: print, audio, and video. Sequence each of the eight items, such as print one week, audio the second week, and video the third week. Marketing progressively educates, informs, and entertains your customers.

All Four. Because of the internet, you now can use all four methods of print, audio, video, and live marketing to get your message out on your own website or to the various marketing channels. Mix and match your various marketing pieces to different channels. People learn different ways. You'll need all four ways to attract customers.

Method: Send your message out

You have a completed core-marketing message that can be tailored to a specific marketing method for the various marketing channels. Now it's time to distribute it.

How often do you send out your marketing? If you're sending out *valuable information* through your marketing, your customer will tell you either that you're boring and drop any further contact with you, or they'll want to know more about what you're saying.

Here's a suggested list of how much and what to send out:

▸ a 2-4 times a week blog, Twitter, or FaceBook fan page entries or posts about your product

▸ a weekly to monthly email announcing events you host or endorse

▸ a monthly publication; vary the subjects:

  • a newsletter featuring subjects about your industry or business, or deals that you find from around the web

  • a planned customer or network contact: holiday theme, article, customer testimonial, Meetup.com event, etc.

▸ slow-leak marketing through an auto-responder offering hints, tips, or secrets

▸ a monthly press release announcement describing organizational news

▸ quarterly information sharing and trend topic webinars

▸ annual conferences

Marketing testing. An essential part of marketing is selecting a small sample of your market materials to get some first feedback. Test different demographics and measure response rates and comments. If you can reach 100,000 people with a direct marketing piece, 350,000 subscribers in one magazine ad and 150,000 in another, then *market to a small sample of the total percentage of people* in your list to see how well they respond to your marketing. Shoot for 10 percent of the total for each channel by concentrating your marketing in certain zip codes with demographics representative of your target audience. This will save your marketing money. You can test and improve your marketing and try again with a larger group.

Lead generation, lists, and qualifying customers

Marketing is about communicating with your potential ideal customers and telling them your story. To get your message to them you need to generate leads to create a marketing contact list. So if you have completed your marketing message above, now you need a person's contact information to send it to.

Building a list, both online and offline, is critical.

It's OK to start a list from scratch, but having or buying a qualified list of ideal clients is better. So here are some ways you can generate a list, and don't hesitate to use more than one:

1. Surveys
2. Opt-In, free trials or offers
3. Podcasts
4. Personal/guest blog posts
5. Audio downloads
6. RSS feed subscriptions
7. Access to cool videos
8. Give a quote
9. Ecards and Ebooks
10. Contests or drawings
11. Coupons
12. Special offers
13. Inside information access
14. Webinars
15. Teleseminars
16. Live event registrations

Some people may want to opt-in for your email list for an Ebook/report. Others may prefer a printed report/CD/DVD of content in exchange for their mailing address. Remember to differentiate each person on your qualified list.

Qualify customers by creating Marketing-to-Sales process "documents." Your marketing, sales, and operations need to be consistent, especially for professional services. Describing how you work and the timeframes you work with sets expectations with your customers. It can also act like a marketing document that customers can send to friends, generating referrals.

Here are some suggestions for communicating with your customer so that each piece of material consistently tells them how you work:

1. **Introduction process "document" piques interest** - It's an informal document to download, listen to or view on your website, or request through email/snail-mail. A one-page document or short two- to five-minute audio or video clip should explain:

   1.1. **Process:** how things are done in a simple, step-by-step illustration

   1.2. **Time:** how much is needed for each step in the process *and* the total amount of time the process takes from beginning to end; sets project boundaries

   1.3. **Customer:** what the customer *gives to you* and what they can *expect from you* at each step

   1.4. **You:** what you will *get from the customer* and what you will *give to your customer* at each step of the process

2. **Work Order, Request For Proposal, or quote process document:**

   2.1. **Work Order document** - This can be a longer three- to six-page document up to a 15-30 page Ebook or a 10-15 minute audio or video clip that your customer downloads or views from your website. Prospects receive it after they have given you their contact information with the intent of working with you. This document goes into more detail about your process. Providing a downloadable document gives a "fill in the blank" worksheet for your customer so they are ready to work with you. If the customer does not want to complete the document and wants to talk to you directly, you can fill it out during the phone call or at a meeting. Make sure the customer receives a copy not only for their records but also to refer to during question and answer time.

   2.2. **Request For Proposal/Quote (RFP/RFQ)** - This is a potentially longer document that goes into more detail with information about what the customer wants and what you intend to do

3. **Legal Contract** - A legally binding document that adds the "legalese" or obligations written in earlier documents. Keep it looking similar to the earlier documents for consistency and so it's "familiar" to them when they sign it.

Reasons for Content Marketing-to-Sales process "documents." Creating a flyer, white paper, small book, free report, audio, video, Ebook, RFP/RFQ, or a contract communicates the basics of what you do. You create these types of print, audio, and video documents because they:

▸ *Educate and qualify your customer.* Rather than having to explain how you work through individual email, phone, or in person to every potential customer, these various documents educate and qualify them. Having 20 qualified customers ready to buy instead of 100 who just want to talk saves you time and energy. Those 20 come ready to pay you.

▸ *Set customer expectations.* The documents reduce confusion with your customer about what is happening during the process of completing the project. You can give your documents away or sell the information. Then they are paying you for your expertise and you have credibility with them.

> Marketing is a matter of being in front of your customers until **they** are ready to buy, not when **you** are ready to sell.

▸ *Make money for your expertise.* If you were to sell this information, you'd be making some money for both your talent and the time you have put into it.

▸ *Become part of your marketing.* By putting your business name and info in and on your document, you are on your way to becoming an expert in what they are looking for. In the right format, potential customers could share your document with others or buy it for their friends.

▸ *The do-it-yourself (DIY) crowd or "sponge person" won't take up your valuable time.* The DIY prospect or "sponge" wants your knowledge and time, the more the merrier. Creating a sample document or video of what you do, available 24/7, so here's how they see your knowledge and time:

- The more they get, the happier they get. Sometimes expecting it to be free, and at your expense: no profit. Even then, a small number never intend to pay, so they'll rarely be a customer.

- Your information shows your expertise without you *personally* trying to convince them about the quality of your product or service.

- If they use your information to do it themselves and then later want you to do it for them, you're less likely to argue over your price.

- If they're cheap way of doing it works, and they come to you with it, you now have a mock-up of what they want to do if they change their mind and seek more professional help or results.

- On the other hand, if their cheap way of doing it works and they make more sales, they'll now have money to pay you for a better product without you having to cut your prices to help a starving business to get up and running.

▸ *Point them to others who might do it differently.* If they decide to go somewhere else, you weren't the one for them and have saved yourself time and money. You can pursue other customers who are interested in what you do.

▸ *Create a call to action.* At the end of your document, audio, or video file, create a specific call to action, so that customers know the steps to take next with you. If they have filled out your downloaded document or filled out an online form and sent it to you, you can begin helping them out.

So, create that marketing white paper, book/ebook, or an audio/ video file to give or sell to a potential customer to help qualify them by way of your marketing. You're now free to do other things.

Action Plan: Track marketing results

If you have done all the work above, you may think you're done, but you're not. You need to know the results of your marketing to see how successful it is. Table 4 illustrates how you would track your marketing. It's in a sequence funnel so that one step feeds into another.

> *If passion drives you, let reason hold the reins. - Benjamin Franklin*

You don't want to spend all of your marketing budget in one month, but you do need multiple channels to market in to see where the greatest responses are from.

Here are a few ways to track your marketing data. One of the interesting diferences between a spreadsheet and a database is that the purpose of a *database* is to be able to manage the data (to find a story within your information), while the purpose of a *spreadsheet* is to take a look at numbers:

▸ iWork Numbers spreadsheet of the data that you collect to crunch the data into different statistical ways.

▸ In a Bento or Filemaker Pro database of the data, you can keep a running tab on the information over time and search the data for more meaningful information for your business growth.

Keep in mind that you may break down the steps further into more detail. Measure to find out where your marketing is failing and improve it. At each step of the process in Table 4, ask yourself questions about why things are happening. For instance:

▸ If you get *no response* whatsoever to any marketing, you need to look at a longer time to send the message, other places to market, or change your marketing message completely.

▸ If you get a *small response*, you need to improve your marketing.

▸ If you get a *large response*, and you get leads but no meetings, then what is wrong with how you were qualifying your leads?

Funnel Step	Metric	Channel #1 Magazine	Channel #2 Website
Target Market	# of people in the ideal market		
Ideal Market	# of people potentially buying your product		
Reach	# of people your marketing reaches, % of ideal market #s		
Lead Generation	# and Types (hot, warm, cold) of Leads, % of Reach #s		
Marketing Budget	$ spent on marketing/# of leads and total sales		

Table 4: Marketing Funnel Steps

▸ Target channels that offer: largest volume of customers (#), lowest cost ($), and best performance (%); this includes websites.

At each step of the process, some potential customers will leave. You need to find out why so you can adjust your marketing and/or product to fit what they are looking for. At each step above, if you have lost a customer, it's an opportunity to learn more about your customer and what you are offering. The critical gap will be between what you are offering and what/why they are buying.

Chapter Eight

Step 8: Sales Plan - Meet The Demand

If Edison had a needle to find in a haystack, he would proceed at once with the diligence of the bee to examine straw after straw until he found the object of his search. I was a sorry witness of such doings, knowing that a little theory and calculation would have saved him ninety per cent of his labor. -- Nikola Tesla, assistant to Thomas Edison

Story: "Kids sell the darnedest things"

Thomas Edison once stated, "Anything that won't sell, I don't want to invent. Its sale is proof of utility, and utility is success."

Erica liked this quote, Edison's reflection on his idea for an electric vote recording machine. Eventually the Massachusetts Legislature, Edison's ideal market for the invention, thoroughly denigrated it, claiming "its speed in tallying votes would disrupt the delicate political status-quo." Edison spent time and money on his invention, which was ahead of his time. People were just not ready for it.[84]

Erica was determined to avoid an Edison-type mistake. Learning from others' mistakes would be less costly, so she sought out those life lessons.

---

[84] thomasedison.com/biography.html

Erica called her parents and told them, "I have to move back home. I'm trying to build up my business and I'm willing to help around the house to help cover my costs. I don't want to be a freeloader, but it would allow me to get my business up and running more quickly if I moved back in and kept my costs low."

Reluctantly, her parents agreed. Erica's mother assured her, "We know you're not lazy. We believe in you, but it's tough love. The tough part is us not helping you with your bills, you paying for rent at less than market prices, and covering your own expenses. The love part is us helping you to save yourself money while you're building your first business."

Her dad said it right, "As any parent learns, we found out that giving you a pat on the back helps develop your character - if we give it *often* enough, *early* enough, and on occasion, *low* enough," he said with a smile and gave her a hug and a kiss on her head. Erica giggled back, "Thanks Dad." At least her parents were beginning to see that she was trying to do something with her life, to make something of it, to make a difference in a customer's life. Erica figured she'd have to make the best of the situation, no matter what happened.

Coming up with a good product design for her newsletter and then a good marketing plan piqued people's interest in the information Erica's newsletter provided. The next step was sales, an extension of the marketing step to further educate her customers about what her information would do for them.

Now she needed to translate her marketing words into a sales demonstration or illustration of how her product would work in each situation. In her case, she needed to send out newsletter samples or give a trial membership to potential clients. Erica's marketing was good enough to generate some leads/web traffic as tracking them in the Mac was beginning to show.

Erica as a business owner was not only the CEO and CFO, but also the CSO, Chief Sales Officer. Like many other beginning entrepreneurs, she caught herself saying: "I'm not a salesperson." But Erica received some valuable advice from a fellow entrepreneur, "If you owned the cure for cancer, would you stop others from buying it? No, you wouldn't. Restate what you're doing; you're really qualifying a right customer who has the right problem that your right product solves." Erica soon realized that her limiting belief was that *she* was deciding for her customer rather than letting *the customer* decide. A great product and then a belief in your product is about changing and improving customer lives for the better, and belief goes far beyond selling.

Erica saw her nieces' and nephews' tenacity in getting what they wanted from their parents at various times in their young little "sales" lives at the local stores. They would persevere with their "sales pitch" of, "C'mon Mom, can I have that candy bar/toy/piece of clothing/iPod," even when it was firmly refused a slew of times.

Erica watched the kids learn how to overcome parental objections and offer counter objections, even before the parents had a chance to offer them. The kids learned over time that overcoming both the conjured up and real objections, and then offering alternative ideas, weaken a parent's objections over time until they hear, "I said, NO! If you don't stop bugging me you're going to be in trouble." Or, until the parents agree, with some added stipulations from Mom and Dad.

Sales are a continuation of truthful marketing, a practice of treating all customers as you would like to be treated by a salesperson. As James's dad told Erica, "You have two ears, two eyes, and one mouth. Listen and watch more than you talk, that's the secret to sales. Ask for the sale and if they say yes, stop talking and ring it up."

After any sale Erica begins to follow-up with her customers in a few days, to counter any "sales remorse." The follow-up includes providing more information about her product and offering extra items that might enhance the customer's buying experience.

Erica had talked with James during her darkest business-growing days; he helped her get over her fear of failure by keeping her focused on her main reasons for producing a great product. James told her, "Everyone sells, no matter who you are, and the emotion of selling begins with a belief in what you are selling. If you don't believe in your product, it shows to your customers."

Erica knew she would have a long friendship with James; his mentorship gave her the confidence to face each challenge as it came up and to develop all of her talents and dreams into a reality, and for that she took a great liking to James.

She may have been through the worst of times, but she saw the best of times in her future.

Sales channels: A fishing line, no fishing net

What is critical about marketing is tracking what you are doing and looking for results of your marketing efforts. Sales is no different in that you track information about each sale to find out how to improve your success rate among your customers. After your marketing has been sent out, it's a matter of checking the market's response to what you are offering and eventually making the sale.

Once you know who your customers are and where they congregate, it's a matter of being able to get your product to them through the various channels. Your marketing and sales channels may be different or the same company, person, or even industry; it truly depends on your product and your customers.

Here are some channels through which you can sell your product:

‣ Brick and mortar retail

‣ Click and mortar or online retail stores

‣ Distributors, VAR (Value Added Reseller), independent sales representatives, and dealers

‣ Niche, out of the norm or speciality retail outlets

‣ Intensive, selective, and exclusive distribution

‣ Joint venture partners and endorsers

‣ Internet affiliates or nontraditional salespeople such as "promoters" or "fans" of your product

‣ Professional partnerships

If you have done your research you'll be able to find the best channel to market and sell to. Once that has been done, now it's up to you to prepare yourself for the sales pitch.

Selling is about you and the relationship

Selling is all about you and your product. If you've done all the right things, such as product development and marketing, then selling should be an easier step. Your discussion with your customer about why your product works for them will be easier, as well.

It begins with You

When it comes to building a business, the one thing that most people don't realize is that selling is all about the relationship between you and your customer. The larger the customer, the more the relationship is based on reputation.

"I'm speechless!" Imagine a business you frequent has a person there that you have had your eye on for a while; it's become a crush. Both of you flirt each time you see each other and after much small talk with that person, one day they walk up and hand you their phone number and ask you to call them when you're not at work. You're excited about the potential. You've always wondered, but now it seems possible.

You call them up and talk and this person decides they want to set up a date with you. You're eager to go out with them. You go out and you enjoy yourself throughout the date. You're having a good time getting to know them more.

Then, right in the middle of the date this person asks, "How would you like to buy one of my products?"

"I'm speechless," is probably what you'd say.

> If I could solve all the problems myself, I would. (-Thomas Edison, when asked why he had a team of twenty-one assistants)

How would you think your relationship would proceed with this person going forward? By not disclosing their intentions up front, they started the relationship on the wrong foot and will have to work extra hard to get back into your good graces.

It begins with you, but you have to be transparent about your intentions (fictional story).

It's always about the relationship first; the sales or numbers come later.

Basic selling steps

No matter what product you come up with, as an entrepreneur you will be selling in person or in your advertising and marketing. When it comes to sales, there is a process that every sales person goes through, whether these steps are in person or through digital means such as email, audio, video, or the web. If you sell in person, you'll go through these steps. Macs can help you manage the sales process. Doing this digitally, you can use any number of tools to communicate with your customer.

> *Genius is one percent inspiration and ninety-nine percent perspiration.*
> *- Thomas Edison*

1. **Prepare.** You have to prepare your product and yourself for the sale. This means that you have all the parts ready to discuss with your customer (features, benefits, and terms) when they buy from you.

2. **Get their permission.** To sell anyone anything you need their permission, otherwise you're SPAMMING or only selling to them. You can just go up to someone and try to sell them something, but you may not get very far. It is best to ask for their permission to sell to them. Otherwise you'll come across as only interested in yourself and not in them, as a customer. Ask them, "If I could show you how to _____, would you be interested in knowing more about it?"

3. **Your offer.** Once you have their permission, present your offer. In many cases, it is a "good, better, best" scenario. Of course you will use more detailed and enticing words when offering them your solutions.

4. **Present.** Presenting means that you are giving your reasons for them to buy what you are offering. State the customer's problem, show the customer that it really is a problem, then share the benefits of your product to solve their problem.

5. **Listen.** As you're discussing your product with your potential customer, listen for their responses to your comments and respond appropriately.

6. **Emotional selling.** When you sell something, you are selling to your customer based on emotion that backs up their logic. You cannot sell based on logic alone.

7. **Ask for the sale.** Closing the sale means that you ask them if they want to buy your product. If you have done the earlier steps correctly, this is easy. Always be willing to ask the customer throughout the sales process if they want your product. If they do, stop talking, give them your product, and take their money! When you ask for the sale, ask a Yes-or-Yes question: "Would you prefer the 10 or 16 pack? Delivered Tuesday or Thursday? Pay the full amount or make payments?" If they don't want to buy, ask: why?

This is not just about the sale or commission; think of the long-term sales prospects of each customer. Could this sale turn into another one: Could I obtain referrals from it? If you were to buy one Mac and loved it, how many more would you buy from Apple in the future? The sale is about relationship, not revenue.

Follow-up. The sale does not end when money is in the bank. That's just the beginning. Following up should be done with a number of approaches depending on your product, industry, and you. Once you have made the sale, you need to follow up with your customer. Why? First and most essential is to tell your customers "Thank You" for their business. How would you feel if you bought something and no one said thank you for your business? Second, you also want to see how well you solved the customer's problem

> *People often say that motivation doesn't last. Well neither does bathing, that's why we recommend it daily. - Zig Ziglar*

and to see if there is anything else you can do for them. Eliciting customer comments keeps you in touch with your customers and helps you keep your product fresh as the market changes.

If you are a startup company, marketing (casting your line) and selling (setting the hook) are the two most important steps in making a living. If you can't sell, then you won't eat! It's that simple. Become a student of the sales profession, so that you can get better over time.

Selling ABCs: Always Be Closing? No, but…

From the old school of hard selling, the ABCs of sales is "Always Be Closing," and it's still around in older, more traditional businesses to "get the numbers." Today, the new sales model is "Always Be Charming" (polite, friendly, likable). You would not *always be closing* on a future potential spouse without getting to know them, would you? Would you walk up to the first person you saw and say, "Will you marry me?" No! This is hard selling.

> Innovation comes from the producer, not from the customer.
> - W. Edwards Deming

Some companies see a customer in terms of the current transaction, not someone who can be influenced into the future. If you have a great product, it makes the sales courting process easier. This is especially true if your product is a *good catch* and your customers are ready to say *yes* to you. So, always woo them to pop the *right question* to your *customer for life* because you always want to keep *charming your customer* with your great products and offers. It's all about the relationship.

Capture customer information

There are two ways of collecting a customer's contact information: they give it to you through your marketing or you purchase it through a purchased marketing list. It is essential that if your customer gives you their contact information that you do not "violate" this gift of information by treating it with indifference. Treat their information like you would want your information to be treated, with respect! Never give or sell it to anyone, ever, period!

Why? Because it could hurt or ruin the relationship you're trying to build. You can sell purchased contact information for direct mail campaigns if needed, but not if they give you their contact information.

Once you have sent out your marketing information or put it on your website, you now need to be able to capture your customer's information. At the very least, you'll want to collect their name and email address. If you intend to sell and ship to them, you'll need their business, home, and/or shipping street address and any credit card information to ring up the sale. If you are in larger sales, such as real estate which requires more customer information, then you'll need to track birthdays, business information, and more on your Mac.

To market to your ideal customer, you must include them on your list, or invite them. Check out LinkedIn.com, Facebook.com, or Twitter.com and other social media sites for additional connections and contact information.

> *Stop selling.*
> *Start helping.*
> *- Zig Ziglar*

Customer information can be gained by asking for a business card, fax, email, mail, mailing list, or through the internet. Taking a business card is a quick way of getting the information, but sometimes having customers hand their information to you is not the best use of your time. Having a website where your customer can enter contact information can save you time and money.

Confirm the accuracy of your customer's information by utilizing a verification process. Nothing is more frustrating than a customer waiting for a response from you, but never receiving it because of incorrect information on your end. It may be the customer's fault, but they may not know it.

Mac solution: Your Mac's Address Book is the place to start to enter in your contact information. Make sure that you have a backup of the information in the event your hard drive fails. If you have a CRM program that an ISP hosts and manages, make sure that you keep copies/backups of this information. Even under the best circumstances, hosting companies can lose your data and you'd hate to give your customers a bad experience because of your systems. It's possible to export Address Book contacts into the vCard format and convert them to a CSV (Comma Separate Value) MS Excel or iWork Numbers file, or import the vCards directly into a contact management program.

Gauging interest and improvement feedback

You have created a product to alleviate someone's pain; now listen to them! Receiving a specific response, let alone any response, from your customers is the first step to getting a sale. It means that someone has expressed an interest in what you are selling and that you are providing a solution to their problem. Now you need to gauge their interest.

Once you have gathered your customer's comments, you may alter your product in a variety of ways, based on their comments:

▸ *Do nothing.* Considering the market, you may not want to change anything about your product. There are three reasons why you do not need you to change: trying to please every customer at every price level, changing your business processes based on just one complaint, or if one person objects to something you do, you abandon what you are doing. If you offer a Saks-Fifth-Avenue level of quality and your customer wants Target quality, it's a no brainer: don't change, even if they say it's "too expensive" for them to buy. Not everyone can afford a Rolls Royce.

▸ *Change it.* You could change the product, price, marketing, or some other aspect of what you are selling based on overwhelming feedback. Listen to all comments. If you do see a large benefit to changing, of course change to improve if there is truth in the customer complaints/suggestions. The change *needs to make business sense* for both you and the customer.

▶ *Sell it.* Give them what they came for and take their money, then follow-up with them to see how they like it and get further comments and testimonials.

Make the sale, parlay the sale

This is probably the simple part: just ring the sale up. Take their money, deliver their product, and most importantly, thank them for their business.

Then, begin to parlay each of your current sales into bigger numbers (numbers of transactions) and amounts (higher transaction amounts) of sales. It's about continuing to find out what the customer wants and satisfying more of their needs and wants. That's why you are in business, to find out what your customers are hungry for and feed them that.

Deliver your products

Once you have received their money, it's now a matter of delivering on what you promised to them. Delivering your product could mean packaging and then shipping it to them, allowing them to download it from your website, showing them how to do something, doing the job for them, or even getting someone else to do the job.

Follow-up: essential to business building

Buying Customers. Getting a customer is more than half the battle; keeping them takes follow-up. You need to under-promise and over-deliver on all of your sales transactions. Follow a 3/30/365-day guideline to reduce these problems:

▶ *3 days.* You follow up to see how their purchase was. Do not assume that things went well. Don't assume anything. Ask them:

• Did we do what we said we'd do?

- Are you satisfied?

- How was your experience dealing with our complete buying process?

- What can we do more of? Less of?

- Can we have a referral or testimonial?

▸ *30 days.* Ask again and see if there is anything that you could further help them with. Repeat the earlier questions.

▸ *365 days.* See how things are. Repeat the earlier questions.

When a customer buys something from you, you need to keep in regular contact with them with valuable information that could help them with their use of your product. Or you can give them information about something you are involved with: If you sell bath products, send them some.

When it comes to following up with a customer who buys from you:

1. **Thank them for their business.** Continue to keep in contact with them through email or letters. Check on their purchase, letting them know about other products in your line. Ask them a "Do you need anything else?" question.

2. **Offer something of value for free.** Invite them to attend any free seminars, events, trade shows, or conferences that you may be putting on that might benefit them in the future.

3. **Offer them free information.** Keep them informed of changes to technology, laws, or other aspects of your product that might affect them and their life. If you sell carpet, discuss carpet-industry issues that affect their purchases.

4. **Present seasonal/special event offers.** Look at seasonal or other special times, such as birthdays or holidays, when you can offer additional products.

5. **Offer something else.** Loyalty cards, the opportunity to trade in old products for something new, surveys, rewards for referrals, onsite classes, or other freebies will help continue your business relationship with your customers.

By tracking and recording multiple ways of contacting your customer, you avoid sending them analog or digital SPAM. You're doing this to keep your company's name and/or product in front of the customer, and to see what else you can do for them. It's also about listening to your customers' interests. If you're giving them something of value each time you contact them, they're more likely to allow you to keep sending

> Forget about the business outlook, be on the outlook for business.
> - Paul J. Meyer

them information. Not everyone will buy the first time you send something out; it takes repetition with customers.

Non-buying customers and ways to follow up. Following are a few ways to follow up with your non-buying customers:

▸ Obtain customer contact info before you give them something so you can follow up.

▸ Create an opt-in newsletter or VIP membership that gives them an incentive to stay in contact, such as announcements of upcoming sales or new products.

▸ Give a free offer for lost sales to find out why they don't like your product.

▸ Be creative soliciting comments and be outrageous about it.

▸ Give away your product in exchange for a 30-minute review or comments session.

▸ Pitch your product to local groups, such as user groups, various associations, or Meetup.com groups.

Action plan: Track sales results

When it comes to collecting your customer's information, seek more than just the name and address. Depending on your industry and market, it can be useful to know birthdays, anniversaries, children's birthdays, company associates or colleagues, holidays, or special occasions to keep in touch with them.

When you want some information from them, it's OK to ask, but if you give something in return for their information they're much more likely to share their contact or other information.

From the moment your marketing begins obtaining new customer leads/web traffic, find out how successful your efforts are. Consult Table 5 and, based on the numbers you collect, you'll have some questions to answer:

Funnel Step	Metric	Channel	Channel	Channel
		Magazine	Website	Phone Calls
Lead Generation	# of Leads, % of Reach #s			
Lead Qualifications/ Meetings	# of meetings, % of Lead Generation			
Lead Conversion/ Sales	# of Sales, % of Lead Meetings			
Sales	# and $ of Sales			

Table 5: Sales Funnel Steps

▸ If you're pulling *small numbers* of interested customers, but they abandon your website or only want information, why?

▸ If you're creating *small numbers* of meetings from your marketing leads/web traffic and not making the sale, why?

▸ If you're making the sale, what is the conversion rate? Are you making small numbers of sales or large numbers of sales based on the number of leads/web traffic? Why?

▸ If you're making the sale, can you make larger *numbers* of sales, increasing the volume?

▸ If you're making the sale, can you make larger *amounts* of sales, i.e., can you make more amount per sale transaction?

Once you begin to analyze your sales numbers, break each sale down from the customer level to see what they buy from you (see Table 6). The idea is to find out more about the customer and what reasons they want to buy from you. The more you know about your customer, the more you'll understand your market.

Also find out what products and services are liked and disliked. When a product does not sell, maybe it is time to change or drop the customer, change the product, or discontinue the product.

Funnel Step	Metric	Product #1	Product #2	Product #3
Customer	which product			
Fulfillment	# of orders to fill, # of days to fill each order			
Follow-up	# of follow-ups after the sale			

Table 6: Follow Funnel Steps

Chapter Nine

Step 9: Operation Plan - Work it

In the end, all business operations can be reduced to three words: people, product, and profits. -- Lee Iacocca

Monitor your customers

Your job as a business owner is to check all of your customer comments so you can judge your efforts at marketing, sales, and general customer follow-up. This means looking for and tracking responses to what you do so that you can change or improve to increase your success rate, make more money, and grow your business.

Selling to a customer is a result of a number of comments on the success of all the other work that you have done with product development and marketing. It is not the end of the line; it is just the beginning. You are just beginning to move your business forward and you need to know what your customers think about your product or service.

Every comment, suggestion, and complaint is an opportunity to listen to customers tell you want they like and don't like about your product. It is up to you to listen and decide whether the information is valid and worthwhile to your business. Some of your customers may not even begin to tell you, but you need to be proactive and seek them out to see what they think.

Handle customer service issues

Good business means treating your customer like you would treat yourself. In Christine Comaford's book *Rules for Renegades,* she says that good business manners like saying, "Please," "Thank You," "I'm sorry," and "I don't know" are great ways to show a human being behind your company branding. I'd add to her comments by modifying "I don't know" to "I don't know, but I'll find out." This approach means that you don't give up trying to serve. It means you'll find them another direction, even if it's to a competitor.

> A business absolutely devoted to service will have only one worry about profits. They will be embarrassingly large.
> - Henry Ford

Every business will encounter customer disputes. Returns occur for various reasons and each return is an opportunity to obtain feedback about what you are creating and selling to your ideal customers.

- *Setting expectations.* When it comes to disputes, the first step is prevention by setting correct expectations in your branding, marketing, and sales before you ever interact with your customers.

- *Planning of pricing.* It's a matter of planning and pricing your product so well that your profits offset your costs of returns. Mistakes are one thing; refunds are something else.

- *Buyer's remorse.* Price your product so well that buyer remorse is nonexistent or greatly reduced. Every return takes time away from another sale and reduces the total number of sales you can make.

Negative feedback about what you do is an opportunity to listen, learn, and decide if it's legitimate to the improvement of your product. While nearly all customers are honest and are willing to pay good money for something good, some are not so honest. Still, treat them as you would like to be treated.

"The customer is not always right, but they are still the customer." A gentleman walks into the Apple store to replace his "defective" product. The salesperson responds, "Let me confirm that this unit is defective." The gentleman angrily responds, "This is poor customer service. If I went to any other store, I'd have it replaced *immediately!*" The salesperson replies, "Sir, my first responsibility is to determine if it's defective. If you are correct and it is defective, then we'll gladly replace it according to our warranty with no questions asked. However, if this unit isn't defective and I give you a new unit, you'll be back in a very short time with the same problem. You'll have told all your family and friends about how lousy our products and customer service are. Once I'm positive that you have a good unit, then we need to make sure you are knowledgeable about its proper operation. We really want you to have a good experience with our products" (true story). Each customer interaction is a chance to learn and educate more, on both sides of the sale.

Monitor product quantity and quality

Getting to know your customer also gives you knowledge of what your customers are saying about your products and services. If you leave that to others, you can become detached from what you are creating. Every comment gives you an opportunity to decide what your future product or service will be. Maybe their comments will lead you to create a totally different product or service. Don't detach yourself 100 percent from this aspect of your job; it'll keep you in business longer.

Monitor your vendors

Monitor what your vendors are charging and what they're delivering in products. If you have a fixed expense and they increase, find out why. If there is a jump in your variable expenses, you'll need to pinpoint the trouble area. It's not only the expense of the product, but also the quality of the product, as well.

Monitor your money

The money you make from your business tells the story about how well you're doing. If you can't figure out how much you're making, how can you become more successful?

"How's your vehicle's gas level?" When you get into your vehicle, how accurate is your fuel gauge? If your gas tank holds 10 gallons of gas and you get 25 mpg, when the gauge reads exactly half a tank, can you really go 125 miles based on the accuracy of the gauge? Does your vehicle's gas gauge have evenly spaced marks but is not accurate, i.e. ½ reading means it's really ⅔ full? Do you have to guess when you really have a half tank of gas left? Do you measure your business actions like this? If your measurements are not giving you accurate information, how will you make a good decision? Your business actions determine your business finances (compilation story).

If you don't take the responsibility to manage your money, who will? Have you read about the successful Hollywood stars or recording artists who have had to take their managers to court because of all the money that was misappropriated? It is essential for any business to understand and manage money well. If an accountant or CPA won't tell you how things work in simple language, it's time to hire better experts. Anyone who works for you who is not willing to explain what is happening in simple terms is not the consultant for you.

> *Success in business requires training and discipline and hard work. But if you're not frightened by these things, the opportunities are just as great today as they ever were.*
> *- David Rockefeller*

Money Secrets - Effective Money Management Steps

If you can't manage your personal finances, how are you going to manage your company's finances? If you have difficulty managing small amounts of income, how are you going to handle larger amounts? Connect with a bookkeeper, financial planner, and other financial mentors that can help guide your finances.

Since this is *your* company, *always* know where your money is going, to the penny, by signing every check that goes out for every bill that comes in. Look at each bank statement *and* bill that you get. Even though you may pay a bookkeeper to handle the paperwork, you still need to keep your hands in every phase of the making *and* spending of your company's money.

Here are the wealth-creating *money skills in sequence* you need to learn to grow your financial future:

> *The principle of spending money to be paid by posterity, under the name of funding, is but swindling futurity on a large scale.*
> *- Thomas Jefferson*

1. **Value Money** - Learn the value of money, including finance and accounting. Each penny saved is a seed to produce greater amounts of wealth. Poor money managers see only how much things cost. Good managers seek a Return On Investment (ROI). Wealthy people know the value of both time and money; they've learned to have a head for money. Which is better, spend $100 to earn $50, or spend $1000 to earn $3,000? Of course, the latter. How much would you spend, or invest, to earn $1,000,000? If you're earning a ton of money, a rainy day will come, so sock it away for that day. Great entrepreneurs work in multiples of their marketing funds; for every $1 invested, $2 or more comes back in new business.

2. **Earn Money** - This is where you have a job or have started a business and are earning income from a single source. Later, you aim to earn, not make, more income, including from multiple sources. Increase your income, you get paid in direct proportion to what you bring to the table.

3. **Share Money (10%)** - Sharing your money with others with gifts or charities takes you "outside" yourself, allowing you to think abundance and not scarcity of wealth. It also keeps you grounded with those who have less than you do, reminding you to be appreciative of what you have.

4. **Control Money (50%)** - These are your personal and business necessities, preferably spend no more than 55% of

your income on your necessities as a start. Controlling each penny that goes out can help create savings and lengthen your time in business. This means watching your expenses over time, especially for vendor creep, prices and fees that are increased or added to your bill without notifying you. You have to decide when to grow and expand. Have enough cash on hand, "float," to cover "Big Company" customers that take 60-120 days to pay.

5. **Invest Money (10%)** - Pay yourself first; *make your money work for you.* This is your golden goose; when you retire, you spend the golden eggs (interest), never the goose (principle). Invest your money so that it multiplies in various vehicles, including investments, savings, passive income, "bank on yourself" life insurance, or real estate. Start investing with conservative investment strategies, then on to more aggressive investments, and finally into very aggressive investment money accounts or "buckets."

6. **Save Money (10%)** - Put some of your earnings into a separate accounts. First, create a contingency fund account of six to 12 months worth of income. Once that account is filled, funnel 10 percent into large items such as a new car, equipment, or other items that you will need in the future. It's a good habit to have it automatically deducted because you won't miss it if you never see it.

7. **Multiply Money (10%)** - Education and learning is crucial here; *learn to earn.* The goal is to create multiple streams of income. At first, it may mean having two or more jobs and saving money from the second job to fund your business startup. For an entrepreneur, this means moving from your first product to another item or line. Once this business gains momentum, create multiple businesses. Finally, move on to various income-producing streams, like real estate investments that have positive cash flow.

8. **Spend Money (10%)** - This is money that you and your family get to spend, with no strings attached. Do with as you please and without feeling guilty. You have to *spend it all!*

9. **Shield Money** - After you have created multiple income streams, you'll need to begin creating tax and legal entities to shield your money. There are three types:

9.1.   protection of assets against lawsuits

9.2.   estate planning against income taxes

9.3.   and tax planning to retain wealth and offset death taxes.

All the wealthy entrepreneurs do it; why not you?

You must constantly learn about money matters. Never stop learning about money matters. The better you are at learning about money, the more you'll make, have, keep, and share with others.

"Setting yourself up for retirement." Some of the best retirement advice I got came from my grandfather (see Illustration 5). About seven years before he retired, he figured out what his retirement income was going to be from Social Security and his various other sources of income. For the next few years, he funneled more of his take-home pay into investments so that about three years before he retired, he and my grandmother were living on the level he was going to get from his

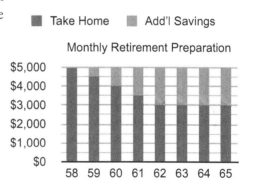

Illustration 5: Monthly retirement graph

retirement. For example, if he was making $5,000 a month before he retired, and his retirement was going to provide about $3,000 a month, he increased his savings until he take home pay was $3,000 a month at age 63. They lived at that pay until he finally retired at 65. The extra $2,000 per month was put into his retirement accounts that he and my grandmother used later. His reasoning? Too often retirement income does not match working or earning income and the retirement shock can be tough to take if you are not ready for the "loss" of income (true story).

Define the ways your customer pays you

How are your customers going to pay you: cash, check, credit or debit card, PayPal, or other means? Even though there are conveniences of various payment methods, they may not all be in your best business interest. Even though more payment options are available for your customers, they also create more complexity with all the various processes that you have to follow with each form of payment.

When do you expect payment from your customers? Depending on the work that you do, such as a consultant or a retail store, you expect to be paid the moment someone walks out with the product or service. However, in some cases this may not be possible.

As a rule, the larger the customer, the longer it takes to get paid, especially for services that you perform. It can take from 60 to 120 days to get paid, so keep enough cash on hand or enough cash to float during this time to cover the cash flow gap. If you have large numbers of customers, be aware that a small percentage of your customers may not pay you or may want to return your product. This will also affect your cash flow.

Business money rules to work by: Always obtain a signed credit application. Always check credit. Always set up credit limits. Always call when customers are late. Always assume that you are going to have some losses. Always, always, always be on top of your personal and business finances.

Cash flow is king

Once you understand the value of money you'll next need to understand the flow of cash through your business so that you can understand if you are making or losing money. It is an irrefutable fact that the longer a customer does not pay you, the less of a chance you'll get paid. Be your own collection agency, unless you have a spouse or employee do the dirty work of collecting what is owed.

Numbers for startups, basic financial statements

There are two number-crunching aspects to starting a business. First, *startup metrics* measure your forward financial motion; second, *traditional accounting* numbers measure historical financial motion.

Startup measurements/metrics. Startup numbers are about acquiring customers, retaining (returning visitors), obtaining referrals (fans), and collecting sales revenue. Some numbers you need to know include:

▸ *CPL* (Cost Per Lead): $500/ad getting 10 customers = $50 per customer)

▸ *CPS* (Cost Per Sale): all expenses added divided by # of customers)

▸ *ATS* (Average Transaction Size): transaction amount in dollars

▸ *CVs* (Customer values): you invest differently in your A, B, and C list customers

▸ *LTV* (Life Time Value): how long to keep customers active

▸ *CTP* (Contribution To Profit): drop your least profitable customers)

▸ *RM* (Revenue Metrics): break down 100% of revenue; how much from A, B, or C?

▸ *QA* (Quality Assurance): low quality and returns affect profits

▸ *EC* (Expense Creep): how expenses and prices creep upward

Traditional accounting. This includes the financial statements below, which are snapshots of your businesses health. They show you how you are doing. Accountants and financiers use them; startups rarely do.

▸ *Income statement:* Revenue - Expenses = Net Income. The Income, or Profit and Loss (P&L), statement measures all of your revenue with all of your expenses for a specific period.

▸ *Balance sheet:* Liabilities + Equity = Assets. The Balance sheet gives a snapshot of a business's assets, liabilities, and the owner's equity for a given time. This statement is important for investors to help in the valuation of the business.

▸ *Cash Flow statement.* The Cash Flow statement measures the financial activity over a specified time period and tracks the effects of changes in Balance sheet accounts, showing if the business can pay its bills or not.

Monitor your business

This is how most people start their businesses:

▸ *Ready:* You've written a business model/plan, researched the feasibility to make money, and planned to make it happen.

▸ *Set:* From your business model/plan you create an action plan to start your business, prepare to open, and set soft and hard opening dates.

▸ *Go:* Grand Opening Day is here! You execute what you've planned to do, prepared to do, and now you open your doors for business!

There are two phases of running a business are Preparation (Ready, Set) and Execution (Go). Preparation is like practicing for a sports game or designing a winning war strategy. Execution is playing out that game plan or running the missions that can win a war. In sports, you have ready, set, go; in war, you have ready, aim, fire. The ready and set/aim is the preparation phase while the go/fire is the execution phase.

Preparation: Ready, Set. Prior planning prevents poor performance. However, *no model or plan ever survived coming in contact with your customers, competition, opponents, or enemies.* Your assumptions and ideas may not match up to the experience once the whistle is blown for the game to start or the trigger is pulled to begin the war.

Most sports and military analogies used in the business world are very poor. Why? Because both sports games and military wars are based on a certain amount of "down time." In sports there are multiple practices to train the players to win the game based on the coach's game plan, as well as time-outs, giving you time to regroup as needed. In the military, you undergo multiple training sessions and drills to prepare for the war, followed by war plans to win the war. With both sports and wars, there are ends in sight.

In business, however, there is just one serious time when a business practice or drill time is available to an entrepreneur to perfect your business game plan. It's the time between the moment you had your idea of starting your business and the day you open the doors for business! To a lesser degree, it lasts until you release a new product to your customers.

Execution: Go! This is where a strong game day and wartime analogy works. The moment you open for business is similar to the whistle blow at the start of the game, or the first shots fired in war.

In business, once you are open for business, you are on the go all the time.

Once your business bell has rung, it's difficult to un-ring it. There is very little let-up in getting things done and you don't have the luxury to go back over issues repeatedly to get them right. You're learning as you go along and correcting things as they come up, much like during the big game. There is no final game whistle or surrender in business, unless you're ready to sell or fold your business.

That is, unless you're a serial entrepreneur and have the luxury to fail at business, regroup, and try again. It's also a matter of perspective. There is only one final game whistle or last bullet fired in business and that is when you physically die. In business the only time you lose is when the business fails or you quit.

Move your needles: a 10,000-foot business view

There is a familiar saying about management: "What gets measured, gets done." To measure results, you first define a process, especially *a complete cycle*. Defining the process involves:

1. defining a beginning/starting step of the process.

2. defining each step of the process.

3. defining the end of the process.

4. defining a process measurement/needle, then working to move it.

Example: cooking an egg. A generic process would be pulling out the pan, spraying cooking oil, cracking the egg into the pan, cooking the egg, plating the egg, cleaning up, then beginning again. Notice that this is a *complete cycle*, not from clean pan to dirty pan, but from clean pan to clean pan. That is a complete cycle. Measurement would be how much time it takes t cook and egg, how much time to clean the pan/plate?

Define how to measure success. Preferably measure a single item within a multi-step process, i.e., the critical few versus the trivial many. A measurement creates a "needle" on an analog or digital numerical readout. Needles can measure things like total sales, the number of leads or contacts received, or even the number of transactions that have occurred over a specific period, such as hour, day, or week. Then it's up to you to perform an action in the process to move your defined needle number, up or down, good or bad, to achieve better results. In any measurement, it is important to create both quality *and* quantity measurements. If you can get one measurement that satisfies both requirements, you're golden.

> A great man is hard on himself, a small man is hard on others.
> - Confucius

The "10,000-foot Business View" in Table 6 is an example of how a business situational awareness board should look in your office. This is an overall process, but you'll need to further define how things progress from one step to another. Measure only the

10,000-foot Business View			
Step	**Metric/ Output**	**Goal/ Outcome**	**Potential Numbers**
1. Market Research			
2. Market Opportunity Customers			
3. Market Channels			
4. Marketing			
5. Leads/Web Traffic			
6a. Prospect: Qualification			
6b. Prospect: Meeting			
7. Sales/Revenues/Conversions			
8. Billing			
9. Accounting			
10. Customer Service			
11. Follow-up			
12. Referrals/Testimonials			

Table 6: 10,000-foot Business View Measurement/Metric

essential parts at each step. You can define more details about the process that you have designed, but you have to find one critical point that affects each step to measure for overall improvements.

Below are the essential steps to measure your business and to understand the reasons for success, failure, and needed improvements through your business funnel.

1. **Market research and potential** - researching and finding the size and type of market potential for your product

2. **Market opportunity** - the potential for your product to solve your ideal customer's problem

241

3. **Market "pipes," paths, or channels** - the various channels that you'll use for both getting your marketing message and your product out to your customer

4. **Marketing** - attracting ideal customers, sending your marketing message out to paying customers, and setting expectations up front to cut potential customer dissatisfaction

5. **Leads** - customer interest in your product or service; leads progress from the number of hits to your website to getting a customer's contact information

6. **Prospects** - the potential of a client/customer lead: prospects can be hot (buy now), warm (looking to buy), or cold (buying later, but you need to market to them); marketing moves them from cold to hot

   6.1. **Lead/Prospect qualification** - Determine if the customer lead is right for your product. Ask a few questions or let them tell you what they are looking for.

   6.2. **Lead/Prospect meeting** - In certain businesses, you'll need a meeting with the prospect to discuss how your product will benefit them.

7. **Sales/Revenue** - ringing up the sale, taking their money, and giving them your product

8. **Billing** - getting paid for your product or service

9. **Accounting** - tracking your cash flow into and out of your business; preparing to pay taxes

10. **Customer service** - meeting customer expectations and handling returns, defective merchandise, or poor service

11. **Follow-up** - contacting prospects and soliciting feedback from both interested leads and former customers

12. **Referrals/Testimonials** - obtaining (asking for) referrals and testimonials that:

12.1. are brief, truthful, and reflect positively on you or your company

12.2. include brief information about your company (such as your market or industry)

12.3. talk about how your product or service helped their business with their results or benefits

12.4. will be included in your marketing materials along with your business address, website, and other information

Pinpoint your problem areas. These essential steps are laid out with Table 6 above so that you can begin measuring how your business is doing. For instance, if you are not obtaining any leads, you need to check out the leads step, as well as the steps above it, to see where the problem lies. If you are not making any sales from your leads, then examine your sales techniques and the steps above that.

> You don't get paid for the hour. You get paid for the value you bring to the hour.
> - Jim Rohn

It's important to find out why you are not making forward progress. If you are not making any sales despite having leads, maybe your marketing is not setting correct expectations. Maybe your market research is bad and you need to start again to reexamine your assumptions. If you're making sales that are often returned, ask why? Always ask *why* to decide where the problem lies.

At each step in the above twelve steps, you can also get more detailed as to where things are failing and are the beginning of measuring for success.

Business, financial, priority management

Your doors are open and customers are beginning to shop around to see what you are offering and decide if they will part with their money for your product.

Business versus financial management

Business management is running your business to take care of your customers, adding value to vendor resources, and using your time and resources effectively and efficiently. Business management is the "top dog" of business processes. Project management and task management are different. Project management is the discipline of planning, organizing, motivating, and controlling resources to achieve specific goals. Task management is the process of managing tasks through its life cycle. It involves planning, testing, tracking and reporting.

Financial management controls the finances of your business to keep cash flowing, so that you can make a profit, stay in business, prosper, and grow. It's about understanding the costs of doing business, how much profit you're making, and what the market will bear for your product. It also includes tax strategies to cut your tax burden.

Balancing time, priority, and money management

Time management gurus say that time management is essential to running a successful business. This is not completely accurate. Being aware of time is the start to building a successful business. Time lost just a few minutes ago cannot be recovered. It's gone forever. Everyone is given the same 24-hour period to do with as they please. How time is spent is what differentiates one person from another, one culture from another, one nation from another. Time stops for no one, no business, no culture, no state, or country.

Who you are and how you choose to use your time determines the results of your efforts and your life. Imagine that you are a coin. Each coin has two sides: one side is designated time and the other is designated priorities. The value *you* place on both your time *and* your priorities determines the *value of the coin of you*. Do not let selfish people decide your value, no one should

> *The key is not to prioritize what's on your schedule, but to schedule your priorities.*
> - Stephen Covey

decide your value but you. Let only those that have your best interest at heart influence you and add value to your life.

Time management also includes spending time to rest, to recuperate, to begin again. Expending energy without the necessary rest leads to burnout and complications later on, so it is imperative that you allot time for rest and rebuilding one day a week.

> *You can always make more money, but you can NEVER make more time!*
> *- Dani Johnson*

Priority management is about doing triage on your life and business and finding what is important and what is not. When you say yes to something, you are automatically saying no to something else. When you say yes to starting your own business you are saying yes to doing more in life and potentially no to working for someone else.

Here are four perspectives of time and priority management:

1. **Random tasks, jobs, and time.** Let time slip by and fill up your time with whatever comes along or what is decided by someone else – *neither effective nor efficient*. In this way you become a dead leaf in the wind, slow or fast, wherever the situation blows you.

2. **Fill up your day.** Fill up your time with all sorts of activities regardless of needs or wants with no outlined or defined direction – *efficient, but not very effective*. Following this path, you find things to do, but there is no bearing. As the saying goes, all speed and no bearing get you no where fast.

3. **Focus on business goals only.** Establish only business goals, break them down into smaller pieces, and divide them up into the time you have during each day. This leaves little or no time for your family, friends, and community – *partially effective and partially efficient*. You set a direction, but it is incomplete because it does not take into account your whole life. It takes into account only your business life and is unbalanced. Burnout is sure to follow.

4. **Focus on Business Goals + Life Goals.** Establish long-term life goals for ALL areas of your life. Break them down into smaller pieces, and divide those pieces into your available time ensuring that you give time for each – *both effective and efficient*. Break down big or yearly goals into monthly or weekly goals until you get to your day: then set your priorities for the day as Crucial, Very Important, and Less Important. Prioritizing your day according to your long-term vision allows you to be more proactive and less random. Planning your life allows you control over your life as you see fit versus allowing others to control it as they see fit.

5. **Business leadership goals.** Leadership goals are about you, realizing you own your own business and focus on the right priorities of your time. What's your time worth as a business owner? $50 an hour? $250 an hour? How about $1000 an hour? Do you spend two hours (at $200 an hour) calling around to save $100 in your cell phone bill? Could a Virtual Assistant (at $10-15 per hour) do that instead of you?

Money management. When it comes to startups, you either have time or money, but usually not both at the same time.

Startup companies usually have time and not much money. However, if you do have money, you often don't have the time to do what you want. The important thing is that you do not necessarily have to spend money to make money. You can do things cheaply, if not for free, if you think through what you are trying to do and be creative.

Tip. Don't buy lunch for a potential customer; go to your local coffee shop. Buy coffee instead because prospects may not buy what you are selling and then you have spent money needlessly. Better yet, combine both volunteer time and business time: meet a client or vendor at a nonprofit to discuss business first and helping others second. If they object, would you want to work with someone who does not share your values?

Decision making and performance

When I was a young USAF Lieutenant, Col. Robin Wohnsigl told a small group of us one day, "You always have to maintain situational awareness, even when you're bogged down in the details of getting things done. You need to 'pop your head up' to see what's happening all the time." In other words, always keep an eye on the big picture. In the case of your business, you have to keep seeing your business from your customer's and market's needs and wants all the time.

Performance. Fighting all battles yourself is a brawl; picking your battles wisely is your best course of action. Let others fight your specific fight if they are better at it than you are. How do you decide?

> *Creating wealth is not a zero-sum game, so you don't have to stab people in the back to win.*
> *- Paul Graham*

Ask: Will my personal and business efforts matter in the next few years, five years? If yes for your personal efforts, then do them! If yes for the business efforts, outsource or delegate them. If no, quit what you are doing! Now to further define your task list, here are some additional steps:

1. **List goals to be done.** Make a list of the three to five things that are most important and make sure that you define what success or "done" means. There are three views of results:

    1.1. **Output results** - The *known, measured, and/or proven results* of a specific and defined process, such as driving a golf ball down the fairway and reaching consistently the 250 yard mark, running a seven minute mile, or creating sales of $10,000 your first month in business. Output results are normally historical in nature, i.e., last year, last month, yesterday, or even the last hour, but it is *based on a known measurement.*

    1.2. **Expected results** - An expected is your *desired, chosen, and/or stretch results or goals* that you want to achieve, such as wanting to drive a golf ball 600 yards from your average of 250 yards, wanting to run a two-minute mile from your best of a six-minute mile, or sales of $100,000 your second year in business. Notice that a goal of running a two-minute mile may not be a realistic goal; based on physics, it's not humanly possible to run it, unless there are changes to the process (using a bike or car). Expected results are future-oriented in nature and are considered unknown, but may or may not be achievable based on a current level of knowledge. **"Eight-cylinder engine block."** Henry Ford decided to get his engineers to produce an eight-cylinder engine block. His engineers said it was impossible. He said to work on it; they came back and still said it could not be done. He told them to work it until they did it. It took them over a year, but eventually, with much trial and error, they were able to produce it. Why? Because even though the engineers said it was impossible, Ford replied, "Produce it anyway" (true story).[85]

1.3. **Results gap** - The gap or distance between the output and expected results. A narrow, stretch, Big Hairy Audacious Goal (BHAG), or out-of-this-world goal is an expected decided upon to shoot for. Running a three-minute mile is unachievable on a human scale, but a two-minute mile while riding a bike or in the car is; these results can be achieved if you change the process. **"The Fosbury Flop."** In 1968, because Dick Fosbury changed the high jump *process*, all future jumpers' *output* changed the *results* of later high jumps contests (true story).

2. **Decide on a priority.** Gather as much information as time and money will allow, and when decision time comes, make one. Don't second guess yourself because problems will inevitably occur no matter what you decide, and there are no perfect plans.

---

[85] *Think and Grow Rich* by Napoleon Hill, pg 28-29

3. **Commit to that goal.** Once you have made a decision, commit to finishing the goal until it's done. The only reason to change is if the information or situation changes and seriously affects the outcome of your efforts.

4. **Plan how to reach that goal.** Figure out the steps needed to complete the goal, in the correct sequence, to be effective and efficient with your time, money, and resources.

5. **Work it out.** Get it done! Keep your actions moving forward toward your goals.

6. **Adjust and pivot as necessary, moving forward.** You probably will miss some things along the way; just work through them, as well.

Too often companies see people as machines in their quest for cost efficiencies. The book *Slack*, by Tom DeMarco, suggests that larger corporations are hurting their workers by pushing more work with less time, and without any process improvement. People switching between one large project and another slows one down because the mental readjustments take time. Too much switching causes a person's productivity to fall.

"Pop goes the…" I had a friend, Pete, who was a programmer. We worked together and became fast friends. One day, I came up behind him in his cubicle and, as usual, he had his headphones on, listening to music. Not realizing that he was deep in thought, I nudged his shoulder and startled him to death! He was a little upset with me and told me never to do that again. Why? He was reprogramming a large database in his head and because I had startled him, he "lost" all of his mental work! While we can all chuckle that he should have "saved his work" by writing it down, that he and others do such intense mental work that requires total concentration can be just as strenuous as physical work (true story).

> *You are the same today that you are going to be in five years from now except for two things: the people with whom you associate and the books you read.*
> *- Charles Jones*

Improve, automate, get lean

There are two ways of making more money in your business: selling more or reducing or controlling your costs by being more effective and efficient with your time and money. Reducing your operating costs potentially means more money in your pocket; cutting your prices may increase the market share of your product. Even during a recession, selling more is always the better way of staying in business.

Most businesses see only one way of reducing costs: cutting or quit doing something altogether. It might be quick, but can be painful in many ways.

There is another approach.

How does one improve, automate, and get lean? By following the steps below:

1. **Define** - First, define what it is that you are doing. Set boundaries for what you intend to do. As your business grows, you'll redefine what you will do with customers, technology, and other parts of your business as things change.

2. **Change** - Once you have defined what you are doing, the process needs to be *stabilized,* i.e. get consistent, over time using the Plan, Do, Check, Act process described above. This is the most essential principle to follow in any business because of the changes that you'll need to take a look at in the future. You'll need to figure out how to improve it. While not everything needs changing, you need to keep a sharp eye out for opportunities to improve. Also be aware that some changes may not improve, may improve little, or may not be worth the effort. Change in this context means getting "more bang for your buck" in building your business, or a better Return On Investment (ROI).

   2.1. **Simplify** - Cut tasks to their smallest parts so that the more complex tasks are made easier and faster, costing you less. Over-complicating increases the time it takes to get things done. Make sure that you do not over-design products. Perfect is one thing, but good enough can be good enough and may be better than perfect for what the customer needs.

2.2. **Eliminate** - Eliminate processes that do not add value to your business, or products that are not selling well. This also means that you, as a business owner, cut tasks you do, which leads to the next step.

3. **Delegate** - Delegation can be done two ways: outsourcing, and contracting your work or delegate and empower someone in your business to take over some of your tasks. Outsourcing to another small business can keep your business lean and focused on your core competencies. The work is now out of your hands, but you're still responsible for its completion. Delegation also means that, as the business owner, you cut tasks *you* do by handing them to an administrative or virtual assistant, so that you can concentrate on strategy and business relationships.

> *If you can't describe what you are doing as a process, you don't know what you're doing.*
> - W. Edwards Deming

4. **Automate** - Automating your business includes tasks that are repeatable. There are three basic approaches to automating:

4.1. **Automate from "manual or analog" labor to Mac labor.** From a sales perspective, this means moving from an ad hoc mode of selling to designing sales scripts for what needs to be said to customers. From an operations perspective, this can mean computerizing follow-up correspondence to your customers. Lead generation means reducing cold calls through phone or visits or designing direct mail pieces to select customers so that they call you ready to buy.

4.2. **Automate workflows on the Mac.** Automating on a Mac means using its built-in technologies found in the Automate business workflows with your Mac section above and applying it to your specific business situation. This could mean changing how and where you store your business information. In the case of Address Book, it might mean migrating its information into a Filemaker Pro database for a more complex manipulation or a more secure backup plan.

4.3. **Automate outsourced tasks.** In certain circumstances you may want to hire a company to outsource some of your tasks, such as mass marketing. Make sure that you are constantly in the loop with what is happening and check the results you are paying for.

The previous steps are in a somewhat logical order, but there are times that a logical order may not be best. There is no right or wrong way of doing things here, just as long as you work on it.

Manage your business on a Mac

Paper or plastic: Analog or digital

The term analog in this case refers to a "paper trail" of your business while digital is keeping track of it in electronic form. Both paper and digital files need to be tracked, but not everything in your business needs to be in both analog and digital form. You can get along with just pure paper/analog files such as a DayTimer or Franklin Planner. If you have a digital file you *absolutely need* a paper backup copy of your company's critical business information that's stored in a safe and secure place.

In some cases you need both, especially financial records.

The purpose of having digital copies is to be able to quickly find information. The purpose of having paper records is to back up your digital versions.

You keep a paper trail for when a digital archive is destroyed. Digital archives can be easier to transport and can be restored from the paper or analog version if the digital data is corrupted.

Contact management

Keeping track of all of your customer's information is crucial to running a business. A customer list is *gold* to any business. Whether you keep track of hundreds or millions of contacts, ensure their information is safe and accurate. Continuing solid relationships means having secure and reliable data management of your contact's information.

Address Book. Using Apple's Address Book is a simple way to keep a contact list of thousands. Beyond a list of thousands, you'll need to export into the vCard format and convert the data into a CSV (comma-separate value, or a tab or comma delimited) file to import into a Numbers or Excel spreadsheet, a Filemaker Pro database, or a hosted application for contact management.

> *Any fool can criticize, condemn, and complain – and most fools do.*
> *- Dale Carnegie*

▸ *Smart Groups* - If you are a construction general contractor, you can add into the note field the type of your subcontractors, vendors, or customers. Now create a Smart Group for each title, issue, or other factor, such as birthdate, and you have all of your contact information displayed with one click.

▸ *Travel tip* - Enter all the vendors that you use, such as airline, hotel, or car rental companies into Address Book. Then create a separate group naming it "July 4th Atlanta Trip" and drag and drop the vendors you use during that trip into the newly created group. This can be synched with your iPhone. Now you have all of their addresses and contact info in one place and do not have to hunt for them.

▸ *vCards* - Apple's Mail program allows you to add a vCard into your email or email signature so that any new customer or vendor can drag and drop your import information into their Address Book. It saves you and your customer time and increases the accuracy of sharing your contact information.

To-do list and Calendar

Use your calendar to monitor, focus, and balance your life. If you are a solo entrepreneur, you may need to track only your information. If you have multiple vendors and clients that are involved with your tasks and meetings, you may need to track other people, as well.

To-do list and calendar. Tracking a to-do list should be done two ways: in a list and in a calendar. The reason? From a process standpoint, you want to know the steps necessary to get the task, project, or job done. Tracking in a calendar helps you plan out your work days, weeks, and months. You also should add in your personal life goals.

▸ Apple's Calendar keeps track of a basic set of to-dos by priority, due date, completed, web address, and note fields.

▸ Apple's Mail program allows you to select a word, a data-detected date or address, or highlighted text; right-click or CNTL click on the selected item and create a new to-do that is posted in Calendar. You don't have to worry about retyping. Just select it and create the new to-do item in Calendar.

▸ In Apple's Mail application you can use its basic to-do listings. Create a Smart Mailbox and use the Flag/Unflag function as the criteria. Then click the Flag/Unflag button on the icon bar. You now can begin flagging emails that require your actions and unflag items when they are completed.

Time Blocking. Time blocking is setting aside blocks of time, an hour or two for example, so you can focus and reduce or eliminate distractions. *Identify your top priority*, the one thing which will make everything else you do easier or unnecessary. *Event time* is flex time around an event or your tasks, not clock time, leaving work at 5 p.m. *Planning time* is having time to work on your business to see if you're reaching your goals. *Time off* is having fun time like a full day off to recharge your work batteries.

> Time blocking: If it's not on my calendar, it doesn't get done.

Tip. Use four to six calendars in iCalendar: yellow for business planning; blue for education/seminars/Meetups; green for making money (blue + yellow = green); orange for vacations, birthdays and anniversaries; and red for hot or important items. In the event title, add keywords ("Meeting:" "Phone:," or even "Planning:") or special characters: ? (tentative), $ (money), or even characters styled after Twitter.com #hashtags for quick visual reference. Use the Calendar search function to list all of your occurrences.

Sales/Order processing and e-commerce

Each sale you make requires you to process an order using an invoice, sales receipt, or note listing what the customer ordered and the price paid.

If your sales are processed through e-commerce or a web shopping cart, these sales systems usually take care of this process and allow you to track and download this information for your records or import into an accounting system.

Pricing and delivering your product. Do some research to see how your competitors are pricing their products. Let your buyers know your terms: It is better to get your money sooner than later. In case of customers not paying you when you agreed, appeal to their ethics and sense of fairness: "That's the deal we made."

Tip: pricing discounts plus special offers, not. Beware of customers who want it all, such as discounts and special offers, then pay you late because they want to be able to do both. It costs *you* money. Plan with your experts on how to handle this situation to prevent further costs to your business.

Finances: Billing and accounting

Billing is keeping track of what you are owed for products you sell, communicating to your customers what they owe, and in some cases, tracking sales. Do what you can to be paid on time. The longer that a bill is not paid, the greater the chance of it not being paid at all.

Accounting is accurately putting the right dollars in the right chart of accounts in the right timeframe. If you don't have the right billing system set up, your accounting won't be right either. This is very important as errors in finances can cause bad customer experiences and problems when dealing with vendors and government agencies.

Bookkeepers and Accountants are different: Bookkeepers enter your data into your accounting system, while accountants make sure you're accounting for your finances according to government rules.

A *bookkeeper* may be a person without an accounting degree. They enter revenue and expenses into the proper chart of accounts, pay bills, process payroll, and prepare sales invoices.

An *accountant* will prepare adjusting journal entries to record prepaid expenses or accrued expenses, calculate and record depreciation and amortization, and establish allowances for uncollected accounts. After making the adjusting entries, the accountant prepares and reviews the company's financial statements (income statement, balance sheet, statement of cash flows). The accountant also assists the company's management in understanding the financial impact of past and future decisions.

Record keeping: finance, legal, notes

Documentation, such as contracts, legal paperwork protecting your intellectual property (patents, trademarks, copyrights), press releases, marketing materials, your day planner notes, invention drawings, and other communications, is essential to have if you ever get into legal trouble. Even notes from your day planner can be admitted as evidence in a trial. So you'll need to have a digital or analog (hand written) record-keeping system in place to handle all the documents you'll be producing as you build your business.

Tip: The organization of your digital files should mirror your paper files. Why? So it's easy to find things. It requires more upfront organization, but the extra effort means less time doing tasks.

Record retention. Certain business and personal records are required to be retained anywhere from three years to indefinitely. Check with your hired professional to find out these timeframes. If you can print images of these records as PDFs, you can speed things up if you need to research answers in your documentation. Everything that can be printed on a Mac can become a PDF, so take advantage of its technologies if you need quick answers. Have paper back-up of essential files for when of digital failures including sealing paper files against the elements such as fire, sun, heat, freezing, and water damages.

Yearly, monthly, and daily tasks

You have critical tasks that need to be done to keep your business afloat. You have taken your goals from your business plan and broken them down into daily, weekly, and monthly goals.

It's essential to be able to plan out your work so that you can deliver what your customer wants when they want it, within reason. Plan your work so that you don't shortchange yourself in earning an income and plan for mistakes that happen. If you can, charge a premium for rushing a job. Most good businesspeople recognize they can charge a premium for faster or better.

Task priorities simplified. Fill in the blanks to this statement at the beginning of every month:

I will achieve _____ (pick a number above 0 and below 1,000,000 and a subject), by _____ (date)!

Do this for three separate areas or one area with three issues that you need to work on per month and post it so that you and

257

ROAR: Defining Critical Tasks / Month _____			
Results (# + subject)	Owner	Action	Resources
1. 1000/10,000 Sales Leads	**CEO**	Marketing	Website budget
2. Hire an editor			
3. Increase number of words written per day.			

Table 7: Monthly Tasks Form Measurement/Metric

others can see it every day. See Table 7 for what a chart would look like.

In addition, here's a few things every business needs to do:

Yearly tasks: Strategy. One of the aspects of assessing your strategy yearly is that you revisit the tasks you've set to achieve your strategic goals. You look at them broken down into monthly tasks. If you're keeping up with your documentation, this should not be much more than gathering each monthly task report and consolidating them into yearly numbers. If you have designed a business plan and written an action plan from that, you can build a yearly task plan from that.

If a year is too far out to work on your strategy, then work on it monthly or quarterly. The goal is to think ahead.

▸ *Plan for taxes.* If you are just starting out, you need to plan how your income and spending will affect your taxes and decide how to pay quarterly taxes, sales taxes, and year-end taxes. Setting aside some money can help offset the year-end burden.

▸ *Review of your earlier marketing/sales/performance goals.* Review your goals to see how well you kept to what you had planned. Learn where you missed things and where you were on the right track. If you are just starting your business, you'll need to know how well you do according to your business plan.

▸ *Plan this year's goals.* After you have reviewed your business plans or last year's goals, adjust your results and be realistic with what you are able to do, based on last year's performance.

▸ *Plan personal and family time.* Don't miss out on the things that ground you, including yearly birthdays, anniversaries, doctors and dentists meetings, auto mechanics, or oil changes, etc.

If you are just starting your business, you'll still need to plan your attack. Your strategy/vision/mission determine how you intend to get things done.

Weekly/Monthly tasks: Tactics. Running your business well sometimes means breaking down your larger tasks into smaller steps. For example, following up with delinquent customers may require multiple tries to reach them. It's important that you make the effort. Why? You have to know where you stand financially to account for such losses, so that you can adjust your efforts to focus on the important things.

> *Everything that can be invented has been invented.*
> *- Charles H. Duell, Commissioner, U.S. Office of Patents, 1899*

▸ *Marketing your business.* Market your business; it is the lifeblood of staying in business. Track your marketing results and stop doing things that aren't bringing you revenue.

▸ *Follow-up with customers.* Late-paying customers may require multiple visits or phone calls to collect payments for finished work. If a customer has paid, follow-up with them as well to get an opinion of your work, both positive and negative.

▸ *Reconcile your bank statements monthly.* Reconciling your bank statements ensures that you are accurate with your finances. Do it within the first few days of the new month. Why? Because otherwise you may be making a decision on incorrect information.

▸ *Check your Profit and Loss (P&L)/Income Statement.* Here you can view how you are doing financially. Review your other financial statements. Do this in the first few days of the month.

▸ *Review your goals.* Keep track of where you are in reaching your monthly goals and objectives.

Daily task priorities. Being productive means getting things done in the time that both you and your customer need. Below are some of the important daily tasks for a small business owner:

▸ *Marketing every day.* Marketing entails getting your company and your product in front of a customer. Marketing can improve your customer base, so do some form of it every day to keep your sales pipelines filled with potential customers. Make no excuses! Marketing is crucial to growing your business. If you find yourself getting too busy, great! Then outsource your less critical work to others. You can then concentrate on the more critical work, including marketing.

▸ *Contact at least three vendors and customers a day.* Marketing is priming the pump to attract customers to your business. To keep customers, you should touch base with at least three customers a day, whether a new customer, an old customer, or a prospect.

▸ *Cash flow questions: End of cash date.* Cash is king in a small business. You have to know the details of your cash flow to understand your business. Create your break-even equation: Based on current expense trends and your available cash on hand, when will you run out of money?

▸ *Tracking sales toward goals.* Find the answer to the question: where are you, now, in reaching your goals?

▸ *Adjustments of various business tasks.* Be flexible and learn to adjust your tasks each day. Unforeseen emergencies or troubles could crop up.

▸ *Back up your Mac's data.* You would be surprised how many companies lose their valuable data because they failed to adequately back it up. Do you know how to recover from a backup when it does happen? You need to understand the complete process that gets you back to operational stability.

▸ *Keep your meetings.* Your work is your advertisement to others, so keep meetings with your customers regardless of what happens elsewhere. It also means it's also OK to say *no* to things.

▸ *Miscellaneous tasks.* Go through your mail and email. Answer voicemail and phone calls, file, invoice, perform bookkeeping, procure/update a website, enter data, and write marketing and sales copy, letters, press releases, and articles. These are all necessary to your business.

> I think it's wrong that only one company makes the game Monopoly.
> - Steve Wright

When it comes to deciding on your various timed tasks, such as repetitive tasks, it is important that you spend time "sharpening your saw" so you won't get to the point that your business fails.

Monitor your Mac

Take time to maintain your Mac to prevent future problems. Taking care of your computer is no different from taking care of your car; the Mac has maintenance requirements, as well.

Mac Training and Help

While Apple provides the ability to get things done using your Mac out of the box, there are times that you need help. As with any learning, it helps get your tasks done faster, saving you time and money. Sometimes spending money to learn something is money well spent. Here are some avenues for getting better at using a Mac:

▸ *Apple's General Online Support.* apple.com/support/

▸ *Apple's Support Communities.* discussions.apple.com

▸ *Apple Retail's onetoone.* apple.com/retail/onetoone/

▸ *Apple Certified Training.* training.apple.com/

▸ *Apple Consultant's Network.* consultants.apple.com/

▸ *Third-Party Consultants.* Search for local Mac experts.

Preventive and routine Mac maintenance

Preventive Maintenance. Maintenance on your Mac keeps you and your business humming. This adage still stands: If you take care of the cents, the dollars will take care of themselves. If you keep your Mac maintained, you'll keep yourself out of more costly upkeep, maintenance, and repairs.

Follow this list of maintenance tips to keep you in business.

▸ *Buy insurance (assurance).* You can buy Apple's AppleCare (not technically insurance), add a rider on your homeowner's insurance to cover a lost or stolen Mac, or use a credit card's insurance policy, if yours has one. AppleCare provides technical support either on the phone or at the Genius Bar at the local Apple store. As a small business, coverage of your Mac can be a lifesaver after an ill-timed problem. Having a spare Mac can also make life a little easier.

▸ *Protecting your Mac.* Buy a UPS (Uninterruptible Power Supply) for brown-outs and power surges or a surge protector for your laptop to protect your Mac from unintended power spikes. Even though you may not see a spike, over time surges produce wear and tear on your Mac's internal parts and cut its effectiveness.

▸ *Backup your Mac's, ISP's, and website's data.* There is no excuse for not backing up your Mac's hard drive using DVDs or an external hard drive. This also includes your hosted data – if you have an ISP that hosts your website or blog, make sure that you regularly back up your website and other hosted data. Apple's Time Machine and a Firewire or USB external hard drive can handle nearly all the needs of a lone entrepreneur. Other backup applications are available, as well.

▸ *Apple and third-party firmware/software updates.* Apple generally takes care of this for you with automatic updates for its products. You have to manually install firmware and software updates from some third-party hardware vendors. If you use many third-party software and hardware applications, on occasion some of their updates can create performance issues with other applications. This includes your Mac's peripherals' drivers for printers or scanners. Research firmware updates for all of your hardware, as well, before installing.

▸ *iOS and third-party updates.* Updating your operating system, such as moving to Snow Leopard or Lion, can cause issues with your current list of software. With any major version improvements, you want to make sure you check with your software vendors to verify that your current software will run on the new version of your operating system. You should stay on top of your Mac software updates, as well. Letting your software get too far out of date may cause trouble with converting files and other glitches.

Note. An ounce of prevention is worth a pound of cure. Not all software updates fix everything, especially if you use many third-party software applications. Updates can cause software conflicts that can make matters worse. So for every major Mac OS update, such as from Snow Leopard to Lion, if you're not a Mac fan and want to be conservative, wait a few months until the 10.x.1 or 10.x.2 comes out so that third-party vendors have time to resolve Apple changes and bugs.

Routine Mac Maintenance. You should do these tasks on a regular basis, just like changing the oil or rotating the tires on your car. Before doing any serious maintenance on your Mac, backup your data and consult Apple documentation support at its website (apple.com/support/), or a certified technician to make sure you are taking the correct actions.

▸ *Check the Mac's S.M.A.R.T hard disk status.* Every Mac has a built-in status update of your hard drive (older Macs may have limited status or none at all). Software such as SMARTReporter or other hard drive utilities can check the health of your hard drive and show the possibility that you might be heading toward hard drive problems.

▸ *Organize your hard drive and empty your trash.* Keeping your files organized and off the desktop, and keeping your trash emptied will keep your Mac running smoothly. Too many files left on your desktop, and not emptying your trash regularly, can slow down your Mac. Try the application Grand Perspective (grandperspectiv.sourceforge.net) or Disk Inventory X (derlien.com). Each will give you a graphical representation of your hard drive files. *Warning:* Ensure that you know what you are deleting; once the file(s) is gone, it is nearly impossible to get it back without costing hundreds if not thousands of dollars in hard drive recovery fees.

▸ *Repair Permissions.* Under the Applications > Utilities > Disk Utility there is a button "Verify Permissions" and "Repair Permissions." You can do the verify first, but most of the time just hit the repair button, unless you want to know what is being repaired. It is recommended that you repair permissions every time you update, add, or delete your Mac OS or apps/programs.

▸ *Maintenance scripts run automatically on your Mac.* Because the Mac OS is based on FreeBSD UNIX (see UNIX lineage here: http://www.levenez.com/unix/), it has scripts that run on a regular basis. *Daily* scripts run at 3:15 AM; *weekly* scripts run at 4:30 AM on Saturday; and *monthly* scripts run at 5:30 AM the first day of each month. Keep your Mac cleaned up to run efficiently. Software such as OnyX or Macaroni allow you to select each of these scripts and run them when you want. The more often you add and delete files or applications, the more often you would do this task. See this Mac website for more info about these scripts: http://www.thexlab.com/faqs/maintscripts.html or check with a Mac professional if you have any questions.

▸ *Defrag your Mac's HD: Not.* Ever since Mac OS 10.3, there is little need for the average user to defrag their hard drive. However, if you have large numbers of files, it may be a good idea.

▶ *Keep your Mac physically clean.* Keeping your Apple products free of dust prevents heat buildup that can wear down internal components and shorten its useful life. Visit Apple's Support site and search for "How to Clean Apple products" or check out cyberclean.tv to clean out crevices in your Mac keyboards and other products.

Troubleshoot your Mac

The basics of troubleshooting your Mac are based on the idea of divide and conquer. Divide the problem into parts so that you can isolate it. For example, is it a hardware or software problem? In some cases it might be difficult to pin down the exact problem, such as the motherboard going bad. This is one of the only ways to narrow down the problem and solve it.

Your Mac is slow, start here. Your Mac's Applications > Utilities > Activity Monitor application will give you clues why your Mac is slowing down. There are three areas to check to help determine the problem: memory, disk use, and hard drive. They can all be related at some point. Open Activity Monitor and follow these steps:

1. The **System Memory tab** is the first place to look for issues such as not having enough memory to handle your applications and files. Click on the System Memory tab.

   > *The only problem with troubleshooting is that sometimes trouble shoots back.*

   If the Free: or green memory slice of the pie chart is at 10 percent or less, then there is a high probability that you will need more memory. If your memory is at its maximum, then you'll have to quit some memory-hogging applications. If your free memory is at 75 percent or more, the slowness may be caused by another issue.

2. The **Hard Disk usage.** When you click on the *Disk Activity tab* and it shows a steady stream of spikes of both of red and green, two situations may be slowing your Mac: 1) having many, many files on your Mac's desktop, or 2) having background applications, such as the Mac's maintenance

scripts or an online storage backup program, that is running, especially if you have just turned on your Mac for the day. If you click on the *Disk Usage tab* and you're approaching 10 percent or less of free hard disk space you'll need to remove files from your hard drive. You could also get a larger internal hard drive or add an external one for archived files.

3. The **CPU usage tab** will display software running in the background while you're doing something important. One of the columns of information on the Activity Monitor window is %CPU. Click to make the arrow point down. If an application is above 30 percent usage or more consistently, there may be a problem with the application.

4. The **Network** tab will give you indications if your Mac is using the network such as an online backup.

Troubleshooting 101: Check obvious stuff first. This may sound simple, but you can find simple solutions more often than you think when things go wrong. Here are some tips to keep your Mac running smoothly:

▸ *Hardware* - Some hardware issues can be easily determined:

- *Power On.* Make sure power is on at the wall outlet, like turning on the light switch. Next, ensure the unit is turned on, or turn the unit off and on again, sometimes this may reset the unit.

- *Connections.* Check the connections for the power, monitor, ethernet, audio input and output, USB, and Firewire cables. You may want to swap the peripheral, or change USB ports or cable and watch for any changes. Occasionally, cables or your Mac's ports do go bad, so you may need to change out a Firewire cable, laptop power adapter, or laptop battery to fix your problem.

▸ *Hardware/Software* - It can get tricky here.

- *Connection path.* A common problem, especially switching between audio applications or different printers, is configuring the correct path between a Mac's hardware and software. Physically plugging in the hardware to your Mac is the first step. The Mac OS and the software you intend to use should be configured to send the signal *along the right path and connections* from the software application, through the Mac OS, and out to your hardware.

- *Disconnect/reconnect.* Occasionally, you might need to unplug and replug or even logout and restart your Mac to reset your Mac's ports.

▸ *Software* - A basic list of things look out for:

- Check your software installation requirements.

- Check for hardware firmware and software updates.

- Check your configuration settings.

- Check for typos or misspellings in configuration settings.

- Delete and reinstall the software, if needed.

- Login to your Mac under a different user account to see if the problem still occurs under an isolated account.

- Quit problematic programs and restart or, if needed, force quit an application that is frozen (CMD + ESC + OPT).

- Restart your Mac.

- Reinstall your Mac OS and other software. To save time, backup a new or pristine Mac OS to your backup hard disk.

Tip. Occasionally, updating computer hardware or software can cause issues where there were none before. Make sure that you have a backup of your Mac before embarking on any significant updates.

When it comes to older computer equipment you have four choices: reuse, recycle, trade in, or discard. While most companies may want to keep older computer equipment as backups in case of breakage of newer computers, holding onto very old computer equipment is not only economically unfeasible, it also takes up valuable space in your organization.

Reduce, redeploy, recycle; and ruined Macs

Reduce your Mac. Using the word "reduce" means that you find the right Mac to get the job done. You don't need a Mac Pro with a large hard drive for an administrative assistant, nor do you use a Mac Mini to handle all of your video editing for a major Hollywood studio. Find the right Mac for the job, no more, no less than you need.

Redeploying (reusing) older Mac equipment. The one thing you may want to do with that old computer, that has been replaced by your new one, is get rid of it. But wait, you can still use it. The single most important part is that if, for some reason, your new one goes down, you have a backup computer that can get you along until it gets fixed. Many a small business has gone down because it did not have a backup plan for using an older computer. So, don't throw away that old computer just yet.

Redeploying older computer equipment within the organization can save valuable resources. When it comes to getting a new computer, the consensus among the Small and Medium Business (SMB) market is that the older computer is "given" to others, or in the case of a growing business, relegated to a less-demanding part of the business. In an SMB business, an older computer can be turned into a file/printer server since most of the time the SMB server needs are minimal, although the storage and backup may be more important. Since most start-up companies have workstations as their first order of business when new computers are purchased, the older ones turn into file servers or "production" machines for the less creative work.

Giving or donating old computers to employees and non-profits, selling them on eBay or other auction houses, or even shipping them overseas to less fortunate countries may provide a tax benefit that may not have been realized. Most organizations won't accept non-working computers because of the time and effort to fix them. When giving or donating the computer, keep the original software on the hard disk and only delete the necessary company or organizational files from prying eyes. This also means keeping the original CDs and documentation, if at all possible.

In addition, while a computer may not be fully working, it can be used for spare parts much like used or "totaled" cars in junk yards. These organizations will take out the working components of computers and build a working computers. Organizations that help out are: cristina.org, techsoup.org, the ever growing diyparts.org, and pcsforschools.org.

Recycle or Trade-ins. Recycling or trading in your older computer is another way to get rid of them.

When it comes to trading in an old computer, many of the larger manufacturers have trade-in or recycling policies that offer ways in which to properly dispose of your older computers. Go to your manufacturer's web site and type in "recycle" or other key terms to find out how to properly dispose of computer equipment.

Apple recycles its products (apple.com/recycling/). Other sources of recycling: metech-arm.com, recycle.net, and earthpro.com, just to name a few. The Environmental Protection Agency (EPA) has some info about recycling and reusing computers, along with a host of other organizations that can assist you in doing the right thing: epa.gov/epaoswer/hazwaste/recycle/ecycling/donate.htm

Ruined. Macs that can no longer be used need to be properly disposed. If, after using a computer as a backup computer or as a file/print server for a few more years, you find that computer is starting to give up the computer ghost, you need to dispose of it properly, not only to protect your private information on the hard drive, but to also protect our environment.

The steps to be taken to discard that old computer are as follows:

Remove Essential Files. Move, copy, and then remove all essential files from the hard drive, including word processing or spreadsheet files that you need to keep. Move the files to another hard drive or burn them to a CD or DVD.

Reformat Hard Drive. Reformat or completely physically destroy your old hard drive in each computer. You can purchase any number of programs that can securely delete your data from your hard drive, or you can use Terminal to DIY on your old Mac using OS X. You can find Terminal under Applications > Utilities. The Terminal program uses BASH shell and has two commands that can be of assistance to you at this point. The command "rm" which is the UNIX shortcut for "remove" will remove the files and directories that you choose. However, "srm" stands for "secure remove," which provides a simple level of data deletion, DOD level of protection at 7 levels of overwriting, all the way up to 35 levels of overwriting. Secure remove overwrites the hard drive with garbage a number of times to erase data. Normal deletion of files only removes the hard drives "Table of Contents" but still leaves the data in its last known location.

Remove Company Insignias/Labels. Removing your company's insignia or labels prevents crackers from gaining valuable information about your company. This includes removing your login data, as well, such as your name and address.

Document Donations and Disposals. Document your gifts of old computer equipment, whether to company employees, non-profits, or other agencies, not only for tax advantages but also for "legal issues" concerning disposal of hazardous materials.

Recycle It. Finally, find a place to take your old computer equipment. Check out your local listings of recycling organizations, including state organizations. Disposing of computers has become a rather large business because of the various materials in the computers themselves, but also because of the sensitive information contained on computer hard drives.

Action plan: Track business results

You've done the marketing and you've made the sale, now it's a matter of making sure you manage your business right and keep your costs low. You need to track your complete end-to-end business processes to understand your business and Table 8 below is the last lap of completing your business measurements.

Chapter Ten

Step 10: Next Steps

Whatever your past has been, you have a spotless future. --
Anonymous

Now that you understand what to do and how you intend to move forward, you need to possess a long-term vision of what you want your business to look like. As an entrepreneur, one of the goals of your business is keeping costs under control. Don't be stingy. There are certain functions, like marketing, which you cannot avoid that require constant testing and verification. Spending marketing dollars is a continual "plan, do, check, then change" to improve each response.

Startup milestones

One of the first milestones is making a profit or "being in the black" early in your business. The sooner you're in the black and making profit, the better off you are. One's startup date can be hazy, it could be the date you had the idea, make the decision to take action, or the day you incorporate. What ever date, it's your startup date.

1. **"Startup date"** + **"Making your First Sale."** There is nothing like selling to your very first customer.

2. **"Startup date" + six months.** From the date of your startup you should be able to handle your business operationally within six months: clearly defined processes, ideal customers, and most of all, proper pricing of your products. Solo entrepreneurs should be making a profit soon after starting or toward the end of the six-month period.

3. **"Startup date" + 12-18 months.** Larger businesses should reach a break-even point or begin profitability at this point and everyone should concentrate on gaining more ground in revenue.

4. **"Startup date" + three to five years.** Continually improve what you are doing to gain more customers and check your growth plans to see if you are on track.

5. **"Startup date" + five to ten years.** Delegate some or all of your tasks so that you can do other things, including taking a vacation, thinking of your next business idea, or non-profit work.

If you have moved beyond the years of being in business, it's now time to take a look at your longer-term prospects by seeing how you intend to move forward.

Are you on track based on the ideas listed below?

Long-term thinking: Where are you heading?

At first, all you envision is getting your product out the door and making sales. Eventually your business will require a long-term view, direction, and strategy. As your business grows, you may even create a new market, then you'll have to switch your focus from a single product to a product line or service repertoire. Entrepreneurs who create new markets have changed the industry rules and will have competitors trying to unseat their place in that market. Long-term growth principle: never let growth erode the corporate culture; grow only as large or fast as the culture can support.

It's not about you

In the beginning of this book, I said, "It's about you!" and asked the questions: What is your passion? What do you love to do? As you grow your passion into building a business and build your confidence as you become successful, the need arises to transition from passions to business sense. You should never completely lose your passion, but shift your focus to "it's about the business."

The purpose of any business is not to fuel your ego; it's to serve your customer. It's a matter of taking your raw emotions out of the business. If you intend to sell your business, you need to take *you* out of the business and concentrate on the future of the business.

Business on the side

Start by building a small business on the side to create a second stream of income. Having a second stream of income while you still have your job is great place to start. Sometimes you're thrown out of the boat and you have to sink or swim for survival.

Out the corporate door and on your own

Once you've started your business, start putting aside some of the second income for the day that you intend to leave your main job or you plan to retire. Place the money in a liquid account (easily converted to cash) so that you can access it without penalty, if the need arises.

Lifestyle or purposeful living

Your business is now making a good living for you. You're saving a large amount of the profits to live a good lifestyle. You intend to funnel some of these profits into a non-profit organization that matches your life's purpose. Keep in mind that taking tons of profit out as a salary from your business might be good for a short time, but does it fulfill your life's purpose? Some entrepreneurs love the thrill of starting their own business and becoming serial entrepreneurs by starting, growing, and then selling businesses multiple times. Others like to become parallel entrepreneurs, operating two or more businesses at the same time.

Maintain or build your business

Once you have started your business, you decide to grow it to even bigger heights. Be aware that the level that you want to grow it may stretch your capabilities. It is essential that you get mentoring help as you grow. Find help from someone who has been there. If you make $100,000 in sales and want to make $500,000 in sales, find someone who is achieving these numbers and seek their advice on what to do to get there.

What will those new heights be? A certain amount of sales per year? A certain number of employees? To keep the quality of your product level high?

At this point you do not have to offer an IPO and make millions, but you want to keep doing what you're doing and are comfortable with what you're doing. There is no problem with this approach to building a business. In Bo Burlingham's book *Small Giants,* he writes that there are some companies that are content keeping their business small and of high quality to keep loyal customers coming back and not growing too large or selling it outright to another company.

Acquisition or sale

Some serial entrepreneurs plan for the day when they sell their company or negotiate an acquisition. Others consider it only when things get tough. If you are considering getting out of the business, first consider the tax implications of taking money versus stock options if someone acquires it.

The best case is to be acquired by a larger company for money or stock options. Your lawyer and accountant are to give you sound advice, but ultimately it's your decision. They do not know everything, so take responsibility for your decisions.

Failure: Out of business, then starting again

While we've all heard the admonitions to "never quit," there are times that you do need to shut down the computer and close the doors of your business. As in poker, you need to know when to hold 'em and know when to fold 'em.

Most of us have heard the statistic that most startups fail within the first five years. You rarely hear about what happens after they close up shop. Failed entrepreneurs often record their experiences on startup blogs and websites. What happens to them?

True entrepreneurs begin again!

In John C. Maxwell's great book *Failing Forward,* he says that the average number of failures for serial entrepreneurs is 3.8 times before they are successful in business. Entrepreneurs do not get deterred or see themselves as failures. They see failure as a part of growing and learning, necessary to becoming better entrepreneurs producing better products and competing in the world of business. Failure is really redefined as "testing." You test and keep testing until you succeed. Re-read the long quote by Napoleon Hill in the above business planning section.

> *How to break free from generations of failure?* **Studying** *the biographies of successful people. Chase your passion, not your pension, and associate with optimists.*
> *- Dennis Waitley*

Some people look at failure as "damaged goods;" that once a failure, always a failure. Hogwash! As long as you are still breathing, you have the opportunity to begin again, to strike out to other pastures, and to move forward. Listen to constructive criticism, but only to criticism that truly benefits your future, not when it benefits only another person. If you change yourself, you can change others' perceptions of you and what you do. You have to make the change first before they'll change their perceptions of you.

Business people who do not come back never had the talent or the guts to make it back. Those businesses that are able to create a second act for have the talent to continue and will make it. Donald Trump, Steve Jobs, Martha Stewart came back, just to name a few. Their talents separated them from the rest of the pack, hence the business comeback.

Lastly, you may need to go out of business only as your last choice. You may find a willing buyer for your business, especially if you have a loyal following and you're tired of the business you're in and want to get out. At some point you may have to go out of business, but it's not the end of you. As Zig Ziglar has stated, "Failure is a detour, not a dead-end street."

Get back up and into the game

If you have failed, do not feel bad, everyone has done it and many will do it again. Did you know that a great baseball hitter hits over .300? That's one hit out of three at-bats. Filing for bankruptcy? Henry Ford, P.T. Barnum, Sam Walton, Frank Lloyd Wright, David Buick (founder of Buick Motors), Donald Trump, and J.C. Penney have all gone through bankruptcy. Business comebacks are not easy, but business failures are not etched in stone, either.

> One of the hardest parts of life is deciding whether to walk away or try harder.

There are three ways of looking at a failure:

▸ *Dwelling on it ("Pity Party")* - Don't get "stuck" in the failure and forever hold onto the past. When it comes to failure, expect it to happen, but never, never, never allow it to become a self-fulfilling prophecy.

▸ *Dealing with it ("Man/Woman Up")* - Take ownership and learn what went wrong; make changes, so you can *redefine what failure is*. Getting a vaccination inoculates you from certain diseases; learning from failure inoculates you for future failures. Focus on the positive experience to make you stronger and grow from it.

▶ *Denying it ("Macho Man/Woman")* - By not facing your problem, you will potentially and repeatedly fail in the same way in the future. Failure should be defined as failing to learn from failure.

J. C. Penney began his retail career as a boy entrepreneur. His family was so poor that, at the age of eight, he had to earn money to buy his own clothes. So, he bought, raised, and sold pigs to buy himself some new shoes. Later, he became a partner in a store and it became so successful that he bought them out and expanded his company until the stock market crash of 1929. Penney wanted to die – his wealth was wiped out at age 57. In the deepest part of his loss, he found his life's purpose and started again with renewed vigor. Within a few short years, he was again "whole." While never achieving his past wealth, he used his time to help others until his death at age 95 in 1971.[86]

In the book *The Millionaire Next Door,* author Thomas Stanley states that statistically, "hitting it big" or "winning the Lotto" are windfalls that are truly rare. Millionaires who slug it out, day by day, customer by customer, and whose wealth is honorably achieved, maintained, and earned, have a higher success rate at maintaining their earned wealth over the course of their lifetime. Included in this is the personal learning, growth and understanding of *what wealth is* that is acquired as the money is earned. Truly wealthy people have learned the skills of the wealthy, how

> *Pain Shared = Pain Divided,*
> *Joy Shared = Joy Multiplied*
> *- Lt. Col Grossman*

to be rich, and the difficulties of working through what being rich really means. *Anyone* can learn these facts and skills; they are not limited to any person, group, or segment of people. It's just a matter of being willing to search out and learn these skills.

What do you call a failed entrepreneur in Silicon Valley? Experienced. They become a veteran of the various business conflicts in the marketplace, of customers, and other businesses. Anywhere else in the U.S. a failed entrepreneur would have to

---

[86] http://en.wikipedia.org/wiki/James_Cash_Penney

change their name, move to another town, and watch their parents hang their heads in shame. In Silicon Valley, after hearing about your first failure, they ask, "What's your next company going to be?"

The culture of the U.S. should be innovative, believing that change is inevitable, that leasing office space to 20-year-olds is not unheard of, that taking a $2 million check and building a company around solving a problem is *the* most important part of a startup culture. This culture needs to be in the U.S. schools, colleges and universities, businesses, and government institutions.

When Napoleon Hill talked with Thomas Edison about his over 10,000 failed experiments to perfect the incandescent lamp, he asked him, "What would you have done if you had not finally uncovered the secret?"

With a merry twinkle in his eyes, Edison replied, "I would be in my laboratory working now, instead of wasting my time talking with you."[87]

Successful people speak in the *future tense* of unattained milestones and objectives which they intend to accomplish or achieve. Failures speak in the *past tense* of their defeats and disappointments and they allow failure to rule their lives.

Do not close your door to both good and bad experiences; both will help mold your life's journey. As Napoleon Hill and Edison both knew, there is no such reality as "failure."

There are only blessings in disguise, forcing us to change course in our lives leading us to greater opportunities, happiness, and understanding.

No pain, no gain.

---

[87] *A Year of Growing Rich* by Napoleon Hill, pg 126

Chapter Eleven

Resources

If a man empties his purse into his head, no man can take it away from him. An investment in knowledge pays the best return. -- Benjamin Franklin

Even if you have never graduated from any school, you can still become a millionaire business owner by starting a personal learning program to develop yourself. Henry Ford only had a third-grade education. Microsoft's Bill Gates, Apple's Steve Jobs, and Galileo Galilei (who confirmed our planets moved around our sun) each never finished college. Don't let a lack of a formal education be a hindrance to your success.

Your Learning Program: Books, movies, etc.

Where do you go to learn more? There are two ways: Learn from your life experiences and learn from other's life experiences. Both ways can come in many different forms.

Books. The point of reading is to gain more insight into the subjects that interest you. Reading books is one of the best routes to take. Everyone is familiar with amazon.com, but most are not aware of half.com. You can also visit your local used book store to get what you're looking for or check a book out at your local library/university's library.

Some suggested books to read are:

1. **The Bible (Christian and Jewish)** - The Good Book is about how to live your life, including the morality of business and the reason for business: to serve others.

2. Rabbi Daniel Lapin, **Thou Shall Prosper: Ten Commandments for Making Money** - Rabbi Lapin offers a advice, including that everyone is in business for themselves, to never retire, and businesses *have to be* moral.

3. Erik Wesner, **Success Made Simple** - Wesner gives an inside look at why Amish businesses thrive with a 95% success rate.

4. Rabbi Levi Bachman, **Jewish Wisdom for Business Success: Lessons from the Torah and Other Ancient Texts** - This book discusses the purpose of business and morality, as well as spirituality entrepreneurship versus classic and social entrepreneurship from the Jewish perspective.

5. Thomas DiLorenzo, **How Capitalism Saved America** - DiLorenzo describes how various government actions precluded American citizens from their right to earn a living.

6. Andrew Carnegie, **Triumphant Democracy** - Written in 1886, he outlines what it took for America to become, within 100 years of our nation's birth, equal to, and in some cases, surpassing Old World Europe's economy.

7. Simon Sinek, **Start with Why** - It's about your purpose, your reason for being: *why* are you doing what you're doing, which will next determine the *how* and the *what*.

8. Leonard E. Read, **I, Pencil** - How futile it is for any one mind or even a group of great minds to try to undertake the task of bringing into existence everyday goods and services that we take for granted.

9. Adam Smith, **The Wealth of Nations** - THE book that changed Americans' view of entrepreneurship and the role of government in guiding a nation's prosperity.

10. Napoleon Hill, **Think and Grow Rich** - Think less about just *doing* a job and more about *doing better* on your job. Think less about getting a *job* and more about getting *work*.

11. Napoleon Hill, **The Laws of Success** - Hill was tasked by Andrew Carnegie to find concrete answers to success, thus this book is he basis of 25 years of research.

12. Ayn Rand, **The Fountainhead** - This story, made into a movie, sums up entrepreneurial passion and spirit. The question isn't who is going to let me, it's who is going to stop me.

13. Thomas Sowell, **Basic Economics: A Citizen's Guide to the Economy** - Sowell shows how the free enterprise system works the best for earning a living.

14. Clayton Christensen, **The Innovator's Dilemma: The Revolutionary Book that Will Change the Way You Do Business** - Disruptive organizations create a threat to large companies.

15. Walter Isaacson, **Steve Jobs** - This is THE unvarnished biography of the CEO of Apple.

16. Daniel H. Pink, **Drive: The Surviving Truth About What Motivates Us** - Forget the carrots and sticks; it's all about someone's internal motivation

> *If you feed your mind as often as you feed your stomach, then you'll never have to worry about feeding your stomach or a roof over your head or clothes on your back.*
> *- Albert Einstein*

17. Robert Coram, **Boyd: The Fighter Pilot Who Changed the Art of War** - Boyd's system of "observe, orient, decide, and act" (OODA) is the cornerstone of adapting to change in your environment.

18. T. Harv Eker, **Secrets of the Millionaire Mind** - Your money "blueprint" from growing up will tell you how far you can go in making it and gives steps for change.

19. Tom Rath, Donald Clifton, **How Full Is Your Bucket?** - Your insides are reflected on your outside.

20. Ken Blanchard, **Gung Ho!** - This book teaches how to motivate people.

21. Chris Gardner, **Start Where You Are: Life Lessons in Getting from Where You Are to Where You Want to Be** - Dare to begin right where you are.

22. Marcus Buckingham, Donald O. Clifton, Ph.D. - **Now, Discover Your Strengths** - Focus on what you do best and don't "shore up" your weaknesses.

23. Steven Gary Blank, **The Four Steps to the Epiphany** - Blank offers a roadmap to achieving Product/Market Fit.

24. W. Clement Stone, **The Success System That Never Fails** - Personal success begets business success.

25. Mark Sanborn, **The Fred Factor** - Even the most simple forms of work can make all the difference in your world.

26. Mark Victor Hansen and Robert G. Allen, **The One Minute Millionaire** - This book shows how to approach being a millionaire.

27. Mark Victor Hansen and Robert G. Allen, **Cracking the Millionaire Code** - The same idea as the previous book, but their 32 views of product development are indispensable to growing your business product line.

28. Adrian Slywotzky, **The Art of Profitability** - There are various ways of seeing profit in a business.

29. Seth Godin, **Tribes** - Be the leader of your own tribe of change; forget big businesses.

30. Tim Ferris, **The 4 Hour Work Week** - Outsourcing some of your business tasks can earn you more money. This book includes a list of various resources startups can use.

31. Seth Godin, **Ideavirus** - Godin shows how to get a product to go viral.

32. Seth Godin, **Purple Cow** - Being remarkable, unique and not ordinary is important in business

33. Chip and Dan Heath, **Made to Stick** - Why do some ideas survive and others die?

34. Robert Pirsig, **Zen and the Art of Motorcycle Maintenance** - This book should be read slowly and savored.

35. Geoffrey A. Moore, **Crossing the Chasm** - Startups get stuck in the "chasm," in between early adopter and mainstream customers.

36. Brian Tracy, **The 100 Absolutely Unbreakable Laws of Business Success** - This book is a personal guide to success.

37. Guy Kawasaki, **Enchantment** - This book illustrates the art of changing hearts, minds, and actions.

38. Guy Kawasaki, **The Art of the Start** - A detailed view of a larger startup business, this book teaches a "swing for the fences" approach.

39. Guy Kawasaki, **Reality Check** - This book provides great information for larger startup businesses.

40. John C. Maxwell, **Failing Forward** - Maxwell explains how to handle and learn from failure.

41. Bo Burlingham, **Small Giants** - You don't need to be the next Microsoft or Apple; small can still be great.

42. John C. Maxwell, **There's No Such Thing As Business Ethics** - Ethics are ethics.

43. Thomas J. Stanley, **The Millionaire Next Door** - What does a millionaire really looks like? It's not about the display or the "bling" of wealth.

44. Michael E. Geber, **The E-Myth Revisited** - Where do startups fail the most?

45. Dennis Waitley, **Seeds of Greatness** - Notice that a seed has great potential of multiplying itself many times over, but not until conditions are met.

46. Rieva Lesonsky and Staff of Entrepreneur Magazine, **Start Your Own Business** - This offers a great summary of most of the issues involved in starting a business.

47. Beth Andrus, **The Essential Business Handbook** - Key ingredients needed to start and run a business are listed.

48. Rhonda Abrams, **What Business Should I Start?** - What are you interested in starting up?

49. Rhonda Abrams, **Successful Business Research** - Do your due diligence and research the feasibility of starting a business.

50. Rhonda Abrams, **Six Week Startup** - Starting a business in a matter of weeks.

51. Jeff Gitomer, **Little Red Book of Selling** - If you don't sell, you won't be in business long.

52. Jeff Gitomer, **Sales Bible** - This book provides even more information about selling.

53. Zig Ziglar, **See You At The Top** - Ziglar is the master at showing how to motivate yourself.

54. Jim Collins, **Good to Great** - This book defines long-range business growth.

55. Jim Collins, **Built to Last** - Collins shows how businesses were defined and how good foundations kept them in business.

56. Christine Comaford, **Rules for Renegades** - She offers a "true grit" account of what it takes to build a large business.

57. Robert A. Watson/Ben Brown, **The Most Effective Organization in the U.S.: Leadership Secrets of the Salvation Army** - You can have an effective and efficient organization doing good for both vendors and customers.

58. Peter M. Senge, **The Fifth Discipline** - How do you view learning?

59. William Manchester, **American Caesar: Douglas MacArthur 1880-1964** - Reading biographies of leaders gives insights into their lives and thinking. In this book you'll find

that Gens. MacArthur and Patton both had personal libraries in the thousands of books! Earners are learners.

60. Max Depree, **Leadership is an Art** - This is oh so true.

61. David Allen, **Getting Things Done** - Allen teaches about being personally productive.

62. Eliyahu M. Goldratt, **The Goal** - What is your goal?

63. Fredrick Brooks, **The Mythical Man-Month** - Here's a view of people and project management.

64. Donald Wheeler, **Understanding Variation: Key to Managing Chaos** - Decisions made with poor data can waste valuable time, people, and financial resources.

65. W. Edwards Deming, **Out of the Crisis** - This American helped Japan overcome their second-place quality showing as evidenced by Honda and Toyota's success.

66. Edward De Bono, **Six Thinking Hats** - This book presents the various viewpoints of problem solving.

67. Tom DeMarco, **Slack** - People cannot switch thinking from one subject to another like a machine; there are delays.

68. Spencer Johnson, **Who Moved My Cheese** - Take your mental and physical blinders off and begin to watch for change.

69. Ken Blanchard, **Raving Fans** - Blanchard is the expert on obtaining raving fans for your business.

> *I cannot live without books.*
> *- Thomas Jefferson*

70. Ken Blanchard, **Whale Done!** - Another of Blanchard's books discusses positively affecting others.

71. Malcolm Gladwell, **Tipping Point** - Most large society changes start slow but occur at a tipping point.

72. Malcolm Gladwell, **Blink** - Keep from over thinking.

73. Malcolm Gladwell, **Outliers: The Story of Success** - This book presents other views of success.

74. Jim Loehr and Tony Schwartz, **Power of Full Engagement** - Monitoring your physical and emotional energy level will enable your productivity.

75. Ed Oakley & Doug Krug, **Enlightened Leadership** - Ask the right questions; get the right answers.

Movies. If you don't want to read, many movies teach about business subjects.

1. **It's a Wonderful Life (1946)** – A small-town banker goes up against a larger tycoon. It's about the customer relationships, not about the almighty bucks.

2. **The Kid (2000)** – An image consultant (Bruce Willis) makes tons of money but is not happy with his life. His childhood dreams and authentic self come back and he leaves his PR firm to follow his dream.

3. **Teacher's Pet (1958)** – This movie discusses both the pros and cons of education versus real life in the trenches of business, especially in the newspaper world. The best scene is when Clark Gable writes a story in class for journalism professor Doris Day that does not follow all of her requirements. It does, however, get the job done for business: classic education versus business scene.

4. **Bottle Shock (2008)** – It's the story of the early days of California wine making, featuring the now infamous, blind Paris wine tasting of 1976 that has become known as "Judgment of Paris." Up and coming entrepreneurs shocked the world wine establishment.

5. **The Pursuit of Happyness (2006)** – Chris Gardner rose from being homeless to becoming a multimillionaire.

6. **Tucker: The Man and His Dream (1988)** – Preston Tucker dreamed of building a car to beat the Big Three auto makers at their game. He was forced into bankruptcy stemming from legal battles, but was later found innocent of all charges.

7. **Door to Door (2002)** – This film won six Emmy Awards portraying the true life story of J. R. Watkins' door-to-door salesman, Bill Porter, who had cerebral palsy. His parents never let his disability limit him, and he would not let his disability keep him from being productive in business.

8. **12 O'Clock High (1949)** – Required viewing by military officers and corporate leaders, this film illustrates leadership and how to get results. Military leadership, with a similar intensity as police, fire, or emergency medical personnel where a few too many lives are at stake, is different from business leadership. Leadership involves the situation, the leader, and the follower.

9. **Baby Boom (1987)** – A corporate marketing guru leaves the corporate world for the simple life in the northeast United States. She ends up becoming successful at selling organic baby food. Although they offered, she never returned to corporate life. The film was based on the book *Small Giants:* stay small to stay excellent.

> *Learning never exhausts the mind.*
> *- Leonardo da Vinci*

10. **Miracle on 34th Street (1947)** – While not a totally business-oriented film, this story shows Santa's customer service.

11. **Citizen Kane (1941)** – This is the classic "business" film, voted #1 film of all time by the American Film Institute.

12. **The Devil Wears Prada (2006)** – This story is about a new hire working for a demanding fashion magazine editor boss.

13. **Stand and Deliver (1988)** – Teaching math to high school kids in the inner city and making them whiz kids, despite their environment.

14. **What Women Want (2000)** – A great film, it shows a chauvinistic marketer trying to understand what women want in products and the change that occurs within him.

15. **Other People's Money (1991)** – This film depicts the struggle between love and money.

16. **Pirates of Silicon Valley (1999)** – Apple and Microsoft duke it out during the beginning of the personal computer era.

17. **Freedom Writers (2007)** – An inner-city school teacher encourages L.A. kids to write about themselves, while learning the world is full of people with similar experiences.

18. **Erin Brockovich (1988)** – This film is based on a true story about a legal assistant who helps take down Energy Big Business in one of the largest court battles against a big company.

19. **The Aviator (2004)** – Howard Hughes makes a run for the money-making airplanes and ultimately leaves all of his estate to the Howard Hughes Medical Institute, not succumbing to political pressure.

20. **Barbershop (2002)** – A small barbershop experiences the ups and down between big business and small business, illustrating the "life" of a small business.

21. **Clerks (1994)** – This film digs into customer psychology.

22. **Hudsucker Proxy (1994)** – An inexperienced business graduate gets involved with a stock scam.

23. **Rocky (1976)** – Motivation can overcome big odds. Read how Sylvester Stallone sold the movie on page 122 of *The One Minute Millionaire*.

24. **Patton (1970)** – Even though this movie discusses war, business is really about war between multiple enemies, your competitors. The movie is also about leadership. What most people do not know is that both General Patton and Eisenhower were students of history and warfare; both had tens of thousands of volumes in their personal libraries. How many of today's CEO can boast of this claim?

25. **Big Night (1996)** – Two brothers run a restaurant in the 1950s facing tough issues.

26. **Mildred Pierce (1945)** – Business success is used to gain a daughter's love, but it fails.

27. **In Good Company (2004)** – An older advertising exec deals with a younger boss.

28. **Pretty Women (1990)** – A business liquidator breaks up businesses just for money and has a change of heart and finds that a win/lose situation creates a different result than a win/win one.

29. **Jerry MacGuire (1996)** – A struggling sports agent finally achieves success despite being seen as a "loser" by those in his career field.

30. **The Bucket List (2007)** – Don't leave this life without doing something from your bucket or "shoulda" list.

31. **Click (2006)** – When a TV remote allows people to "fast forward" over boring periods of life, they still miss out.

32. **Working Girl (1988)** – A secretary works for a boss who steals her ideas and sells them as her own. Karma never felt so good.

33. **You've Got Mail (1998)** – A small book store gets gobbled up by Big Business; the story focuses on the relationship between the two owners.

34. **Tin Men (1987)** – A door-to-door aluminum siding salesmen will do anything to get a sale.

35. **Office Space (1999)** – Software programmers are fed up with their jobs and decide to do something about it.

36. **Being There (1979)** -- A mentally deficient gardener learns business/life lessons from a wealthy king-maker industrialist. Because he doesn't understand his own limitations, this mentally retarded man ends up a contender for the U.S. presidency. "Life is a state of mind."

Books about Macs. There are some books that will help you with your Mac; here are a few that work well. As a side note, some of the books below are in a series of books, so if you like one series style you might like the others.

▸ Robin Williams, **The Little Mac Book, Snow Leopard Edition** - About 1990, Robin self published *The Little Mac Book* and *The Mac is not a Typewriter*. A larger publishing company, QUE, published a similar, competing book, *The Big Mac Book*. When Robin's book began selling, they changed the title to be similar to hers. Guy Kawasaki picked up on the story and wrote about it in his MacUser column, publishing the publisher's fax number because, as Robin stated in her open letter to QUE, they "were just not nice." In turn, QUE's book just faded away and hers took off. Thanks Guy and Robin, for the inspirational success for the little guy against "not nice" big companies (true story).

> *If we all did the things we are capable of, we would astound ourselves.*
> *- Thomas Edison*

▸ David Pogue, **Mac OS X Snow Leopard: The Missing Manual**.

▸ Dwight Spivy, **Mac OS X Snow Leopard Portable Genius**.

▸ Guy Hart-Davis, **iWork '09 Portable Genius**.

▸ Josh Clark, **iWork '09: The Missing Manual**.

▸ Guy Hart-Davis, **iLife '09 Portable Genius**.

▸ Adam Angst, **iPhoto 09 for Mac OS X: Visual Quickstart Guide**.

▸ Matt Neuburg, **Take Control of Exploring & Customizing Snow Leopard**.

▸ Joe Kissell, **Take Control of Mac OS X Backups, Fourth Edition**.

▸ Ernest Rothman, Brian Jepson, Rich Rosen, **Mac OS X for UNIX Geeks**.

Mac Web and Software sites

▸ macsurfer.com is a daily aggregation of Mac information on the web.

▸ macworld.com is THE Mac magazine, since day one.

▸ myfirstmac.com has entry-level information about your Mac.

▸ maclife.com is another magazine about Mac products.

▸ macdirectory.com is a listing of companies that deal with a Mac.

▸ tidbits.com is one of the oldest and best email newsletters about Apple and Mac products.

▸ apple.com/downloads has listings of Mac software; see also the Mac App Store.

▸ macupdate.com shows updated Mac software.

▸ macupdate.com is another site for Mac software.

▸ versiontracker.com is still another listing of updated software releases.

▸ macforge.net is a geek-level site of software projects that are built by programmers for other programmers and those needing specific tools for their jobs, including open source projects that can be downloaded for free and improved, and uploaded for others to improve.

▸ iworkcommunity.com is a source of iWork templates.

Startup help and resources

Below is a list of free and low-cost resources to get your business up and running. Also check out other resources throughout the book.

"Free" should not be misunderstood or misleading, as in no cost to you. There is an implied sense of obligation to give back to the community or to those who help. The best way of getting

> *Give a man a fish and you feed him for a day; teach a man to fish and you feed him for a lifetime. Sell him fishing supplies and you've got a business. Then you can become a land owner and buy a fishing pond.*

help is to offer "free help" to those around you without strings attached, being a "giver" to others, but being aware that you need to set boundaries regarding who and what you give. Non-profits may be places to offer free advice and tips, but with clients you may offer appetizers of what you do to help them understand what you do. Actions precede money. Here is a list of resources:

▸ *Ask* is the number one thing to do because it is important to ask others for help. This includes family, friends, new acquaintances, and other entrepreneurs. Almost every entrepreneur wants to see a fellow entrepreneur become successful, but you have to ask to receive help.

▸ *Give* of yourself in both time and talent if you have received help from someone else. Someone does not have to ask in order for you to give help. Nothing is more important than putting yourself out there to assist others in their endeavor. If all you do is ask for help and rarely give help to others, what type of reputation will you get? Be a giver of your time, tools, and talents. Visit volunteer.org and check out how you can help.

▸ *Feedback* includes saying, "Thank You" to those who have helped you; it's essential to building a good reputation.

▸ *Networking* is about getting out and about meeting others; you make connections with others who know someone who might be able to help you. A great resource is meetup.com.

▸ *Free classes* or seminars are offered by others. Give free classes to help others, and you'll increase your good reputation.

▸ *iTunesU* by Apple (or iTunes University) offers tons of free classes on most any subject including classes from major and Ivy League schools. You can download them into your iTunes application and iPod/iPhone and listen at your leisure.

- *National Federation of Independent Business* (nfib.com) is an organization devoted to entrepreneurs and their issues.

- Facebook.com is a popular social networking site that is becoming just as important for businesses on which you can also buy ads for your business.

- Twitter.com is instant messaging at 140 characters.

- kickstarter.com is the largest funding platform for creative projects.

- LinkedIn.com is a professional online resume, business marketing, and networking site. Has a strong search engine for finding groups of like interests. Never lose that personal contact ever again.

- younoodle.com allows you to get in touch with others in a startup mode.

- PBWorks.com is not only a wiki but also a collaboration tool, document manager, and project management tool.

- startupnation.com gives a list of resources by entrepreneurs for entrepreneurs.

- uservoice.com allows customers to give voice to their concerns.

- getrichslowly.org/blog is a blog about saving dollars and cents, as many an entrepreneur needs.

- lifehacker.com is a DIY site to do just about anything.

- alltop.com has some more sites devoted to small businesses such as: startups.alltop.com, small-business.alltop.com

- partnerup.com is about networking with others and finding partners for your business.

- vator.tv gives a voice of the entrepreneur by uploading your short video about your company.

- wordpress.org is a free blogging site, but you'll need to move to your own domain name at some point if you have your own business. You can also install WordPress on your own website, if needed.

▸ makemineamillion.com lists ideas, but ideas are a dime a dozen; it's all about the execution and taking actions.

Resources and Templates for Businesses. Some of the resources below have plenty of information, people, and resources to help you. Templates are normally Word/Excel or Pages/Numbers that you fill in. These templates give you a head start and give the necessary structure, information, and expected results to show to investors. Here are a few sources of templates:

> *You are never too old to set another goal or to dream a new dream.*
> *- C. S. Lewis*

▸ iStart.org is a premier site for startups, especially those that want to enter business plan competitions with others to get funding.

▸ SCORE.org (Service Corps Of Retired Executives) has templates for startup businesses that can be opened in either Excel or Numbers.

▸ Small Business Development Centers (SBDC, sba.gov) is another great resource for starting a business.

▸ Successmagazine.com is one of the oldest periodicals focused on being successful. Entrepreneur.com has some checklists of things to consider for staring your own business and are free to download. Inc.com magazine also offers online resources.

▸ licensing.org discusses licensing of all sorts. Provides joint venture insights beginning with owning your intellectual property and being paid or paying someone for the rights to sell your/their intellectual property.

▸ microsoft.com also has some templates for business plans and Apple's iWork Pages can read these files.

▸ IONfreshstart.com is a site that has iWork Office templates for business plans for the Mac that are well worth their information and essential questions.

▸ Morebusiness.com is another site that contains prebuilt business plans and about 100 more sample business plans.

▸ Check vendor sites for templates, such as filemaker.com for Filemaker Pro/Bento templates that you can download for free or as a demo.

Parting thoughts

My two favorite quotes follow:

- *You cannot bring about prosperity by discouraging thrift.*
- *You cannot strengthen the weak by weakening the strong.*
- *You cannot help little men by tearing down big men.*
- *You cannot lift the wage earner by pulling down the wage payer.*
- *You cannot help the poor by destroying the rich.*
- *You cannot establish sound security on borrowed money.*
- *You cannot further the brotherhood of man by inciting class hatred.*
- *You cannot keep out of trouble by spending more than you earn.*
- *You cannot build character and courage by destroying men's initiative and independence.*
- *And you cannot help men permanently by doing for them what they can and should do for themselves.*
  - William J. H. Boetcker (often attributed to Abraham Lincoln)

It is not the critic who counts; not the person who points out how strong people stumble, or where the doer of deeds could have done better. The credit belongs to the person who is actually in the arena, whose face is marred by dust and sweat and blood, who strives valiantly; who errs and comes short again and again; because there is no effort without error and shortcomings; but who does actually strive to do the deed; who knows the great enthusiasm, the great devotion, who spends himself in a worthy cause, who at the best knows in the end the triumph of high achievement and who at the worst, if he fails, at least he fails while daring greatly. So that his place shall never be with those cold and timid souls who know neither victory nor defeat.
- Teddy Roosevelt

Two of my favorite films are *The Kid* and *Bottle Shock*. *The Kid* is the story about an image consultant who is not happy with this life making loads of money. He then takes a "trip" back into his childhood and reclaims his real passion, deciding to follow his childhood dreams doing what he loves to do, not what he had decided to do years before.

The movie *Bottle Shock* is a "based on a true story" film about the California winery Chateau Montelena in the 1970s. It is entered into a blind tasting against French wines: the California wines rated best in each category in what has been called the "Judgement of Paris" and the wine was memorialized at the Smithsonian soon after the historic event.

Watch and learn from these movies; you may find that what you "love" has been waiting in the wings for you all of this time.

Here are other quotes that I found interesting and appropriate for this book:

I have never met a man so ignorant that I couldn't learn something from him.
- Galileo Galilei, Italian astronomer, 1564-1642

Tell me and I forget. Teach me and I remember. Involve me and I learn. - Benjamin Franklin

Iron rusts from disuse; water loses its purity from stagnation...even so does inaction sap the vigor of the mind.
- Leonardo da Vinci

The philosophy of the rich versus the poor is this: The rich invest their money and spend what's left; the poor spend their money and invest what's left. - Jim Rohn

Being broke is a temporary situation. Being poor is a mental state. - Mike Todd

People ask the difference between a leader and a boss. The leader leads, and the boss drives. - Theodore Roosevelt

There is only one boss. The customer. And he can fire everybody in the company from the chairman on down, simply by spending his money somewhere else.
- Sam Walton

Gentlemen, enlisted men may be entitled to morale problems, but officers are not. I expect all officers in this department to take care of their own morale. No one is taking care of my morale.
- General George Marshall about leadership

As a young teenager, Uncle Glenn pointed to a rusted piece of metal near his workshop and asked me what I saw. "A piece of junk," I said. "To me, that is potential. I can mill off the rust and make that into something else, then sell it at a profit." - my Uncle, Kevin Cullis

Unless commitment is made, there are only promises and hopes; but no plans. - Peter Drucker

Being busy does not always mean real work. The object of all work is production or accomplishment and to either of these ends there must be forethought, system, planning, intelligence, and honest purpose, as well as perspiration. Seeming to do is not doing. - Thomas Edison

Your time is limited, so don't waste it living someone else's life. Don't be trapped by dogma – which is living with the results of other people's thinking. Don't let the noise of other's opinions drown out your own inner voice. And most important, have the courage to follow your heart and intuition. They somehow already know what you truly want to become. Everything else is secondary.
- Steve Jobs

About this book, about this author

About this book. I wrote this book using iWork and iLife '09. Earlier versions of iLife and iWork may not duplicate the things that are explained here.

The book text and book cover were created 100 percent in iWork Pages '09 and all the tables and graphics were designed using the tools in Pages. Pages was chosen to show that a book could be written and designed completely at a much lower entry cost point than what professionals say to use.

So, it can be done. Because it can be done there is no longer any excuse why someone such as you cannot get published today.

It's a matter of will and putting in the time to write it, publish it, market it, and get it sold. It has truly become a desktop/book publishing revolution.

The main text font is 12 point Garamond with 14 point leading (pronounced like "heading," stated as 12/14, or "12 on 14" leading). Chapter numbers are 24 point Trebuchet MS; chapter titles are 24 point Futura Condensed, and all section and subsection headings are 14 point Helvetica. The heading/footer font is 11 point Garamond and the blocked quotes are 10 point Optima italic.

Garamond Type History. This typeface is based on Roman types cut by Jean Jannon in 1615. Jannon followed the designs of Claude Garamond which had been cut in the previous century. Garamond's types were, in turn, based on those used by Aldus Manutius in 1495 and cut by Francesco Griffo. The italic is based on types cut in France circa 1557 by Robert Granjon. Garamond is a beautiful typeface with an air of informality which looks good in a wide range of applications. It works particularly well in books and lengthy text settings.[88]

The book was then outsourced and printed using an independent Print-On-Demand (POD) publisher. An independent (micro-niche) publishing company is primarily a Just-In-Time (JIT) printing production company, i.e., producing only the number of books that have been ordered, so there is no need to carry inventory. All other services, such as marketing and editing, were outsourced to other people or companies, with the results placed in the Pages document.

Reasons to use an independent publisher:

▸ *Customer demand.* Information in this book was more important and useful to customers today, not later. Time is money, and any delay in finding and applying solutions to making or saving money is money wasted or lost.

▸ *Cost of time and money.* Good entrepreneurs always calculate the cost of time and money. Time lost is money lost.

---

[88] Apple's Font Book Information about Garamond font

- *Defects versus perfection.* A product's "defects" can still be productive if the ROI is good enough, but those defects need to be taken out over time or reviewed later to see if the ROI is still there.

- *Save money today.* Implement a 20-percent savings today versus an 80-percent savings in 12 months. You enjoy the savings over the course of five months and the other seven months you "make money" versus realizing "larger savings" down the road. Why wait, implement now.

- *Invest money today.* Do it and enjoy the Return On Investment (ROI) savings now. If spending $30 will save you $100, it's worth it. If a $19.99 iWork Pages software package can do what you need compared to a $699 Adobe InDesign software package, you've paid enough to get the job done.

▸ *Time to market.* The time it takes for publishing companies to get a new book to market is at least 12-24 months. Independent publishing starts at 12 months, but anyone can get a book out in six months or less depending on the subject and amount of information that the book contains.

▸ *Time to change or update a book.* When it comes to producing an update to a book, a publisher can take months or years to get it done. An independent publisher can take any finished updates and within days have the change available to the market.

▸ *Large publishing companies rarely bank on a new author.* Most companies rarely or never pick up an unpublished author and spend thousands of dollars developing them, especially in a slow economy. If the author's subject is a hot topic in the marketplace, such as how to program an application for an iPad, then maybe they might jump on it. However, there is hope. When you have personally sold thousands of your independently published books, you've shown publishers there's demand for your book and you're willing to do the marketing work to get it out there. You've got skin in the book publishing game, and they like this aspect of new authors.

About the Author. I have helped thousands of small business entrepreneurs for over a decade, from those who were thinking about starting up a business to larger businesses. I helped all select Windows. Linux, and Mac hardware and software solutions. Those entrepreneurs included writers to lawyers to carpet cleaners; from young twenty-somethings to older folks who "can't decide what I want to do when I grow up;" from men looking to ignite their long lost passion to moms wanting to teach their kids to be financially independent.

Taking my own advice and "eating my own dog food," I started my own business to help others use their Mac to the fullest. My experience is showing them not only what is best *on* the Mac, but most important, what is best *for* a business.

Feel free to reach out to me with questions, comments, or ideas about your business idea. You can contact me through email at kevincullis@gmail.com, or you can visit my website at MacStartup.com for more commentary and tips. Connect with me through Facebook, through Twitter (@kevincullis), and LinkedIn (linkedin.com/in/kcullis). I live in Denver, Colorado.

Let's start a conversation.

Index

FREE Bonuses Section

1. **Get Your FREE ebook PDF** of *How to Start a Business: Mac Version.* Email me a copy of your receipt and I'll forward the PDF to you.

2. **Get Your Second FREE Ebook!** Get a FREE classic marketing ebook that the advertising industry has followed since its publication. Just E-mail your book receipt to kevincullis@gmail.com and I'll forward this FREE ebook to you.

3. **FREE SURPRISE if you follow #2 above.**

4. **Need more books?** To order more books, visit http://www.MacStartup.com and click on the "My Book" tab and order as many as you need.

5. **Volume Discounts.** If you are looking for volume discounts, they're available for 10 or more books, so please contact me at kevincullis@gmail.com so we can discuss the transaction.

Made in the USA
Lexington, KY
22 December 2014